An Introduction to

CLIENT/SERVER COMPUTING

An Introduction to CLIENT/SERVER COMPUTING

Subhash Chandra Yadav
M.Sc., M.C.A. and M.Phil. (Computer Science)
Reader
Department of Computer Applications
Rajarshi School of Management and Technology
U.P. College Campus
Varanasi, (U.P.)

Sanjay Kumar Singh
Ph.D. (Computer Science and Engineering)
Reader
Department of Computer Engineering
Institute of Technology,
B.H.U., Varanasi, (U.P.)

PUBLISHING FOR ONE WORLD

NEW AGE INTERNATIONAL (P) LIMITED, PUBLISHERS

New Delhi • Bangalore • Chennai • Cochin • Guwahati • Hyderabad
Jalandhar • Kolkata • Lucknow • Mumbai • Ranchi
Visit us at **www.newagepublishers.com**

Published by New Age International (P) Ltd., Publishers
First Edition: 2009

Branches:

- 36, Malikarjuna Temple Street, Opp. ICWA, Basavanagudi, **Bangalore**. © (080) 26677815
- 26, Damodaran Street, T. Nagar, **Chennai**. © (044) 24353401
- Hemsen Complex, Mohd. Shah Road, Paltan Bazar, Near Starline Hotel, **Guwahati**. © (0361) 2543669
- No. 105, 1st Floor, Madhiray Kaveri Tower, 3-2-19, Azam Jahi Road, Nimboliadda, **Hyderabad**. © (040) 24652456
- RDB Chambers (Formerly Lotus Cinema) 106A,1st Floor, S.N. Banerjee Road, **Kolkata**. © (033) 22275247
- 18, Madan Mohan Malviya Marg, **Lucknow**. © (0522) 2209578
- 142C, Victor House, Ground Floor, N.M. Joshi Marg, Lower Parel, **Mumbai**. © (022) 24927869
- 22, Golden House, Daryaganj, **New Delhi**. © (011) 23262370, 23262368

ISBN : 978-81-224-2689-2

Rs. 195.00

C-09-02-3435

Printed in India at Glorious Printers, Delhi.
Typeset at Inhouse.

PUBLISHING FOR ONE WORLD
NEW AGE INTERNATIONAL (P) LIMITED, PUBLISHERS
4835/24, Ansari Road, Daryaganj, New Delhi-110002
Visit us at **www.newagepublishers.com**

Preface

In recent years there have been significant advances in the development of high performance personal computer and networks. There is now an identifiable trend in industry toward downsizing that is replacing expensive mainframe computers with more cost-effective networks of personal computer that achieve the same or even better results. This trend has given rise to the architecture of the Client/Server Computing.

The term Client/Server was first used in the 1980s in reference to personal computers on a network. The actual Client/Server model started gaining acceptance in the late 1980s. The term Client/Server is used to describe a computing model for the development of computerized systems. This model is based on the distribution of functions between two types of independent and autonomous entities: Server and Client. A Client is any process that request specific services from server processes. A Server is process that provides requested services for Clients. Or in other words, we can say "A client is defined as a requester of services and a server is defined as the provider of services." A single machine can be both a client and a server depending on the software configuration. Client and Server processes can reside in same computer or in different computers linked by a network.

In general, Client/Server is a system. It is not just hardware or software. It is not necessarily a program that comes in a box to be installed onto your computer's hard drive. Client/Server is a conglomeration of computer equipment, infrastructure, and software programs working together to accomplish computing tasks which enable their users to be more efficient and productive. Client/Server applications can be distinguished by the nature of the service or type of solutions they provide. Client/Server Computing is new technology that yields solutions to many data management problems faced by modern organizations.

Client/Server Computing: An Introduction, features objective evaluations and details of Client/Server development tools, used operating system, database management system and its mechanism in respect of Client/Server computing and network components used in order to build effective Client/Server applications.

Last but not the least, this work is primarily a joint work with a number of fellow teacher who have worked with us. My parents, wife Meera, and our children, Akanksha and Harsh. I am particularly grateful to Dr. A. P. Singh, Principal, Udai Pratap Inter College, Varanasi; Dr. D. S. Yadav, Sr. Lecturer, Department of Computer Science and Engineering, IET, Lucknow; Dr. A. K. Naiyak, Director IIBM, Patna, former President of IT and Computer Science Section of Indian Science Congress Association; Prof. A. K. Agrawal, Professor and Ex-Head of Department, Computer Science and Engineering IT, BHU, Varanasi and Mr. Manish Kumar Singh, Sr. Lecturer, Rajarshi School of Management and Technology for providing the necessary help to finish this work.

Suggestions and comments about the book are most welcome and can be sent by e-mail to scy@rediffmail.com.

Subhash Chandra Yadav

Contents

1

Introduction

1.1 WHAT IS CLIENT/SERVER COMPUTING?

According to MIS terminology, Client/Server computing is new technology that yields solutions to many data management problems faced by modern organizations. The term Client/Server is used to describe a computing model for the development of computerized systems. This model is based on distribution of functions between two types of independent and autonomous processes: Server and Client. A Client is any process that requests specific services from the server process. A Server is a process that provides requested services for the Client. Client and Server processes can reside in same computer or in different computers linked by a network.

When Client and Server processes reside on two or more independent computers on a network, the Server can provide services for more than one Client. In addition, a client can request services from several servers on the network without regard to the location or the physical characteristics of the computer in which the Server process resides. The network ties the server and client together, providing the medium through which the clients and the server communicate. The Fig. 1.1 given below shows a basic Client/Server computing model.

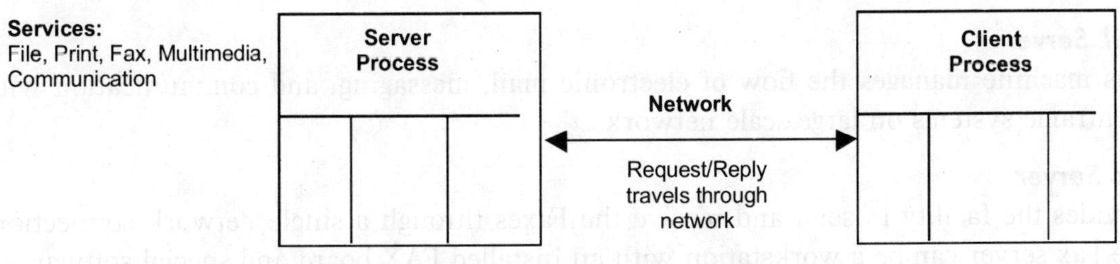

Fig.1.1: Basic Client/Server Computing Model

From the Fig. 1.1 it is clear that services can be provided by variety of computers in the network. The key point to Client/Server power is where the request processing takes place. For example: Client/Server Database. In case of Client/Server database system, the functionality is split between the server system and multiple clients such that networking of computers allows some tasks to be executed on the client system.

1.1.1 A Server for Every Client

A file server can store any type of data, and so on simpler systems, may be the only server necessary. On larger and more complicated systems, the server responsibility may be distributed among several different types of servers. In this section, we have discussed the purpose of various available server:

File Server

All the files reside on the server machine. File Server provides clients access to records within files from the server machine. File Servers are useful for sharing files across a network among the different client process requesting the services. The server process is somewhat primitive because of tends to demand many message exchanges over the network to find the requested data.

The examples of File servers are:

- UNIX: Network File Services (NFS) created by Sun Micro systems.
- Microsoft Windows "Map Drive" e.g., Rivier College's "P-drive".
- Samba: An open Source/Free Software suite that provides seamless file and print services to SMB/CIFS clients (i.e., Microsoft Windows clients).

Print Server

This machine manages user access to the shared output devices, such as printers. These are the earliest type of servers. Print services can run on a file server or on one or more separate print server machines.

Application Server

This machine manages access to centralized application software; for example, a shared database. When the user requests information from the database, the application server processes the request and returns the result of the process to the user.

Mail Server

This machine manages the flow of electronic mail, messaging, and communication with mainframe systems on large-scale networks.

Fax Server

Provides the facility to send and receive the Faxes through a single network connection. The Fax server can be a workstation with an installed FAX board and special software or a specialized device dedicated and designed for Fax Services. This machine manages flow of fax information to and from the network. It is similar to the mail server.

Directory Services Server

It is found on large-scale systems with data that is distributed throughout multiple servers. This machine functions as an organization manager, keeping track of what is stored where, enabling fast and reliable access to data in various locations.

Web Server

This machine stores and retrieves Internet (and intranet) data for the enterprise. Some documents, data, etc., reside on web servers. Web application provides access to documents and other data. "Thin" clients typically use a web browser to request those documents. Such servers shares documents across intranets, or across the Internet (or extranets). The most commonly used protocol is HTTP (Hyper Text Transfer Protocol). Web application servers are now augmenting simple web servers. The examples of web application servers are Microsoft's Internet Information Server (IIS), Netscape's iPlanet IBM's WebSphere, BEA's WebLogic and Oracle Application Server.

Database Server

Data resides on server, in the form of a SQL database. Database server provides access to data to clients, in response to SQL requests. It shares the data residing in a database across a network. Database Server has more efficient protocol than File Server. The Database Server receives SQL requests and processes them and returning only the requested data; therefore the client doesn't have to deal with irrelevant data. However, the client does have to implement SQL application code. The example of database server is: Oracle9i database server.

Transaction Servers

The data and remote procedures reside on the server. The Server provides access to high-level functions, and implements efficient transaction processing. It shares data and high-level functions across a network. Transaction servers are often used to implement Online Transaction Processing (OLTP) in high-performance applications. A transaction server utilizes a more efficient protocol in comparison to a Database Server. The transaction Server receives high-level function request from the clients and it implements that function. Often it needs to return less information to the client than a Database Server. Examples of the Transaction servers mainly categorized as

- TP-Light with Database Stored Procedures like Oracle, Microsoft SQL Server etc.
- TP-Heavy with TP Monitors like BEA Tuxedo, IBM CICS/TX Series.

Groupware Servers

Liable to store semi-structured information like text, image, mail, bulletin boards, flow of work. Groupware Server provides services, which put people in contact with other people, that is because "groupware" is an ill-defined classification protocol differing from product to product. For Example: Lotus Notes/Domino and Microsoft Exchange.

Object Application Servers

Communicating distributed objects reside on the server. The object server primarily provides access to those objects from the designated client objects. The object Application Servers are responsible for sharing distributed objects across the network. Object Application Servers use the protocols that are usually some kind of Object Request Broker (ORB). Each distributed object can have one or more remote methods. ORB locates an instance of the object server class, invokes the requested method, and returns the results to the client object. Object Application Server provides an ORB and application servers to implement this. For example:

- Common Object Request Broker Architecture (CORBA): Iona's Orbix, Borland's Visibroker.
- Microsoft's Distributed Component Object Model (DCOM), aka COM+.
- Microsoft Transaction Server (MTS).

1.1.2 Client/Server: Fat or Thin

A Client or a Server is so named depending on the extent to which the processing is shared between the client and server. A thin client is one that conducts a minimum of processing on the client side while a fat client is one that carries a relatively larger proportion of processing load. The concept of Fat Clients or Fat Servers is given by one of the important criterion, that is, how much of an application is placed at the client end vs. the server end.

Fat Clients: This architecture places more application functionality *on the client machine(s)*. They are used in traditional of Client/Server models. Their use can be a maintenance headache for Client/Server systems.

Fat Servers: This architecture places more application functionality *on the server machine(s)*. Typically, the server provides more abstract, higher level services. The current trend is more towards fat servers in Client/Server Systems. In that case, the client is often found using a fast web browser. The biggest advantage of using the fat server is that it is easier to manage because only the software on the servers needs to be changed, whereas updating potentially thousands of client machines is a real headache.

1.1.3 Client/Server: Stateless or Stateful

A stateless server is a server that treats each request as an independent transaction that is unrelated to any previous request. The biggest advantage of stateless is that it simplifies the server design because it does not need to dynamically allocate storage to deal with conversations in progress or worry about freeing it if a client dies in mid-transaction. There is also one disadvantage that it may be necessary to include more information in each request and this extra information will need to be interpreted by the server each time. An example of a stateless server is a World Wide Web server. With the exception of cookies, these take in requests (URLs) which completely specify the required document and do not require any context or memory of previous requests contrast this with a traditional FTP server which conducts an interactive session with the user. A request to the server for a file can assume that the user has been authenticated and that the current directory and file transfer mode have been set. The Gopher protocol and Gopher+ are both designed to be stateless.

Stateful Server

Client data (state) information are maintained by server on status of ongoing interaction with clients and the server remembers what client requested previously and at last maintains the information as an incremental reply for each request.

The advantages of stateful server is that requests are more efficiently handled and are of smaller in size. Some disadvantages are their like state information becomes invalid when messages are unreliable. Another disadvantage is that if clients crash (or reboot) frequently, state information may exhaust server's memory. The best example of stateful server is remote file server.

Stateless vs Stateful Servers

There are some comparative analysis about stateless and stateful servers.

* A stateful server remembers client data (state) from one request to the next.
* A stateless server keeps no state information. Using a stateless file server, the client must specify complete file names in each request specify location for reading or writing and re-authenticate for each request.
* Using a stateful file server, the client can send less data with each request. A stateful server is simpler.

On the other hand, a stateless server is more robust and lost connections can't leave a file in an invalid state rebooting the server does not lose state information rebooting the client does not confuse a stateless server.

1.1.4 Servers and Mainframes

From a hardware perspective, a mainframe is not greatly different from a personal computer. The CPU inside a mainframe was, however, much faster than a personal computer. In fact, what a mainframe most closely resembled was a LAN. A mainframe was 'larger' in terms of:

* The raw speed expressed in instructions per second, or cycles.
* The amount of memory that could be addressed directly by a program.

Mainframes are the monstrous computer system that deals mainly the business functions and technically these giant machines will run MVS, IMS and VSAM operating systems. There is a common believe that a mainframe is 'database'. There are many reasons behind this belief:

* Many servers are either file or database servers running sophisticated database such as Sybase, Oracle and DB2.

* These servers connect to the mainframe primarily to access databases.
* Organisations use servers specifically to replace mainframe databases.
* Organisations keep applications on the mainframe usually for better database performance, integrity and functionality.

Mainframe users argue that in the long run, a mainframe is at least as good a server as a PC, and perhaps even better. And because the mainframe portrayed as a better server than a PC, the picture is clear: PC servers and mainframe servers compete at the back-end both are essentially databases.

There is some controversy as to whether servers will eventually replace mainframes. They may, but not in the near future. Mainframes still serve the purpose in managing the complex business rules of very large organizations and enterprises that are spread out over a very large area. But the increasing processing power of servers combined with their lower costs makes them the logical replacement to mainframe-based systems in the future.

In the meanwhile, Client/Server networks will often find it necessary to connect to mainframe-based systems. This is because some data can only be found in the mainframe environment, usually because the business rules for handling it are sufficiently complex or because the data itself is massive or sensitive enough that as a practical matter it remains stored there.

Connection to a mainframe requires some form of network – like access. Even if you are using a telephone and modem as your access hardware, you still require special software to make your workstation appear to the mainframe to be just another network terminal. Many vendors can provide the necessary software to handle this type of network extension.

A very natural question at this stage is: How do Client/Server Systems differ from Mainframe Systems?

The extent of the separation of data processing task is the key difference.

In mainframe systems all the processing takes place on the mainframe and usually dumb terminals are used to display the data screens. These terminals do not have autonomy.

On the other hand, the Client/Server environment provides a clear separation of server and client processes, both processes being autonomous. The relationship between client and server is many to many.

Various other factors, which can have, prime considerations to differentiate the mainframe and Client/Server systems:

- **Application development:** Mainframe systems are over structured, time-consuming and create application backlogs. On the other hand, PC-based Client/Server systems are flexible, have rapid application development and have better productivity tools.
- **Data manipulation:** Mainframe systems have very limited data manipulation capabilities whereas these techniques are very flexible in the case of Client/Server systems.

- **System management:** Mainframe systems are known to be integrated systems but in the case of Client/Server systems only few tools are available for system management.
- **Security:** Mainframe systems are highly centralized whether as Client/Server systems are relaxed or decentralized.
- **End user platform:** Mainframe systems comprise of dumb terminals, are character-based, single task oriented and of limited productivity. On the other hand, Client/Server systems are intelligent PC's with graphical user interface having multitasking OS with better productivity tools.

1.1.5 Client/Server Functions

The main operations of the client system are listed below:

- Managing the user interface.
- Accepts and checks the syntax of user inputs.
- Processes application logic.
- Generates database request and transmits to server.
- Passes response back to server.

The main operations of the server are listed below:

- Accepts and processes database requests from client.
- Checks authorization.
- Ensures that integrity constraints are not violated.
- Performs query/update processing and transmits responses to client.
- Maintains system catalogue.
- Provide concurrent database access.
- Provides recovery control.

1.1.6 Client/Server Topologies

A Client/Server topology refers to the physical layout of the Client/Server network in which all the clients and servers are connected to each other. This includes all the workstations (clients) and the servers. The possible Client/Server topological design and strategies used are as follows:

(*i*) Single client, single server
(*ii*) Multiple clients, single server
(*iii*) Multiple clients, multiple servers

(*i*) **Single client, single server:** This topology is shown in the Fig. 1.2 given below. In this topology, one client is directly connected to one server.

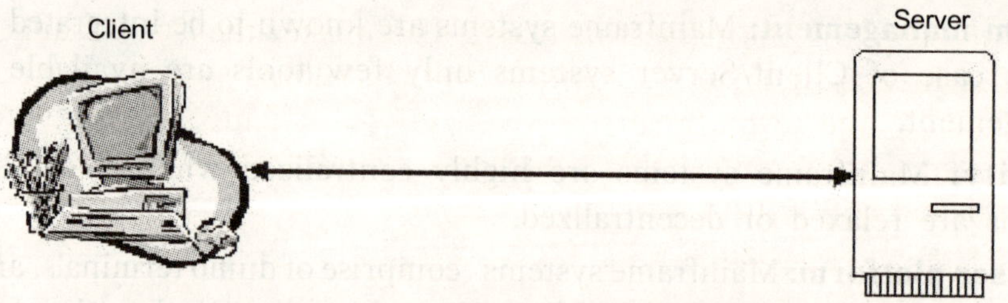

Fig.1.2: Single Client, Single Server

(*ii*) **Multiple clients, single server:** This topology is shown in the Fig. 1.3 given below. In this topology, several clients are directly connected to only one server.

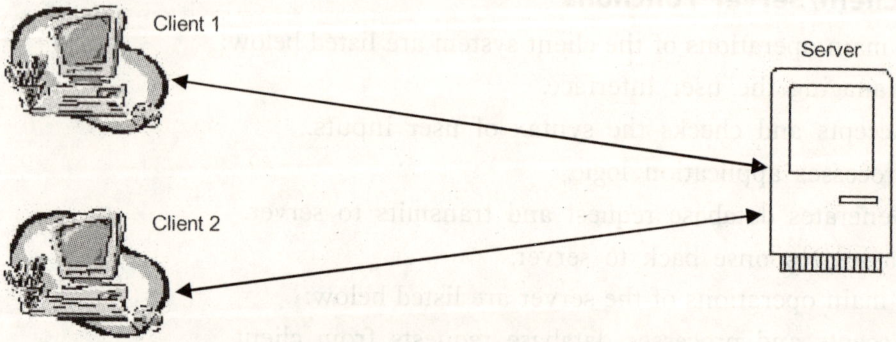

Fig.1.3: Multiple Clients, Single Server

(*iii*) **Multiple clients, multiple servers:** This topology is shown in the following Fig. 1.4 In this topology several clients are connected to several servers.

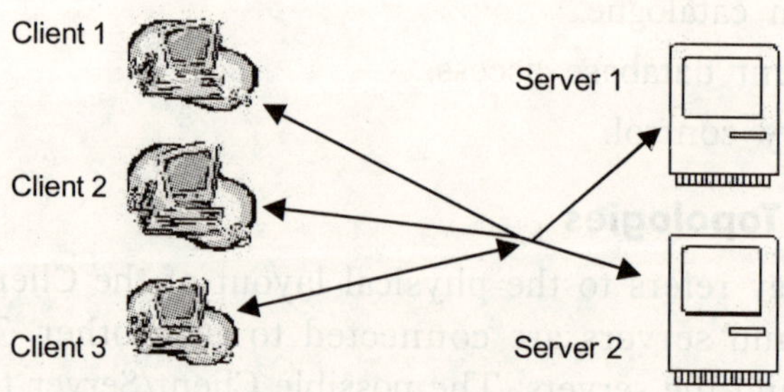

Fig.1.4: Multiple Clients, Multiple Servers

1.1.7 Integration with Distributed Computing

Distributed computing is the term used for implementation of technologies across heterogeneous environments. For operating systems, heterogeneous computing means the ability to communicate with other operating systems and protocols. Distributed computing is a complex architecture. It involves rearchitecture of applications, redevelopment of systems and increased efficiency in maintaining a network as a whole. Many distributed nodes work on behalf of one requesting client. This makes the system fault tolerant and decentralized, which is an obvious advantage over centralized systems. For the technology to become effective and revolutionary, developers of distributed applications have to do everything possible to minimize the complexity of development and maintenance and integrate their software with disparate platforms. Client/Server application designing necessitates the modularization of applications and their functions into discrete components. These components must be bounded only by encapsulated data and functions that may be moved between the systems. This design model gives Client/Server software more adaptability and flexibility.

1.1.8 Alternatives to Client/Server Systems

There are various client/server projects are running in industry by various companies. Before committing a project to Client/Server, some alternatives can be considered that includes:

- Movement of an existing mainframe application to a smaller hardware platforms, for examples IBM's ICCS transaction processing to an AS/400 or an OS/2 LAN Server.
- Replacement of mainframes computer terminals with PCs that is able to emulate terminals.
- Replacing an existing mainframe system with a packaged system that does the job better.
- Beautifying an existing mainframe application by adding a GUI front-end to it. There are programs available specifically to do this.

1.2 CLASSIFICATION OF CLIENT/SERVER SYSTEMS

Broadly, there are three types of Client/Server systems in existence.

(*i*) Two-tier

(*ii*) Three-tier

(*iii*) N-Tier

1.2.1 Two-tier Client/Server Model

The application processing is done separately for database queries and updates and for business logic processing and user interface presentation. Usually, the network binds the back-end of an application to the front-end, although both tiers can be present on the same hardware.

Sometimes, the application logic (the real business logic) is located in both the client program and in the database itself. Quiet often, the business logic is merged into the presentation logic on the client side. As a result, code maintenance and reusability become difficult to achieve on the client side. On the database side, logic is often developed using stored procedures.

In the two-tier architecture, if the Client/Server application has a number of business rules needed to be processed, then those rules can reside at either the Client or at the Server. The Fig. 1.5 below clarifies this situation.

(*a*) Centralized Two-tier Representation:

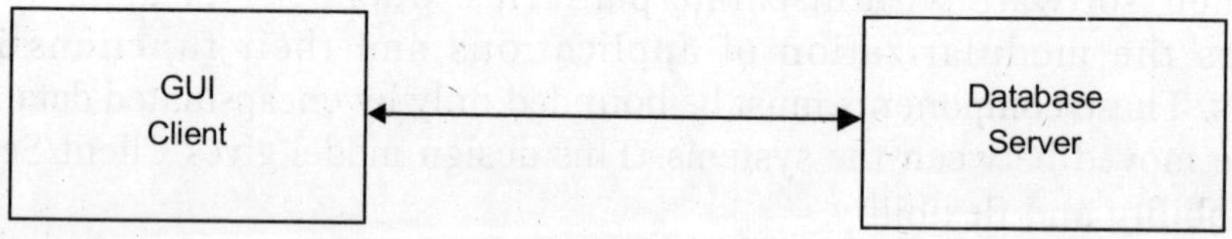

(*b*) Business Rules Residing on the Client:

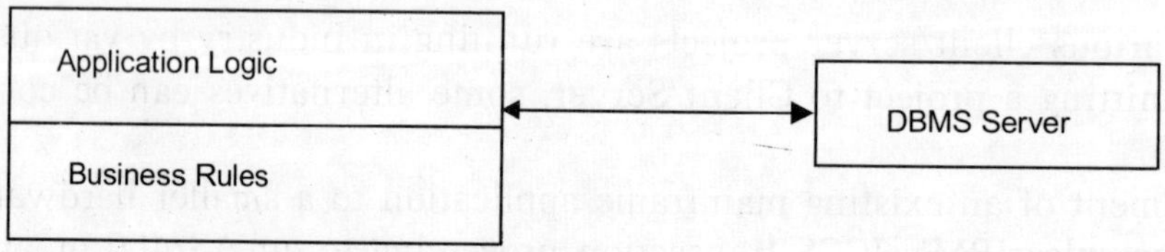

(*c*) Business Rules Residing on the Server:

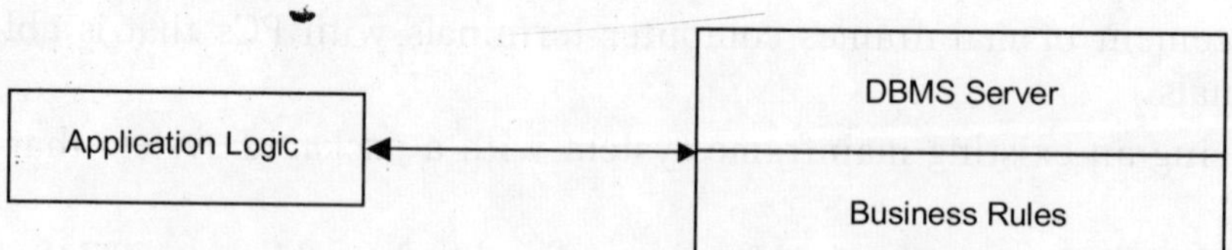

Fig.1.5: The Two-tier Approach Illustrated

The architecture of any client/server environment is by definition at least a two-tier system, the client being the first tier and the server being the second.

The Client requests services directly from server i.e. client communicates directly with the server without the help of another server or server process. The Fig. 1.6 (at the end of this section) illustrates a two-tier Client/Server model.

In a typical two-tier implementation, SQL statements are issued by the application and then handed on by the driver to the database for execution. The results are then sent back via the same mechanism, but in the reverse direction. It is the responsibility of the driver (ODBC) to present the SQL statement to the database in a form that the database understands.

There are several advantages of two-tier systems:

- Availability of well-integrated PC-based tools like, Power Builder, MS Access, 4 GL tools provided by the RDBMS manufacturer, remote SQL, ODBC.
- Tools are relatively inexpensive.
- Least complicated to implement.
- PC-based tools show Rapid Application Development (RAD) i.e., the application can be developed in a comparatively short time.
- The 2-tier Client/Server provides much more attractive graphical user interface (GUI) applications than was possible with earlier technology.

- Architecture maintains a persistent connection between the client and database, thereby eliminating overhead associated with the opening and closing of connections.
- Faster than three-tier implementation.
- Offers a great deal of flexibility and simplicity in management.

Conversely, a two-tier architecture has some disadvantages:

- As the application development is done on client side, maintenance cost of application, as well as client side tools etc. is expensive. That is why in 2-tier architecture the client is called 'fat client'.
- Increased network load: Since actual processing of data takes on the remote client, the data has to be transported over the network. This leads to the increased network stress.
- Applications are loaded on individual PC i.e. each application is bound to an individual PC. For this reason, the application logic cannot be reused.
- Due to dynamic business scenario, business processes/logic have to be changed. These changed processes have to be implemented in all individual PCs. Not only that, the programs have to undergo quality control to check whether all the programs generate the same result or not.
- Software distribution procedure is complicated in 2-tier Client/Server model. As all the application logic is executed on the PCs, all these machine have to be updated in case of a new release. The procedure is complicated, expensive, prone to errors and time consuming.
- PCs are considered to be weak in terms of security i.e., they are relatively easy to crack.
- Most currently available drivers require that native libraries be loaded on a client machine.
- Load configurations must be maintained for native code if required by the driver.
- Problem areas are encountered upon implementing this architecture on the Internet.

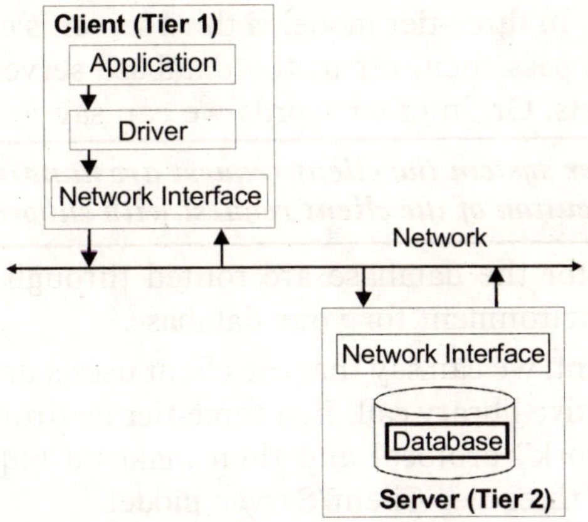

Fig. 1.6: Two-tier Client/Server Model

1.2.2 Three-tier Client/Server Model

Reusability is hard to achieve if pieces of business logic must be distributed across systems and several databases are involved. To avoid embedding the application's logic at both the database side and the client side, a third software tier is inserted in between. In the three-tier architecture, most of the business logic is located in the middle tier (here business logic is encapsulated as a component in a separate tier). In this structure, when the business activity or business rules change, only the middle tier must be modified.

In three-tier architecture application responsibilities are divided into three logical categories (in other words, the business system must provide three types of main services).

- **Presentation (GUI) or user services:** Include maintaining the graphical user interface and generating what users see on the monitor. Presentation Logic dealing with:
  - Screen formatting
  - Windows management
  - Input editing
  - What-if analysis
- **Application services or business rules:** These include executing applications and controlling program flow. Business logic dealing with:
  - Domain and range validation
  - Data dependency validation
  - Request/response architecture of Inter Process Communication level
- **Database services or data server:** Which refers to the management of underlying databases. Server logic deals with:
  - Data access
  - Data management
  - Data security
  - SQL parsing

Based on these three components, the three-tier architecture of Client/Server system is shown in fig. 1.8 below. In three-tier model, a third server is employed to handle requests from the client and then pass them off to the database server. The third server acts as proxy for all client requests. Or, in other words we can say:

"In three-tier client/server system the client request are handled by intermediate servers which coordinate the execution of the client request with subordinate servers."

All client requests for the database are routed through the proxy server, thereby creating a more secure environment for your database.

In two-tier environment, we can say that the client uses a driver to translate the client's request into a database native library call. In a three-tier environment, the driver translates the request into a "network" protocol and then makes a request via the proxy server. Figure 1.8 represents the three-tier Client/Server model.

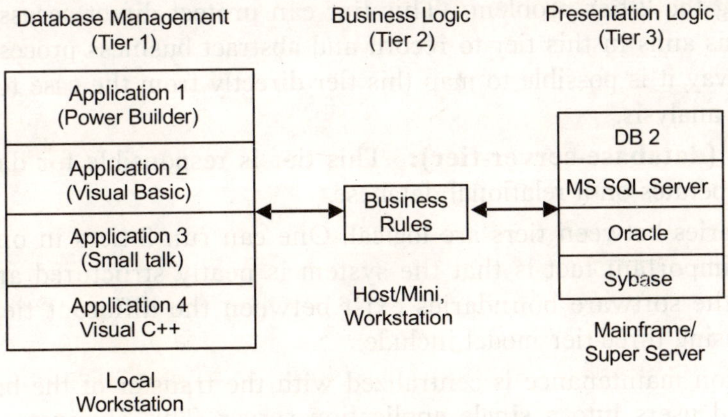

Fig.1.7: Three-tier Architecture

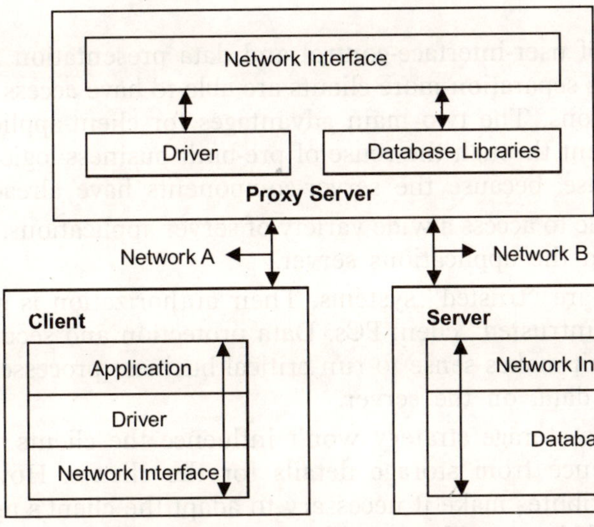

Fig.1.8: Three-tier Client/Server Model

The proxy server makes the database request on behalf of the client and passes the results back after they have been serviced by the database. This approach eliminates the need for DBMS to be located on the same server. There are a couple of drawbacks to this model. One is that it requires that a small server process (listener) be set up on the middle server. Secondly, it requires all your client requests be transmitted into a "network" protocol.

First-tier (client-tier): The main responsibility of this tier is to receive user events and to control the user interface and presentation of data. As most of the software is removed from the client, the client is called "Thin Client". Mainly browser and presentation code resides on this tier.

Second-tier (application-server-tier): The complex application logic is loaded here and available to the client tier on request from client. This level forms the central key towards solving the 2-tier problem. This tier can protect direct access of data. Object oriented analysis aims in this tier to record and abstract business processing in business projects. This way it is possible to map this tier directly from the case tools that support object oriented analysis.

Three-tier (database-server-tier): This tier is responsible for data storage. This server mostly operates on a relational database.

The boundaries between tiers are logical. One can run 3-tiers in one and the same machine. The important fact is that the system is neatly structured and well-planned definitions of the software boundaries exist between the different tiers. Some of the advantages of using three-tier model include:

- Application maintenance is centralized with the transfer of the business logic for many end users into a single application server. This eliminates the concern of software distribution that are problematic in the traditional two-tier Client/Server model.
- Clear separation of user-interface-control and data presentation from application-logic. Through this separation more clients are able to have access to a wide variety of server applications. The two main advantages for client-applications are clear: quicker development through the reuse of pre-built business-logic components and a shorter test phase, because the server-components have already been tested.
- Many users are able to access a wide variety of server applications, as all application logic are loaded in the applications server.
- As a rule servers are "trusted" systems. Their authorization is simpler than that of thousands of "untrusted" client-PCs. Data protection and security is simpler to obtain. Therefore, it makes sense to run critical business processes that work with security sensitive data, on the server.
- Redefinition of the storage strategy won't influence the clients. RDBMS' offer a certain independence from storage details for the clients. However, cases like changing table attributes make it necessary to adapt the client's application. In the future, even radical changes, like switching from an RDBMS to an OODBMS, won't influence the client. In well-designed systems, the client still accesses data over a stable and well-designed interface, which encapsulates all the storage details.
- Load balancing is easier with the separation of the core business logic from the database server.
- Dynamic load balancing: if bottlenecks in terms of performance occur, the server process can be moved to other servers at runtime.
- Business objects and data storage should be brought as close together as possible. Ideally, they should be together physically on the same server. This way network load for complex access can be reduced.
- The need for less expensive hardware because the client is 'thin'.
- Change management is easier and faster to execute. This is because a component/program logic/business logic is implemented on the server rather than furnishing numerous PCs with new program versions.

- The added modularity makes it easier to modify or replace one tier without affecting the other tier.
- Clients do not need to have native libraries loaded locally.
- Drivers can be managed centrally.
- Your database server does not have to be directly visible to the Internet.

An additional advantage is that the three-tier architecture maps quite naturally to the Web environment, with a Web browser acting as the 'thin' client, and a Web server acting as the application server. The three-tier architecture can be easily extended to N-tier, with additional tiers added to provide more flexibility and scalability. For example, the middle tier of the three-tier architecture could be split into two, with one tier for the Web server and another for the application server. Some disadvantages are:

- The client does not maintain a persistent database connection.
- A separate proxy server may be required.
- The network protocol used by the driver may be proprietary.
- You may see increased network traffic if a separate proxy server is used.

1.2.2.1 Transaction Processing Monitors

It is the extension of the two-tier Client/Server architecture that splits the functionality of the 'fat' client into two. In the three-tier Client/Server architecture, the 'thin' client handles the user interface only whereas the middle layer handles the application logic. The third layer is still a database server. This three-tier architecture has proved popular in more environments, such as the Internet and company Intranets where a Web browser can be used as a client. It is also an important architecture for TPM.

A Transaction Processing Monitor is a program that controls data transfer between client and server in order to provide consistent environment, particularly for online transaction processing (OLTP).

Complex applications are often built on top of several resource managers (such as DBMS, operating system, user interface, and messaging software). A Transaction Processing Monitor or TP Monitor is a middleware component that provides access to the services of a number of resource managers and provides a uniform interface for programmers who are developing transactional software. Figure 1.9 illustrates how a TP Monitor forms the middle tier of three-tier architecture. The advantages associated with TP Monitors are as given below:

Transaction Routing: TP monitor can increase scalability by directing transactions to specific DBMS's.

Managing Distributed Transaction: The TP Monitor can manage transactions that require access to data held in multiple, possibly heterogeneous, DBMSs. For example, a transaction may require to update data item held in an oracle DBMS at site 1, an Informix DBMS at site 2, and an IMS DBMS at site 3. TP Monitors normally control transactions using the X/Open Distributed transaction processing (DTP) standards. A DBMS that support this standard can function as a resource manager under the control of a TP Monitor acting as a transaction manager.

Load balancing: The TP Monitor can balance client requests across multiple DBMS's on one or more computers by directing client services calls to the least loaded server. In addition, it can dynamically bring in additional DBMSs as required to provide the necessary performance.

Funneling: In an environment with a large number of users, it may sometimes be difficult for all users to be logged on simultaneously to the DBMS. Instead of each user connecting to the DBMS, the TP Monitor can establish connections with DBMS's as and when required, and can funnel user requests through these connections. This allows a large number of users to access the available DBMSs with a potentially smaller number of connections, which in turn would mean less resource usages.

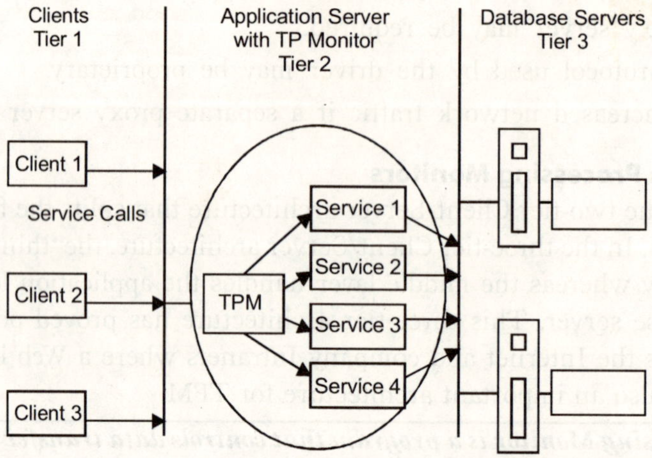

Fig.1.9: Middleware Component of TPM

Increased reliability: The TP Monitor acts as transaction manager, performing the necessary action to maintain the consistency of database, with the DBMS acting as a resource manager. If the DBMS fails, the TP Monitor may be able to resubmit the transaction to another DBMS or can hold the transaction until the DBMS becomes available again.

A TP Monitor is typically used in environments with a very heavy volume of transaction, where the TP Monitor can be used to offload processes from the DBMS server. Prominent examples of TP Monitors include CICS and Encina from IBM (which are primarily used on IBM AIX or Windows NT and bundled now in the IBM TXSeries) and Tuxido from BEA system.

1.2.2.2 Three-tier with Message Server

Messaging is another way to implement the three-tier architecture. Messages are prioritized and processed asynchronously. Messages consist of headers that contain priority information, and the address and identification number. The message server connects to the relational DBMS and other data sources. The difference between the TP monitor technology and the message server is that the message server architecture focuses on intelligent messages, whereas the TP Monitor environment has the intelligence in the monitor, and treats transactions as dumb data packets. Messaging systems are good solutions for wireless infrastructures.

1.2.2.3 Three-tier with an Application Server

The three-tier application server architecture allocates the main body of an application to run on a shared host rather than in the user system interface client environment. The application server does not drive the GUIs; rather it shares business logic, computations, and a data retrieval engine. Advantages are that with less software on the client there is less security to worry about, applications are more scalable, and support and installation costs are less on a single server than maintaining each on a desktop client. The application server design should be used when security, scalability, and cost are major considerations.

1.2.2.4 Three-tier with an ORB Architecture

Currently, work is going on in the industry towards developing standards to improve interoperability and determine what the common Object Request Broker (ORB) will be. Developing client/server systems using technologies that support distributed objects holds great promise, as these technologies support interoperability across languages and platforms, as well as enhancing maintainability and adaptability of the system. There are two-prominent distributed object technologies at present:

- Common Object Request Broker Architecture (CORBA).
- COM/DCOM (Component Object Model/Distributed Component Object Model).

Standards are being developed to improve interoperability between CORBA and COM/DCOM. The Object Management Group (OMG) has developed a mapping between CORBA and COM/DCOM that is supported by several products.

Distributed/collaborative enterprise architecture: The distributed/collaborative enterprise architecture emerged in 1993. This software architecture is based on Object Request Broker (ORB) technology, but goes further than the Common Object Request Broker Architecture (CORBA) by using shared, reusable business models (not just objects) on an enterprise-wide scale. The benefit of this architectural approach is that standardized business object models and distributed object computing are combined to give an organization flexibility to improve effectiveness organizationally, operationally, and technologically. An enterprise is defined here as a system comprised of multiple business systems or subsystems. Distributed/collaborative enterprise architectures are limited by a lack of commercially-available object orientation analysis and design method tools that focus on applications.

1.2.2.5 Three-tier Architecture and Internet

With the rapid development of Internet and web technology, Client/Server applications running over Internets and Intranets are becoming a new type of distributed computing. A typical web application uses the following 3-tier architecture.

- The user interface runs on the desktop as client.
- The client is connected (through one or more immediate server links) to a web server, which may be a storehouse for downloadable applets (Software components).
- This web server is, in turn, is supported by a database server which keeps track of information specific to the client interest and history.

These web applications rely on Internet standards (HTTP, HTML, XML etc.) as well as distributed objects programming languages.

1.2.3 N-tier Client/Server Model

N-tier computing obliges developer to design components according to a business schema that represents entities, relationship, activities roles, and rules, thereby enabling them to distribute functionality across logical and physical tiers, allowing better utilization of hardware and platform resources, as well as sharing of those resources and the components that they support to serve several large applications at the same time.

Another aspect of splitting tiers is that application developers and administrators are able to identify bottlenecks and throw hardware at them to enable load-balancing and fail-over of certain nodes. The splitting may be between application logic components, security logic, and presentation logic, computational-intensive and I/O-intensive components and so on. The most common approach used when designing N-tier system is the three-tier architecture. Three-tier and N-tier notations are similar, although N-tier architecture provides finer-grained layers. Architectures often decide to layout much more than three -tiers to deploy services (An infrastructure that supports three-tier is often made of several machines and services whose functionalities aren't part of the three-tier design).

Figure 1.10 shown below depicts the N-tier architecture.

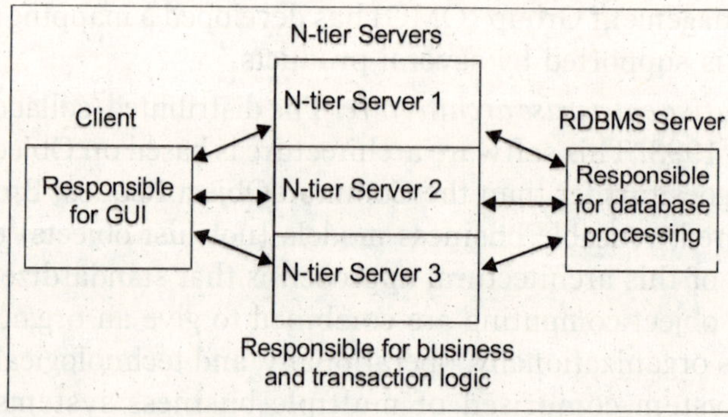

Fig.1.10: N-tier Architecture

N-tier computing provides many advantages over traditional two-tier or single-tier design, which includes the following:

- Overall performance has been improved.
- The business logic is centralized.
- Enhanced security level is attained.

An alternative to N-tier computing includes *fat server/fat client.* A *fat server* locates business logic within the RDBMS on the server. The client issues remote procedure calls to the server to execute the process. Fat servers are the best suited for structured and consistent business logic, such as online transaction processing (OLTP). Modern RDBMS products support fat servers through stored procedures, column rules, triggers, and other methods.

A *fat client* embeds business logic in the application at the client level. Although a fat client is more flexible than a fat server, it increases network traffic. The fat client approach is used when business logic is loosely structured or when it is too complicated to implement at the middle-tier level. Additionally, fat client development tools, such as 4GL languages, sometimes offer more robust programming features than do middle-tier programming tools. Decision support and ad-hoc systems are often fat client based.

1.3 CLIENTS/SERVER—ADVANTAGES AND DISADVANTAGES

1.3.1 Advantages

There are various advantages associated with Client/Server computing model.

(i) **Performance and reduced workload:** Processing is distributed among the client and server unlike the traditional PC database, the speed of DBMS is not tied to the speed of the workstation as the bulk of the database processing is done at the back-end. The workstation only has to be capable of running the front-end software, which extends the usable lifetime of older PC's. This also has the effect of reducing the load on the network that connects the workstation; instead of sending the entire database file back and forth on the wire, the network traffic is reduced to queries to and responses from the database server. Some database servers can even store and run procedures and queries on the server itself, reducing the traffic even more.

(ii) **Workstation independence:** Users are not limited to one type of system or platform. In an ORACLE-based Client/Server system the workstations can be IBM – compatible PCs, Macintoshes, UNIX workstations, or any combinations of the three. In addition, they can run any of a number of operating systems such as MS-DOS, Windows, IBM's OS/2, Apple's System 7 etc. That is, application independence is achieved as the workstations don't all need to use the same DBMS application software. Users can continue to use familiar software to access the database, and developers can design front-ends tailored to the workstation on which the software will run, or to the needs of the users running them.

(iii) **System interoperability:** Client/Server computing not only allows one component to be changed, it also makes it is possible for different type of components systems (client, network or server) to work together.

(*iv*) **Scalability:** The modular nature of the Client/Server system may be replaced without adversely affecting the rest of the system. For example, it is possible to upgrade the server to a more powerful machine with no visible changes to the end user. This ability to change component system makes Client/Server systems especially receptive to new technologies in both hardware and software.

(*v*) **Data integrity:** Client/Server system preserves the data integrity, DBMS can provide number of services that protect data like, encrypted file storage, real time backup (while the database is being accessed), disk mirroring (where the data is automatically written to duplicate database on another partition of same hard disk drive), disk duplexing (where the data is automatically written to a duplicate database on a different hard disk drive), transaction processing that keeps the track changes made to the database and corrects problems in case the server crashes. (Transaction processing is a method by which the DBMS keeps a running log of all the modifications made to the database over a period of time).

(*vi*) **Data accessibility (enhanced data sharing):** Since the server component holds most of data in a centralized location, multiple users can access and work on the data simultaneously.

(*vii*) **System administration (centralized management):** Client/Server environment is very manageable. Since data is centralized, data management can be centralized. Some of the system administration functions are security, data integrity and back up recovery.

(*viii*) **Integrated services:** In Client/Server model all information that the client is entitled to use is available at the desktop, through desktop interface, there is no need to change into a terminal mode or to logon into another processor to access information. The desktop tools – e-mail, spread sheet, presentation graphics, and word processing are available and can be used to deal with the information provided by application and database server's resident on the network. Desktop user can use their desktop tools in conjunction with information made available from the corporate systems to produce new and useful information using the facilities DDE/OLE, Object-oriented design.

(*ix*) **Sharing resources among diverse platforms:** Client/Server model provides opportunities to achieve open system computing. Applications can be created and implemented without much conversance with hardware and software. Thus, users may obtain client services and transparent access to the services provided by database, communications, and application servers. There are two ways for Client/Server application operation:

- They can provide data entry, storage, and reporting by using a distributed set of clients and servers.
- The existence of a mainframe host is totally masked from the workstation developer by the use of standard interface such as SQL.

(*x*) **Masked physical data access:** SQL is used for data access from database stored anywhere in the network, from the local PC, local server or WAN server, support with the developer and user using the same data request. The only noticeable difference may be performance degradation if the network bandwidth is inadequate. Data may be accessed from CD-ROM, HDD, Magnetic disk, and optical disk with same SQL statements. Logical tables can be accessed without any knowledge of the ordering of column. Several tables may be joined to create a new logical table for application program manipulation without regard to its physical storage format.

(*xi*) **Location independence of data processing:** Users log into an application from the desktop with no concern for the location or technology of the processors involved. In the current user centered word, the desktop provides the point of access to the workgroup and enterprise services without regard to the platform of application execution. Standard services such as login, security, navigation, help, and error recovery are provided consistently amongst all applications. Developers today are provided with considerable independence. Data is accessed through SQL without regard to the hardware or OS location providing the data. The developer of business logic deals with a standard process logic syntax without considering the physical platform.

(*xii*) **Reduced operating cost:** Computer hardware and software costs are on a continually downward spiral, which means that computing value is ever increasing. Client/Server computing offers a way to cash in on this bonanza by replacing expensive large systems with less expensive smaller ones networked together.

(*xiii*) **Reduced hardware cost:** Hardware costs may be reduced, as it is only the server that requires storage and processing power sufficient to store and manage the application.

(*xiv*) **Communication costs are reduced:** Applications carry out part of the operations on the client and send only request for database access across the network, resulting in less data being sent across the network.

1.3.2 Disadvantages

There are various disadvantages associated with the Client/Server computing model.

(*i*) **Maintenance cost:** Major disadvantages of Client/Server computing is the increased cost of administrative and support personnel to maintain the database server. In the case of a small network, the network administrator can usually handle the duties of maintaining the database server, controlling the user access to it, and supporting the front-end applications. However, the number of database server users rises, or as the database itself grows in size, it usually becomes necessary to hire a database administrator just to run the DBMS and support the front-ends.

(*ii*) **Training cost:** Training can also add to the start-up costs as the DBMS may run on an operating system that the support personnel are unfamiliar with.

(*iii*) **Hardware cost:** There is also an increase in hardware costs. While many of the Client/Server database run under the common operating systems (Netware, OS/2 and Unix) and most of the vendors claim that the DBMS can run on the same hardware side by side with the file server software. It usually makes sense from the performance and data integrity aspects to have the database server running on its own dedicated machine. This usually means purchasing a high-powered platform with a large amount of RAM and hard disk space.

(*iv*) **Software cost:** The overall cost of the software is usually higher than that of traditional PC based multi-user DBMS.

(*v*) **Complexity:** With so many different parts comprising the entire Client/Server, i.e., the more are the pieces, which comprise the system the more things that can go wrong or fail. It is also harder to pinpoint problems when the worst does occur and the system crashes. It can take longer to get everything set up and working in the first place. This is compounded by the general lack of experience and expertise of potential support personnel and programmers, due to the relative newness of the technology.

Making a change to the structure of database also has a ripple effect throughout the different front-ends. It becomes a longer and more complex process to make the necessary changes to the different front-end applications, and it is also harder to keep all of them in synchronization without seriously disrupting the user's access to the database.

1.4 MISCONCEPTIONS ABOUT CLIENT/SERVER COMPUTING

Client/Server technology can be stated to be an "architecture in which a system's functionality and its processing are divided between the client PC (Front-end) and database server (back-end)." This statement restricts the functionality of Client/Server software to mere retrieval and maintenance of data and creates many misconceptions regarding this technology, such as:

(*i*) Graphical user interface is supposed to be a necessity for presentation of application logic. As in the case of X-Windows graphical user interface, the implementation comprises both client and server components that may run on the same and different physical computers. An X-Windows uses Client/Server as architecture. This however, does not imply that Client/Server must use GUI. Client/Server logic remains independent of its presentation to the user.

(*ii*) Client/Server software is not always database centric. Client/Server computing does not require a database, although in today's computing environment Client/Server is synonymous with databases. RDBMS packages are the most popular Client/Server applications. A major disadvantage of Client/Server technology is that it can be data centric and the developers can exploit these capabilities.

(*iii*) Client/Server technology does not provide code reuse. Tools that help create Client/Server applications may provide this benefit. Client/Server application build on component-based modeling enhanced code reusability.

(*iv*) Client/Server designing is not event-driven. Client/Server technology merges very well with event-driven systems but the latter are not a requirement for Client/Server. Client/Server application designing involves architecture of software that has innate features of portability with respect to communication pattern, and a well-build non-monolithic code with division of functionality and processing into different components.

EXERCISE 1

1. Client server is modular infrastructure, this is intended to improve Usability, Flexibility, Interoperability and Scalability. Explain each with an example, in each case how it helps to improve the functionality of client server architecture.
2. Explain the following.
   (*a*) Computing in client server architecture over Mainframe architecture has certain advantages and disadvantages. Describe atleast two advantages and disadvantages for each architecture.
   (*b*) Client/Server architecture could be explained as 2-tier architecture. Explain.
   (*c*) Explain the working of three-tier architecture with an application server.
   (*d*) How does the client server interaction work? Explain with a sketch.
   (*e*) Describe the server function and client responsibility in this architecture.
3. Differentiate between Stateful and Stateless servers.
4. Describe three-level schema architecture. Why do we need mapping between schema levels?
5. Differentiate between Transaction server and Data server system with example.
6. In client server architecture, what do you mean by Availability, Reliability, Serviceability and Security? Explain with examples.
7. How client/server computing environment is different from mainframe based computing environment?
8. In the online transaction processing environment, discuss how transaction processing monitor controls data transfer between client and server machines.

2

Driving Forces Behind Client/ Server Computing

2.1 INTRODUCTION

A rapidly changing business environment generates a demand for enterprise – wide data access, which, in turn, sets the stage for end user productivity gains. Data access requirements have given rise to an environment in which computers work together to form a system, often called distributed computing, cooperative computing, and the like.

To be competitive in a global economy, organizations in developed economies must employ technology to gain the efficiency necessary to offset their higher labour costs. Re-engineering the business process to provide information and decision-making support at points of customer contact reduces the need for layers of decision-making management, improves responsiveness, and enhance customer service. Empowerment means that knowledge and responsibility are available to the employee at the point of customer contact. Empowerment will ensure that product and services problems and opportunities are identified and centralized. Client/Server computing is the most effective source for the tools that empower employees with authority and responsibility.

However, Client/Server computing has become more practical and cost-effective because of changes in computer technology that allow the use of PC-based platforms with reliability and robustness comparable to those of traditional mainframe system. In fact, the accelerating trend toward system development based on Internet Technologies, particularly those supplied by Web, has extended the Client/Server model's reach and relevance considerably. For example, to remain competitive in a global business environment, businesses are increasingly dependent on the Web to conduct their marketing and service operations. Such Web-based electronic commerce, known as E-commerce, is very likely to become the business norm for businesses of all sizes.

Even a cursory examination of Websites will demonstrate the Web's search. Organizations that range in size from Microsoft, IBM, GM, and Boeing to local arts/craft and flower shops conduct part – or even most – of their business operations via E-commerce. There are various forces that drive the move to client/server computing. Some of them are:

(*i*) The changing business environment.

(*ii*) Globalization: The world as a market.

(*iii*) The growing need for enterprise data access.

(*iv*) The demand for end user productivity gains based on the efficient use of data resources.

(*v*) Technological advances that have made client/server computing practical like microprocessor technology, data communication and Internet, Database systems, Operating Systems and Graphical User Interface, PC-based and end user application software.

(*vi*) Growing cost and performance advantages of PC-based platforms.

(*vii*) Enterprise network management.

2.2 DRIVING FORCES

Forces that drives the move to Client/Server computing widely can be classified in two general categories based on:

(*i*) Business perspective.

(*ii*) Technology perspective.

2.2.1 Business Perspective

Basically the business perspective should be kept in mind for obtaining the following achievements through the system:

- For increased productivity.
- Superior quality.
- Improved responsiveness.
- Focus on core business.

The effective factors that govern the driving forces are given below:

The changing business environment: Business process engineering has become necessary for competitiveness in the market which is forcing organizations to find new ways to manage their business, despite fewer personnel, more outsourcing, a market driven orientation, and rapid product obsolescence.

Due to globalization of business, the organizations have to meet global competitive pressure by streamlining their operations and by providing an ever-expanding array of customer services. Information management has become a critical issue in this competitive environment; marketing fast, efficient, and widespread data access has become the key to survival. The corporate database has become a far more dynamic asset than it used to be, and it must be available at relatively low cost. Unfortunately, the demand for a more accessible database is not well-served by traditional methods and platforms. The dynamic information driven corporate worlds of today require data to be available to decision makers on time and in an appropriate format. Because end users have become active in handling their own basic data management and data analysis, the movement towards freedom of data access has made Client/Server computing almost inevitable.

One might be tempted to urge that microcomputer networks constitute a sufficient answer to the challenge of dynamic data access. Unfortunately, even the use of networks that tie legions of PC's together is an unsatisfactory solution if request processing overloads the network. The Client/Server model's ability to share resources efficiently by splitting data processing yields a more efficient utilization of those resources. It is not surprising that Client/Server computing has received so much attention from such a wide spectrum of interested parties.

Globalization

Conceptually, the world has begun to be treated as a market. Information Technology plays an important role in bringing all the trade on a single platform by eliminating the barriers. IT helps and supports various marketing priorities like quality, cost, product differentiation and services.

The growing need for enterprise data access: One of the major MIS functions is to provide quick and accurate data access for decision- making at many organizational levels. Managers and decision makers need fast on-demand data access through easy-to-use interfaces. When corporations grow, and especially when they grow by merging with other corporations, it is common to find a mixture of disparate data sources in their systems. For example, data may be located in flat files, in hierarchical or network databases or in relational databases. Given such a multiple source data environment, MIS department managers often find it difficult to provide tools for integrating and aggregating data for decision-making purposes, thus limiting the use of data as a company asset. Client server computing makes it possible to mix and match data as well as hardware. In addition, given the rapidly increasing internet-enabled access to external data through the Internet's inherent Client/Server architecture, corporate Client/Server computing makes it relatively easy to mix external and internal data.

The demand for end user productivity gains based on the efficient use of data resources: The growth of personal computers is a direct result of the productivity gains experienced by end-users at all business levels. End user demand for better ad hoc data access and data manipulation, better user interface, and better computer integration helped the PC gain corporate acceptance. With sophisticated yet easy to use PCs and application software, end user focus changed from how to access the data to how to manipulate the data to obtain information that leads to competitive advantages.

2.2.2 Technology Perspective

Technological advances that have made Client/Server computing practical by proper use of the following:

- Intelligent desktop devices.
- Computer network architectures.
- Technical advances like microprocessor technology, data communication and Internet Database system, operating system and graphical user interface.
- Trends in computer usage like:

(*i*) Standardization: Trend towards open systems and adaptation of industry standards, which includes:

* *de facto* standard: protocol or interface that is made public & widely accepted. (e.g., SNA, TCP/IP, VGA)

* *de jure* standard: protocol or interface specified by a formal standards making body. (e.g., ISO's OSI, ANSI C)

(*ii*) Human-Computer Interaction (HCI): trend towards GUI, user Control.

(*iii*) Information dissemination: trend towards data warehousing, data mining.

- PC-based end user application software together with the increasing power and capacity of workstations.
- Growing cost and performance are advantages of PC-based platforms.

The PC platform often offers unbeatable price/performance ratio compared to mainframe and minicomputer platforms. PC application cost, including acquisition, installation, training, and use, are usually lower than those of similar minicomputer and mainframe applications. New PC-based software makes use of very sophisticated technologies, such as object orientation, messaging, and tele-communications. These new technologies make end users more productive by enabling them to perform very sophisticated tasks easily, quickly, and efficiently. The growing software sophistication even makes it possible to migrate many mission-critical applications to PCs.

The pursuit of mainframe solutions typically means high acquisition and maintenance costs, and chances are that managers are locked into services provided by single source. In contrast, PC hardware and software costs have both declined sharply during the past few years. PC-based solutions typically are provided by many sources, thus limiting single-source vulnerability. However, multi-source solutions can also become a major management headache when system problems occur.

Enterprise Computing and the Network Management

If a business is run from its distributed locations, the technology supporting these units must be as reliable as the existing central systems. Technology for remote management of the distributed technology is essential in order to use scarce expertise appropriately and to reduce costs.

All computing and communications resources are integrated functionally as a single, seamless system. To maximize productivity by providing universal, up-to-date information the technology requirements are that computing technology must be widely deployed. All computers must be networked together in a consistent architecture such that computing and networking resources must be reliable, secure, and capable of delivering accurate information in a timely manner. Maximum capture of information relating to the business and its customers must occur within every business process. That information must be normalized, within reach of all users. To achieve that, mechanics employed to locate, access the data and also for hiding the transmit data. And all the applications must be flexible to user preferences and work styles i.e., applications must interwork with in a common framework.

Client/server technology gives cost-effective, logical, and consistent architectural model for networking that generalizes the typical computer model. Client/Server can simplify network interactions that will give transparent interaction to the users. See the Fig. 2.1 illustrated below:

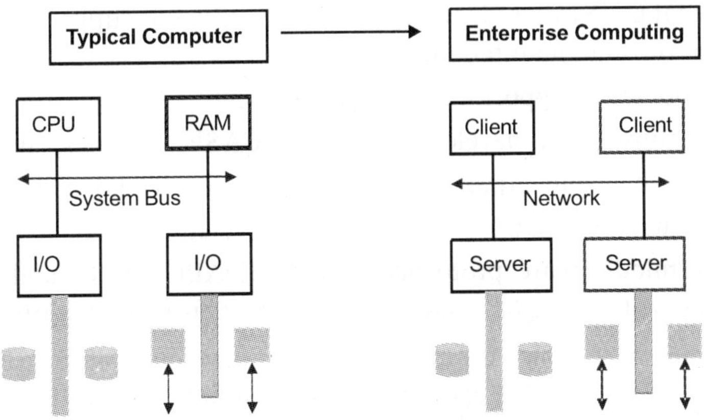

Fig. 2.1: Enterprise Computing

2.3 DEVELOPMENT OF CLIENT/SERVER SYSTEMS

The development of Client/Server systems differs greatly in process and style from the traditional information systems development methods. For example, the systems development approach, oriented towards the centralized mainframe environment and based on traditional programming language, can hardly be expected to function well in a client server environment that is based on hardware and software diversity. In addition a modern end users are more demanding and are likely to know more about computer technology than users did before the PC made its inroads. Then the concerning manager should pertain their knowledge about new technologies that are based on multiple platforms, multiple GUIs, multiple network protocols, and so on.

2.3.1 Development Tools

In today's rapid changing environment, choosing the right tools to develop Client/Server applications is one of the most critical decisions. As a rule of thumb, managers tend to choose a tool that has a long-term survival potential. However, the selection of a design or application development tool must also be driven by system development requirements. Once such requirements have been delineated, it is appropriate to determine the characteristics of the tool that you would like to have. Client/Server tools include:

- GUI-based development.
- A GUI builder that supports multiple interfaces (Windows, OS/2, Motif, Macintosh, and so on).
- Object-oriented development with a central repository for data and applications.
- Support for multiple database (flat file, hierarchical, networked, relational).
- Data access regardless of data model (using SQL or native navigational access).
- Seamless access to multiple databases.
- Complete SDLC (System Development Life Cycle) support from planning to implementation and maintenance.
- Team development support.
- Support for third party development tools (CASE, libraries, and so on)
- Prototyping and Rapid Application Development (RAD) capabilities.
- Support for multiple platforms (OS, Hardware, and GUIs).
- Support for middle ware protocols (ODBC, IDAPI, APPC, and so on).
- Multiple network protocol support (TCP/IP, IXP/SPX, NetBIOS, and so on).

There is no single best choice for any application development tool. For one thing, not all tools will support all the GUI's, operating system, middleware, and databases. Managers must choose a tool that fits the application development requirements and that matches the available human resources, as well as the hardware infrastructure. Chances are that the system will require multiple tools to make sure that all or most of the requirements are met. Selecting the development tools is just one step. Making sure that the system meets its objectives at the client, server, and network level is another issue.

2.3.2 Development Phases

It is important that a marketing plan be developed before actually starting the design and development efforts. The objective of this plan is to build and obtain end user and managerial support for the future Client/Server environment. Although there is no single recipe for this process, the overall idea is to conceptualize Client/Server system in terms of their scope, optimization of resources and managerial benefits. In short, the plan requires an integrated effort across all the departments within an organization. There are six main phases in Client/Server system development.

(*i*) Information System Infrastructure Self-study

The objective is to determine the actual state of the available computer resources. The self-study will generate atleast the following.

- A software and hardware inventory.
- A detailed and descriptive list of critical applications.
- A detailed human resource (personal and skills) inventory.
- A detailed list of problems and opportunities.

(*ii*) Client/Server Infrastructure Definition

The output of Phase One, combined with the company's computer infrastructure goal, is the input for the design of the basic Client/Server infrastructure blueprint. This blue print will address the main hardware and software issues for the client, server, and networking platforms.

(*iii*) Selecting a Window of Opportunity

The next stage is to find the right system on which to base the Client/Server pilot project. After identifying the pilot project, we need to define it very carefully by concentrating on the problem, available resources, and set of ciearly defined and realistic goals. The project is described in business terms rather than technological jargon. When defining the system, we must make sure to plan for cost carefully. We should try to balance the cost carefully with the effective benefits of the system. We should also make sure to select a pilot implementation that provides immediate and tangible benefits. For example, a system that takes two years to develop and another three to generate tangible benefits is not acceptable.

(*iv*) Management Commitment

Top to bottom commitment is essential when we are dealing with the introduction of new technologies that affect the entire organization. We also need managerial commitment to ensure that the necessary resources (people, hardware, software, money, infrastructure) will be available and dedicated to the system. A common practice is to designate a person to work as a guide, or an agent of change, within the organization's departments. The main role of this person is to ease the process that changes people's role within the organization.

(*v*) Implementation

Guidelines to implementation should atleast include:

- Use "open" tools or standard-based tools.
- Foster continuing education in hardware, software, tools, and development principles.
- Look for vendors and consultants to provide specific training and implementation of designs, hardware, application software.

(*vi*) Review and Evaluation

We should make sure that the system conforms to the criteria defined in Phase Three. We should continuously measure system performance as the system load increases, because typical Client/Server solutions tend to increase the network traffic and slow down the network. Careful network performance modelling is required to ensure that the system performs well under heavy end user demand conditions. Such performance modeling should be done at the server end, the client end, and the network layer.

2.4 CLIENT/SERVER STANDARDS

Standards assure that dissimilar computers, networks, and applications scan interact to form a system. But what constitutes standards? A standard is a publicly defined method to accomplish specific tasks or purposes within a given discipline and technology. Standards make networks practical.

Open systems and Client-Server computing are often used as if they were synonymous. It does not make long-term sense for users to adopt a Client/Server environment that is not based on standards. There are currently very few Client/Server technologies based on standards at every level. Proprietary Client/Server technologies (applications, middleware etc.) will always lock you into a particular supplier. The existing costs are always high. Failure to appreciate the spectrum of technologies within the Client-Server model, will always lead to dysfunctional Client/Server solutions. This will result in compromises in key areas of any company's Client/Server infrastructure, such as Usability, Security, and Performance.

There are quite a few organizations whose members work to establish the standards that govern specific activities. For example, the Institute of Electrical and Electronics Engineers (IEEE) are dedicated to define the standards in the network hardware environment. Similarly, the American National Standards Institute (ANSI) has created standards for programming languages such as COBOL and SQL. The International Organization for Standardization (ISO) produces the Open System Interconnection (OSI) reference model to achieve network systems communications compatibility.

Benefits of Open Standards

- Standards allow us to incorporate new products and technology with existing I.T. investments — hardware, operating environments, and training, with minimum effort.
- Standards allow us to mix and match the 'best of breed' products. Thus databases and development tools, and Connectivity software become totally independent.
- Standards allow us to develop modular applications that do not fall apart because the network has been re-configured (e.g., change of topology, or transport protocol etc.), or the graphical user interface standard as changed, or a component-operating environment has changed.
- Standards maintain tighter security.
- Standards reduce the burden of overall maintenance and system administration.
- Standards provide faster execution of pre-compiled code.
- Standards prevent the database and its application and possibly others on the server from having their response time degraded in a production environment by inefficient queries.

2.5 CLIENT/SERVER SECURITY

A security threat is defined as circumstance, condition, or event with the potential to cause economic hardship to data or network resources in the form of destruction. Disclosure, modification of data, denial of service, and/or fraud, waist and abuse. Client/ Server security issues deal with various authorization methods related to access control. Such mechanisms include password protection, encrypted smart cards. Biometrics and firewalls. Client/Server security problems can be due to following:

- **Physical security holes:** These results when any individual gains unauthorized access to a computer by getting some user's password.
- **Software security holes:** These result due to some bug in the software, due to which the system may be compromised into giving wrong performance.
- **Inconsistent usage holes:** These may result when two different usages of a systems contradict over a security point.

Of the above three, software security holes and inconsistent usage holes can be eliminated by careful design and implementation. For the physical security holes, we can employ various protection methods. These security methods can be classified into following categories:

(*i*) Trust-based security.

(*ii*) Security through obscurity.

(*iii*) Password scheme.

(*iv*) Biometric system.

2.5.1 Emerging Client/Server Security Threats

We can identify emerging Client/Server security threats as:

(*i*) Threats to local computing environment from mobile code,

(*ii*) Threats to servers that include impersonation, eavesdropping, denial of service, packet reply, and packet modification.

Software Agents and the Malicious Code Threat

Software agents or mobile code are executable programs that have ability to move from machine to machine and also to invoke itself without external influence. Client threats mostly arise from malicious data or code. Malicious codes refers to viruses, worms (a self-replicating program that is self-contained and does not require a host program. The program creates a copy of itself and causes it to execute without any user intervention, commonly utilizing network services to propagate to other host systems.) e.g., Trojan horse, logic bomb, and other deviant software programs. Virus is a code segment that replicates by attaching copies of itself to existing executables. The new copy of the virus is executed when a user executes the host programs. The virus may get activated upon the fulfilment of some specific conditions.

The protection method is to scan for malicious data and program fragments that are transferred from the server to the client, and filter out data and programs known to be dangerous.

2.5.2 Threats to Server

Threats to server may be of the following types:

(*i*) Eavesdropping is the activity of silently listening to the data sent over the network. This often allows a hacker to make complete transcript of network activity and thus obtain sensitive information, such as password, data, and procedures for performing functions. Encryption can prevent eavesdroppers from obtaining data traveling over unsecured networks.

(*ii*) Denial of service is a situation, where a user renders the system unusable for legitimate users by hogging or damaging a resource so that it can be used. The common forms of this, are:

- **Service overloading:** A server may be rendered useless by sending it a large amount of illegitimate service requests so as to consume up its CPU cycle resource. In such a situation, the server may deny the service request of legitimate requests.
- **Message flooding:** It is a process of increasing the number of receiving processes running over the disk of the server by sending large files repeatedly after short intervals. This may cause disk crash.
- **Packet replay** refers to the recording and retransmission of message packets in the network. Medium tapping can do this. A checker may gain access to a secure system by recording and later replaying a legitimate authentication sequence message. Packet reply can also be used to distort the original message. Using a method like packet time stamping and sequence counting can prevent this problem.

2.6 ORGANIZATIONAL EXPECTATIONS

As we have already discussed the advantages and disadvantages associated with Client/Server computing, from the organizational point of view the managers are looking for the following Client/Server benefits.

- Flexibility and adaptability.
- Improved employee productivity.
- Improved company work flow and a way to re-engineering business operations.
- New opportunities to provide competitive advantages.
- Increased customer service satisfaction.

Flexibility and Adaptability

Client/Server computing is expected to provide necessary organizational flexibility to adapt quickly and efficiently in changing business conditions. Such changes can be driven by technological advantages; government regulations, mergers and acquisitions, market forces and so on. A company that can adapt quickly to changes in its market conditions is more likely to survive than one that cannot.

Multinational companies, whose widely dispersed offices must share information across often-disparate computer platforms, are especially well-positioned to benefit from the flexibility and adaptability offered by the Client/Server infrastructure.

Improved Employee Productivity

Client/Server computing opens the door to previously unavailable corporate data. End users can manipulate and analyze such data on an ad hoc basis by means of the hardware and the software tools that are commonly available with client server environments. Quick and reliable information access enables end users to make intelligent decisions. Consequently, end users are more likely to perform their jobs better, provide better services, and become more productive within the corporation.

Improved Company Work Flow and a Way to Re-engineering Business Operations

Organizations that face problems with their internal data management typically favour the introduction of Client/Server computing. Providing data access is just the first step in information management. Providing the right data to the right people at the right time is the core of decision support for MIS departments. As competitive conditions change, so do the companies' internal structure, thus triggering demands for information systems that reflect those changes. Client/Server tools such as Lotus Notes are designed exclusively to provide corporations with data and forms distribution, and work group support, without regard to geographical boundaries. These workgroup tools are used to route the forms and data to the appropriate end users and coordinate employee work. The existence and effective use of such tools allows companies to re-engineer their operational processes, effectively changing the way they do the business.

New Opportunities to Provide Competitive Advantages

New strategic opportunities are likely to be identified as organizations restructure. By making use of such opportunities, organizations enhance their ability to compete by increasing market share through the provision of unique products or services. Proper information management is crucial within such a dynamic competitive arena. Therefore, improved information management provided by a Client/Server system means that such systems could become effective corporate strategic weapons.

Increased Customer Service Satisfaction

As new and better services are provided, customer satisfaction is likely to improve. Client/Server systems enable the corporate MIS manager to locate data closer to the source of data demand, thus increasing the efficiency with which customer enquiries are handled.

2.7 IMPROVING PERFORMANCE OF CLIENT/SERVER APPLICATIONS

Client/Server-developed applications may achieve substantially greater performance when compared with traditional workstations or host-only applications.

(i) **Offload work to server:** Database and communications processing are frequently offloaded to a faster server processor. Some applications processing also may be offloaded, particularly for a complex process, which is required by many users. The advantage of offloading is realized when the processing power of the server is significantly greater than that of the client workstation. Separate processors best support shared databases or specialized communications interfaces. Thus, the client workstation is available to handle other client tasks. These advantages are best realized when the client workstation supports multitasking or atleast easy and rapid task switching.

(ii) **Reduce total execution time:** The server can perform database searches, extensive calculations, and stored procedure execution in parallel while the client workstation deals directly with the current user needs. Several servers can be used together, each performing a specific function. Servers may be multiprocessors with shared memory, which enables programs to overlap the LAN functions and database search functions. In general, the increased power of the server enables it to perform its functions faster than the client workstation. In order for this approach to reduce the total elapsed time, the additional time required to transmit the request over the network to the server must be less than the saving. High-speed local area network topologies operating at 4, 10, 16, or 100Mbps (megabits per second) provide high-speed communications to manage the extra traffic in less time than the savings realized from the server. The time to transmit the request to the server, execute the request, and transmit the result to the requestor, must be less than the time to perform the entire transaction on the client workstation.

(iii) **Use a multitasking client:** As workstation users become more sophisticated, the capability to be simultaneously involved in multiple processes becomes attractive. Independent tasks can be activated to manage communications processes, such as electronic mail, electronic feeds from news media and the stock exchange, and remote data collection (downloading from remote servers). Personal productivity applications, such as word processors, spreadsheets, and presentation graphics, can be active. Several of these applications can be dynamically linked together to provide the desktop information-processing environment. Functions such as Dynamic Data Exchange (DDE) and Object Linking and Embedding (OLE) permit including spreadsheets dynamically into word-processed documents. These links can be *hot* so that changes in the spreadsheet cause the word-processed document to be updated, or they can be *cut and paste* so that the current status of the spreadsheet is copied into the word-processed document.

Systems developers appreciate the capability to create, compile, link, and test programs in parallel. The complexity introduced by the integrated CASE environment requires multiple processes to be simultaneously active so the workstation need not be dedicated to a single long-running function. Effective use of modern CASE tools and workstation development products requires a client workstation that supports multitasking.

2.8 SINGLE SYSTEM IMAGE

Rapid changes have occurred in computer technology resulting in system of increased capabilities. This indicates that maximum resources are available to accepts all these new products. For the organizations using Client/Server systems the environment is heterogeneous whereas the users prime concern to achieve the maximum functionality. Every Client/Server system should give equal importance to the developers' and users' requirements. For the users, this means the realization of a single-system-image. "A single-system-image is the illusion, created by software or hardware, that presents a collection of resources as one, more powerful resource." SSI makes the system appear like a single machine to the user, to applications, and to the network. With it all network resources present themselves to every user in the same way from every workstation (See the Fig. 2.2, given below) and can be used transparently after the user has authorized himself/ herself once. The user environment with a desktop and often-used tools, such as editors and mailer, is also organized in a uniform way. The workstation on the desk appears to provide all these services. In such an environment the user need not to bother about how the processors (both the client and the server) are working, where the data storage take place and which networking scheme has been selected to build the system.

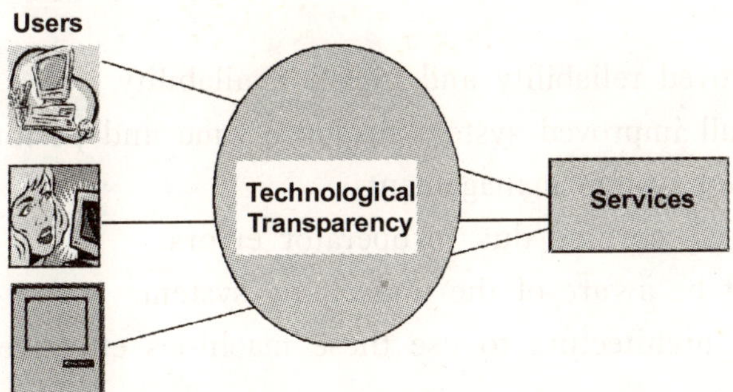

Fig.2.2: Single Image System

Further desired services in *single-system-image* environment are:

- Single File Hierarchy; for example: xFS, AFS, Solaris MC Proxy.
- Single Control Point: Management from single GUI and access to every resource is provided to each user as per their valid requirements.

- Single virtual networking.
- Single memory space e.g. Network RAM/DSM.
- Single Job Management e.g. Glunix, Codine, LSF.
- Single User Interface: Like workstation/PC windowing environment (CDE in Solaris/NT), Web technology can also be used.
- Standard security procedure: Access to every application is provided through a standard security procedure by maintaining a security layer.
- Every application helps in the same way to represent the errors and also to resolve them.
- Standard functions work in the same way so new applications can be added with minimal training. Emphasis is given on only new business functions.

Hence, *single-system-image* is the only way to achieve acceptable technological transparency.

> *"A single-system-image of all the organization's data and easy management of change" are the promises of client/server computing.*

But as more companies follow the trend towards downsized Client/Server networks, some find the promise elusive. Security, scalability and administration costs are three of the key issues. For example, the simple addition of a new user can require the definition to be added to every server in the network. Some of the visible benefits due to *single-system-image* are as given below:

- Increase the utilization of system resources transparently.
- Facilitates process migration across workstations transparently along with load balancing.
- Provides improved reliability and higher availability.
- Provides overall improved system response time and performance.
- Gives simplified system management.
- Reduces the risk covered due to operator errors.
- User need not be aware of the underlying system.
- Provides such architecture to use these machines effectively.

2.9 DOWNSIZING AND RIGHTSIZING

Downsizing: The downward migrations of business applications are often from mainframes to PCs due to low costing of workstation. And also today's workstations are as powerful as last decade's mainframes. The result of that is Clients having power at the cost of less money, provides better performance and then system offers flexibility to make other purchase or to increase overall benefits.

Rightsizing: Moves the Client/Server applications to the most appropriate server platform, in that case the servers from different vendors can co-exist and the network is known as the 'system'. Getting the data from the system no longer refers to a single mainframe. As a matter of fact, we probably don't know where the server physically resides.

Upsizing: The bottom-up trend of networking all the stand alone PCs and workstations at the department or work group level. Early LANs were implemented to share hardware (printers, scanners, etc.). But now LANs are being implemented to share data and applications in addition to hardware.

Mainframes are being replaced by lesser expensive PC's on networks. This is called computer downsizing. Companies implementing business process reengineering are downsizing organizationally. This is called business downsizing. All this would result in hundreds of smaller systems, all communicating to each other and serving the need of local teams as well as individuals working in an organization. This is called cultural downsizing. The net result is distributed computer systems that support decentralized decision-making. This is the client/server revolution of the nineties.

2.10 CLIENT/SERVER METHODOLOGY

Many PC-based developers, particularly those who never knew of any other type of computer, believe that today's methodologies are not only wrong, but also unnecessary. They believe that prototyping based on rapid application development tools make methodologies completely unnecessary. Is this true? If yes, should the methodologies be thrown away? The answer to all these questions depends on the scale and complexity of the application being developed. Small applications that run on a single desktop can be built within hours. The use of methodology in such cases can be waste of time.

However, bigger systems are qualitatively different, especially in term of their design process. Whenever, a system, particularly one involving a database, expands to include more than one server, with servers being located in more than one geographical location, complexity is bound to go up. Distributed systems cross this complexity barrier rapidly. We can say.

- Methodologies are important, and will continue to remain so for the construction of large applications.
- Distributed systems will need these methodologies most of all.
- Today's methodologies will have to change to meet the needs of a new generation of developers and users, accommodate the design of distributed systems, and yield friendly, maintainable systems.

EXERCISE 2

1. Explain various Clients/Server system development tools.
2. Write short notes on the following.
   (*a*) Single system image.
   (*b*) Downsizing and Client/Server computing.
3. Explain Client/Server System development methodology and explain various phases and their activities involved in System Integration Life Cycle (SILC).
4. Explain the following in detail:-
   (*a*) Performance evaluation of Client/Server Application.
   (*b*) Reliability and Serviceability of Client/Server Architecture.
5. Differentiate between Downsizing and Client/Server Computing.
6. Explain different ways to improve performance in Client/Server developed applications.
7. What is client server system development methodology? Explain different phases of System Integration Life-Cycle.
8. How are software's distributed in client server model? In the client server environment, what are performance- monitoring tools for different operating system?
9. What are the various ways to reduce network traffic of client server computing?

3

Architectures of Client/Server Systems

3.1 INTRODUCTION

The term Client/Server was first used in the 1980s in reference to personal computers (PCs) on a network. The actual Client/Server model started gaining acceptance in the late 1980s. The term Client/Server is in reality a logical concept. The client and server components may not exist on distinct physical hardware. A single machine can be both a client and a server depending on the software configuration. The Client/Server technology is a model, for the interaction between simultaneously executing software processes. The term architecture refers to the logical structure and functional characteristics of a system, including the way they interact with each other in terms of computer hardware, software and the links between them.

In case of Client/Server systems, the architecture means the way clients and servers along with the requisite software are configured with each others. Client/Server architecture is based on the hardware and the software components that interact to form a system. The limitations of file sharing architectures led to the emergence of the Client/Server architecture. This approach introduced a database server to replace the file server. Using a Relational Database Management System (RDBMS), user queries could be answered directly. The Client/Server architecture reduced network traffic by providing a query response rather than total file transfer. It improves multi-user updating through a GUI front-end to a shared database. In Client/Server architectures, Remote Procedure Calls (RPCs) or Structural Query Language (SQL) statements are typically used to communicate between the client and server.

> ***File sharing architecture (not a Client/Server architecture):***
>
> *File based database (flat-file database are very efficient to extracting information from large data files. Each workstation on the network has access to a central file server where the data is stored.*

The data files can also reside on the workstation with the client application. Multiple workstations will access the same file server where the data is stored. The file server is centrally located so that it can be reached easily and efficiently by all workstations.

The original PC networks were based on file sharing architectures, where the server downloads files form the shared location to the desktop environment. The requested user job is then run (including logic and data) in the desktop environment.

File sharing architectures work if shared usage is low, update contention is low, and the volume of data to be transferred is low. In the 1990s, PC LAN (Local Area Network) computing changed because the capacity of file sharing was strained as the number of online users grew (it can only satisfy about 12 users simultaneously) and Graphical User Interfaces (GUIs)became popular (making mainframe and terminal displays appear out of data). PCs are now being used in Client/ Server architectures.

Mainframe architecture (not a Client/Server architecture)

With mainframe software architectures all intelligence is within the central host computer. Users interact with the host through a terminal that captures keystrokes and sends that information to the host. Mainframe software architectures are not tied to a hardware platform. User interaction can be done using PCs and UNIX workstations. A limitation of mainframe software architectures is that they do not easily support graphical user interfaces or access to multiple databases from geographically dispersed sites. In the last few years, mainframes have found a new use as a server in distributed Client/Server architectures.

The Client/Server software architecture is a versatile, message-based and modular infrastructure that is intended to improve usability, flexibility, interoperability, and scalability as compared to centralized, mainframe, time sharing computing.

3.2 COMPONENTS

Client/Server architecture is based on hardware and software components that interact to form a system. The system includes mainly three components.

(*i*) Hardware (client and server).

(*ii*) Software (which make hardware operational).

(*iii*) Communication middleware. (associated with a network which are used to link the hardware and software).

The client is any computer **process** that requests services from server. The client uses the services provided by one or more server processors. The client is also known as the **front-end application**, reflecting that the end user usually interacts with the client process.

The server is any computer **process** providing the services to the client and also supports multiple and simultaneous clients requests. The server is also known as **back-end application**, reflecting the fact that the server process provides the background services for the client process.

The communication middleware is any computer **process through** which client and server communicate. Middleware is used to integrate application programs and other software components in a distributed environment. Also known as **communication layer**. Communication layer is made up of several layers of software that aids the transmission of data and control information between Client and Server. Communication middleware is usually associated with a network. The Fig. 3.1 below gives a general structure of Client/ Server System.

Now as the definition reveals, clients are treated as the front-end application and the server as the back-end application, the Fig. 3.2 given below shows the front-end and back-end functionality.

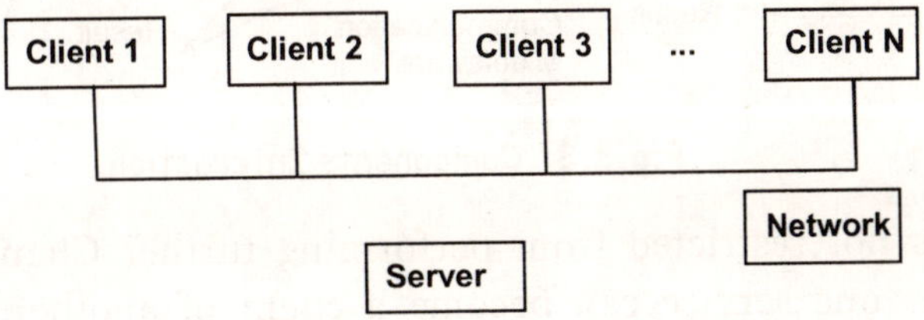

Fig.3.1: Structure of a Client/Server System

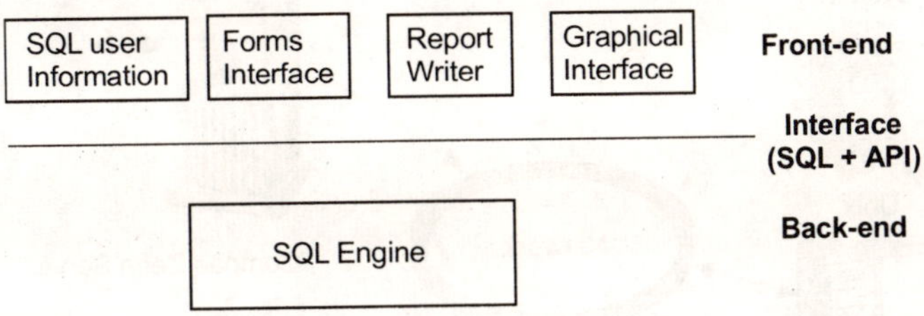

Fig.3.2: Front-end and Back-end Functionality

3.2.1 Interaction between the Components

The interaction mechanism between the components of Client/Server architecture is clear from the Fig. 3.3. The client process is providing the interface to the end users. Communication middleware is providing all the possible support for the communication taking place between the client and server processes. Communication middleware ensures that the messages between clients and servers are properly routed and delivered. Requests are handled by the database server, which checks the validity of the request, executes them, and send the result back to the clients.

3.2.2 Complex Client/Server Interactions

The better understanding about the functionality of Client/Server is observed when the clients and server interact with each other. Some noticeable facts are:

- A client application is not restricted to accessing a single service. The client contacts a different server (perhaps on a different computer) for each service.
- A client application is not restricted to accessing a single server for a given service.

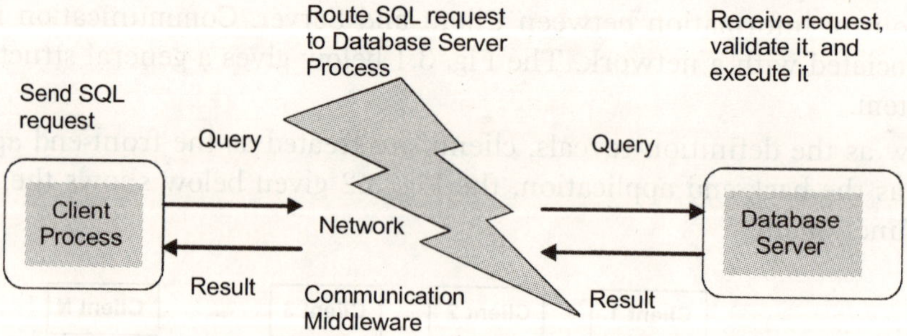

Fig.3.3: *Components Interaction*

- A server is not restricted from performing further Client/Server interactions — a server for one service can become a client of another.

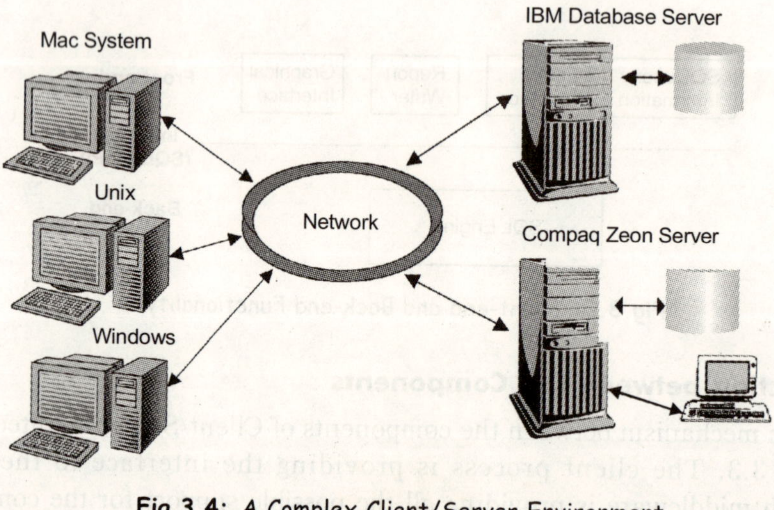

Fig.3.4: *A Complex Client/Server Environment*

Generally, the client and server processes reside on different computers. The Fig. 3.4 illustrates a Client/Server system with more than one server and several clients. The system comprises of the Back-end, Front-end Processes and Middleware.

Back-end processes as: IBM Database server process and Compaq Zeon Server

Front-end as: Application client processes (Windows, Unix and Mac Systems)

Middleware as: Communication middleware (network and supporting software)

The client process runs under different Operating Systems (Windows, Unix and Mac System), server process (IBM and Compaq computers) runs under different operating system

(OS/2 and Unix). The communication middleware acts as the integrating platform for all the different components. The communication can take place between client to client and as well as server to server.

3.3 PRINCIPLES BEHIND CLIENT/SERVER SYSTEMS

The components of the Client/Server architecture must conform to some basic principles, if they are to interact properly. These principles must be uniformly applicable to client, server, and to communication middleware components. Generally, these principles generating the Client/Server architecture constitute the foundation on which most current-generation Client/Server system are built. Some of the main principles are as follows:

(*i*) Hardware independence.
(*ii*) Software independence.
(*iii*) Open access to services.
(*iv*) Process distribution.
(*v*) Standards.

(*i*) Hardware independence: The principles of hardware independence requires that the Client, Server, and communication middleware, processes run on multiple hardware platforms (IBM, DEC, Compaq, Apple, and so on) without any functional differences.

(*ii*) Software independence: The principles of software independence requires that the Client, Server, and communication middleware processes support multiple operating systems (such as Windows 98, Windows NT, Apple Mac system, OS/2, Linux, and Unix) multiple network protocols (such as IPX, and TCP/IP), and multiple application (spreadsheet, database electronic mail and so on).

(*iii*) Open access to services: All client in the system must have open (unrestricted) access to all the services provided within the network, and these services must not be dependent on the location of the client or the server. A key issue is that the services should be provided on demand to the client. In fact, the provision of on-demand service is one of the main objectives of Client/Server computing model.

(*iv*) Process distribution: A primary identifying characteristic of Client/Server system is that the processing of information is distributed among Clients and Servers. The division of the application-processing load must conform to the following rules:

- Client and server processes must be autonomous entities with clearly defined boundaries and functions. This property enables us to clearly define the functionality of each side, and it enhances the modularity and flexibility of the system.
- Local utilization of resources (at both client and server sides) must be maximized. The client and server process must fully utilize the processing power of the host computers. This property enables the system to assign functionality to the

computer best suited to the task. In other words, to best utilize all resources, the server process must be shared among all client processes; that is, a server process should service multiple requests from multiple clients.

- Scalability and flexibility requires that the client and server process be easily upgradeable to run on more powerful hardware and software platforms. This property extends the functionality of Client/Server processes when they are called upon to provide the additional capabilities or better performance.
- Interoperability and integration requires that client and server processes be seamlessly integrated to form a system. Swapping a server process must be transparent the client process.

(*v*) **Standards:** Now, finally all the principles that are formulated must be based on standards applied within the Client/Server architecture. For example, standard must govern the user interface, data access, network protocols, interprocess communications and so on. Standards ensure that all components interact in an orderly manner to achieve the desired results. There is no universal standard for all the components. The fact is that there are many different standards from which to choose. For example, an application can be based on Open Database Connectivity (ODBC) instead of Integrated Database Application Programming Interface (IDAPI) for Data access (ODBC and IDAPI are database middleware components that enables the system to provide a data access standard for multiple processes.) Or the application might use Internet work Packet Exchange (IPX) instead of Transmission Control Protocol/Internet Protocol (TCP/IP) as the network protocol. The fact that the application does not use single standards does not mean that it will be a Client/Server application. The point is to ensure that all components (server, clients, and communication middleware) are able to interact as long as they use the same standards. What really defines Client/Server computing is that the splitting of the application processing is independent of the network protocols used.

3.4 CLIENT COMPONENTS

As we know, the client is any process that requests services from the server process. The client is proactive and will, therefore, always initiate the conversation with the server. The client includes the software and hardware components. The desirable client software and hardware feature are:

(*i*) Powerful hardware.
(*ii*) An operating system capable of multitasking.
(*iii*) Communication capabilities.
(*iv*) A graphical user interface (GUI).

(*i*) **Powerful hardware:** Because client processes typically requires a lot of hardware resources, they should be stationed on a computer with sufficient computing power, such as fast Pentium II, III, or RISC workstations. Such processing power facilitates the creation of systems with multimedia capabilities. A Multimedia system handles multiple data types, such as voice, image, video, and so on. Client processes also require large amount of hard disk space and physical memory, the more such a resource is available, the better.

(ii) **An operating system capable of multitasking:** The client should have access to an operating system with at least some multitasking capabilities. Microsoft Windows 98 and XP are currently the most common client platforms. Windows 98 and XP provide access to memory, pre-emptive multitasking capabilities, and a graphical user interface, which makes windows the platform of choice in a majority of Client/Server implementations. However, Windows NT, Windows 2000 server, OS/2 from IBM corporation, and the many "flavours" of UNIX, including Linux are well-suited to handle the Client/Server processing that is largely done at the server side of the Client/Server equation.

(iii) **Communication capabilities:** To interact efficiently in a Client/Server environment, the client computer must be able to connect and communicate with the other components in a network environment. Therefore, the combination of hardware and operating system must also provide adequate connectivity to multiple network operating systems. The reason for requiring a client computer to be capable of connecting and accessing multiple network operating systems is simple services may be located in different networks.

(iv) **A graphical user interface (GUI):** The client application, or front-end, runs on top of the operating system and connects with the communication middleware to access services available in the network. Several third generation programming languages (3GLs) and fourth generation languages (4GLs) can be used to create the front-end application. Most front-end applications are GUI-based to hide the complexity of the Client/Server components from the end user. The Fig. 3.5 given below illustrates the basic client components.

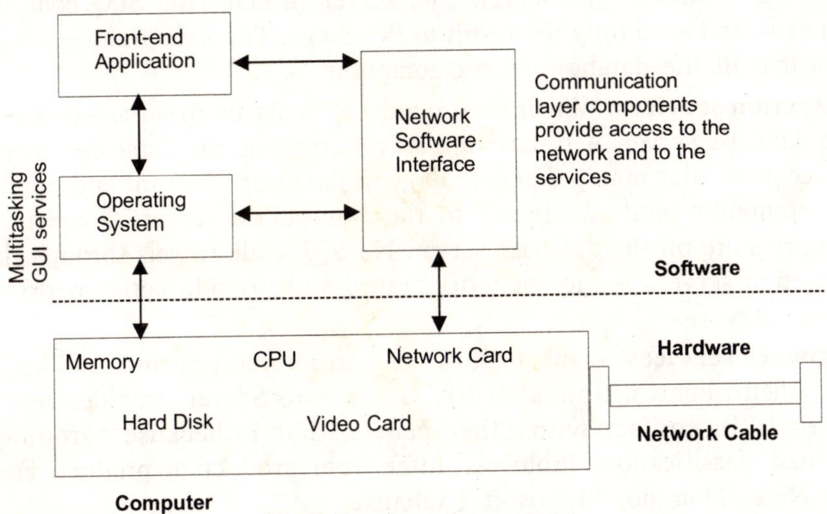

Fig.3.5: Client Components

3.5 SERVER COMPONENTS

As we have already discussed, the server is any process that provides services to the client process. The server is active because it always waits for the client's request. The services provided by server are:

(*i*) **File services**: For a LAN environment in which a computer with a big, fast hard disk is shared among different users, a client connected to the network can store files on the file server as if it were another local hard disk.

(*ii*) **Print services**: For a LAN environment in which a PC with one or more printers attached is shared among several clients, a client can access any one of the printers as if it were directly attached to its own computer. The data to be printed travel from the client's PC to the server printer PC where they are temporarily stored on the hard disk. When the client finishes the printing job, the data is moved from the hard disk on the print server to the appropriate printer.

(*iii*) **Fax services:** This requires at least one server equipped (internally or externally) with a fax device. The client PC need not have a fax or even a phone line connection. Instead, the client submits the data to be faxed to the fax server with the required information; such as the fax number or name of the receiver. The fax server will schedule the fax, dial the fax number, and transmit the fax. The fax server should also be able to handle any problems derived from the process.

(*iv*) **Communication services**: That let the client PCs connected to the communications server access other host computers or services to which the client is not directly connected. For example, a communication server allows a client PC to dial out to access board, a remote LA location, and so on.

(*v*) **Database services:** Which constitute the most common and most successful Client/Server implementation. Given the existence of database server, the client sends SQL request to the server. The server receives the SLQ code, validates it, executes it, and send only the result to the client. The data and the database engine are located in the database server computer.

(*vi*) **Transaction services:** Which are provided by transaction servers that are connected to the database server. A transaction server contains the database transaction code or procedures that manipulate the data in database. A front-end application in a client computer sends a request to the transaction server to execute a specific procedure store on the database server. No SQL code travels through the network. Transaction servers reduce network traffic and provide better performance than database servers.

(*vii*) **Groupware services:** Liable to store semi-structured information like Text, image, mail, bulletin boards, flow of work. Groupware Server provides services, which put people in contact with other people, that is because "groupware" is an ill-defined classification. Protocols differ from product to product. For examples: Lotus Notes/Domino, Microsoft Exchange.

(*viii*) **Object application services:** Communicating distributed objects reside on server. Object server provides access to those objects from client objects. Object Application Servers are responsible for Sharing distributed objects across the network. Object Application Servers uses the protocols that are usually some kind of Object Request Broker (ORB). Each distributed object can have one or more remote method. ORB locates an instance of the object server class, invokes the requested method, and returns the results to the client object. Object Application Server provides an ORB and application servers to implement this.

(*ix*) **Web application services:** Some documents, data, etc., reside on web servers. Web application provides access to documents and other data. "Thin" clients typically use a web browser to request those documents. Such services provide the sharing of the documents across intranets, or across the Internet (or extranets). The most commonly used protocol is HTTP (Hyper Text Transport Protocol). Web application servers are now augmenting simple web servers.

(*x*) **Miscellaneous services:** These include CD-ROM, video card, backup, and so on. Like the client, the server also has hardware and software components. The hardware components include the computer, CPU, memory, hard disk, video card, network card, and so on. The computer that houses the server process should be the more powerful computer than the "average" client computer because the server process must be able to handle concurrent requests from multiple clients. The Fig. 3.6 illustrates the components of server.

The server application, or back-end, runs on the top of the operating system and interacts with the communication middleware components to "listen" for the client request for the services. Unlike the front-end client processes, the server process need not be GUI based. Keep in mind that back-end application interacts with operating system (network or stand alone) to access local resources (hard disk, memory, CPU cycle, and so on). The back-end server constantly "listens" for client requests. Once a request is received the server processes it locally. The server knows how to process the request; the client tells the server only what it needs do, not how to do it. When the request is met, the answer is sent back to the client through the communication middleware.

The server hardware characteristics depend upon the extent of the required services. For example, a database is to be used in a network of fifty clients may require a computer with the following minimum characteristic:

- Fast CPU (RISC, Pentium, Power PC, or multiprocessor)
- Fault tolerant capabilities:
    - Dual power supply to prevent power supply problem.
    - Standby power supply to protect against power line failure.

- Error checking and correcting (ECC) memory to protect against memory module failures.
- Redundant Array to Inexpensive Disk (RAID) to provide protection against physical hardware failures.

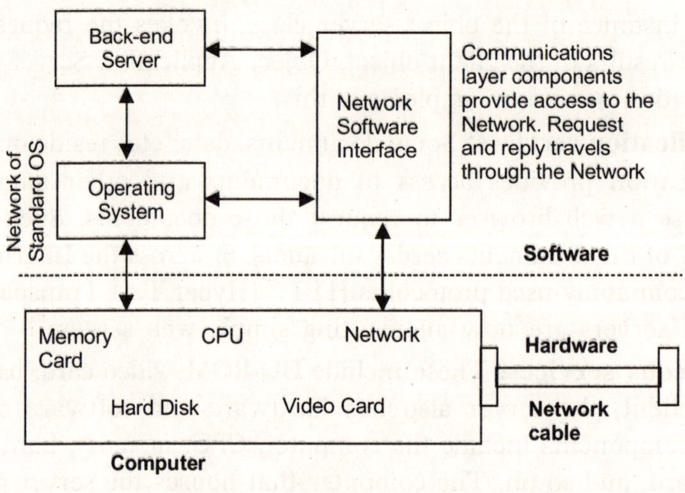

Fig.3.6: Server Components

- Expandability of CPU, memory disk, and peripherals.
- Bus support for multiple add-on boards.
- Multiple communication options.

In theory, any computer process that can be clearly divided into client and server components can be implemented through the Client/Server model. If properly implemented, the Client/Server architectural principles for process distribution are translated into the following server process benefits:

- **Location independence.** The server process can be located anywhere in the network.
- **Resource optimization.** The server process may be shared.
- **Scalability.** The server process can be upgraded to run on more powerful platforms.
- **Interoperability and integration.** The server process should be able to work in a "Plug and Play" environment.

These benefits added to hardware and software independence principles of the Client/Server computing model, facilitate the integration of PCs, minicomputer, and mainframes in a nearly seamless environment.

3.5.1 The Complexity of Servers

The server processes one request at a time; we can say servers are fairly simple because they are sequential. After accepting a request, the server forms a reply and sends it before requesting to see if another request has arrived. Here, the operating system plays a big role in maintaining the request queue that arrives for a server.

Servers are usually much more difficult to build than clients because they need to accommodate multiple concurrent requests. Typically, servers have two parts:

- A single master program that is responsible for accepting new requests.
- A set of slaves that are responsible for handling individual requests.

Further, master server performs the following five steps (Server Functions):

(i) **Open port:** The master opens a port at which the client request reached.

(ii) **Wait for client:** The master waits for a new client to send a request.

(iii) **Choose port:** If necessary, the master allocates new local port for this request and informs the client.

(iv) **Start slave:** The master starts an independent, concurrent slave to handle this request (for example: in UNIX, it forks a copy of the server process). Note that the slave handles one request and then terminates–the slave does not wait for requests from other clients.

(v) **Continue:** The master returns to the wait step and continues accepting new requests while the newly created slave handles the previous request concurrently.

Because the master starts a slave for each new request, processing proceeds concurrently. In addition to the complexity that results because the server handles concurrent requests, complexity also arises because the server must enforce authorization and protection rules. Server programs usually need to execute with the highest privilege because they must read system files, keep logs, and access protected data. The operating system will not restrict a server program if it attempts to access a user files. Thus, servers cannot blindly honour requests from other sites. Instead, each server takes responsibility for enforcing the system access and protection policies.

Finally, servers must protect themselves against malformed request or against request that will cause the server program itself to abort. Often it is difficult to foresee potential problems. Once an abort occurs, no client would be able to access files until a system programmer restarts the server.

> ***"Servers are usually more difficult to build than clients because, although they can be implemented with application programs, server must enforce all the access and protection policies of the computer system on which they run, and must protect themselves against all possible errors."***

3.6 COMMUNICATIONS MIDDLEWARE COMPONENTS

The communication middleware software provides the means through which clients and servers communicate to perform specific actions. It also provides specialized services to the client process that insulates the front-end applications programmer from the internal working of the database server and network protocols. In the past, applications programmers had to write code that would directly interface with specific database language (generally a version of SQL) and the specific network protocol used by the database server. For example, when writing a front-end application to access an IBM OS/2 database manager database, the programmer had to write SQL and Net BIOS (Network Protocol) command in the application. The Net BIOS command would allow the client process to establish a session with the database server, send specific control information, send the request, and so on. If the same application is to be used with a different database and network, the application routines must be rewritten for the new database and network protocols. Clearly, such a condition is undesirable, and this is where middleware comes in handy. The definition of middleware is based on the intended goals and main functions of this new software category.

Although middleware can be used in different types of scenarios, such as e-mail, fax, or network protocol translation, most first generation middleware used in Client/Server applications is oriented toward providing transport data access to several database servers. The use of database middleware yields:

- **Network independence:** by allowing the front-end application to access data without regard to the network protocols.
- **Database server independence:** by allowing the front-end application to access data from multiple database servers without having to write code that is specific to each database server.

The use of database middleware, make it possible for the programmer to use the generic SQL sentences to access different and multiple database servers. The middleware layer isolates the program from the differences among SQL dialects by transforming the generic SQL sentences into the database server's expected syntax. For example, a problem in developing a front-end system for multiple database servers is that application programmers must have in-depth knowledge of the network communications and the database access language characteristic of each database to access remote data. The problem is aggravated by the fact that each DBMS vendor implements its own version of SQL (with difference in syntax, additional functions, and enhancement with respect to the SQL standard). Furthermore, the data may reside in a non-relational DBMS (hierarchical, network or flat files) that does not support SQL, thus making it harder for the programmers to access the data given such cumbersome requirements, programming in Client/Server systems becomes more difficult than programming in traditional mainframe system. Database middleware eases the problem of accessing resources of data in multiple networks and releases the program from details of managing the network communications. To accomplish its functions, the communication middleware software operates at two levels:

- The physical level deals with the communications between client and server computers (computer to computer). In other words, it addresses how the computers are physically linked. The physical links include the network hardware and software. The network software includes the network protocol. Recall that network protocols are rules that govern how computers must interact with other computers in network, and they ensure that computers are able to send and receive signal to and from each other. Physically, the communication middleware is, in most cases, the network. Because the Client/Server model allows the client and server to reside on the same computer, it may exist without the benefit of a computer network.
- The logical level deals with the communications between client and server. Process (process to process) that is, with how the client and server process communicates. The logical characteristics are governed by process-to-process (or interprocess) communications protocols that give the signals meaning and purpose. It is at this level that most of the Client/Server conversation takes place.

Although the preceding analogy helps us understand the basic Client/Server interactions, it is required to have a better understanding of computer communication to better understand the flow of data and control information in a client server environment. To understand the details we will refer to Open System Interconnection (OSI) network reference model which is an effort to standardize the diverse network systems. Figure 3.7 depicts the flow of information through each layer of OSI model.

From the figure, we can trace the data flow:

- The client application generates a SQL request.
- The SQL request is sent down to the presentation layer, where it is changed to a format that the SQL server engine can understand.
- Now, the SQL request is handed down to session layer. This layer establishes the connection to the client processes with the server processes. If the database server requires user verification, the session layer generates the necessary message to log on and verify the end user. And also this layer will identify which mesaages are control messages and which are data messages.
- After the session is established and validated, the SQL request is sent to the transport layer. The transport layer generates some error validation checksums and adds some transport-layer-specific ID information.
- Once the transport layer has performed its functions, the SQL request is handed down to the network layer. This layer takes the SQL request, identifies the address of the next node in the path, divides the SQL request into several smaller packets,

and adds a sequence number to each packet to ensure that they are assembled in the correct order.

- Next the packet is handed to the data-link layer. This layer adds more control information, that depends on the network and on which physical media are used. The data-link layer sends the frame to the next node.
- When the data-link layer determines that it is safe to send a frame, it hands the frame down to the physical layer, which transmits it into a collection of ones and zeros(bits), and then transmit the bits through the network cable.
- The signals transmitted by the physical layer are received at the server end at the physical layer, which passes the data to the data-link layer. The data-link layer reconstructs the bits into frames and validates them. At this point, the data-link layer of the client and server computer may exchange additional messages to verify that the data were received correctly and that no retransmission is necessary. The packet is sent up to the network layer.
- The network layer checks the packet's destination address. If the final destination is some other node in network, the network layer identifies it and sends the packet down to the data-link layer for transmission to that node. If the destination is the current node, the network layer assembles the packets and assigns appropriate sequence numbers. Next, the network layer generates the SQL request and sends it to the transport layer.
- Most of the Client/Server "conversation" takes place in the session layer. If the communication between client and server process is broken, the session layer tries to reestablish the session. The session layer identifies and validates the request, and sends it to the presentation layer.
- The presentation layer provides additional validation and formatting.
- Finally, the SQL request is sent to the database server or application layer, where it is executed.

Although the OSI framework helps us understand network communications, it functions within a system that requires considerable infrastructure. The network protocols constitute the core of network infrastructure, because all data travelling through the network must adhere to some network protocol. In the Client/Server environment, it is not usual to work with several different network protocols. In the previous section, we noted that different server processes might support different network protocols to communicate over the network.

For example, when several processes run on the client, each process may be executing a different SQL request, or each process may access a different database server. The transport layer ID helps the transport layer identify which data corresponds to which session.

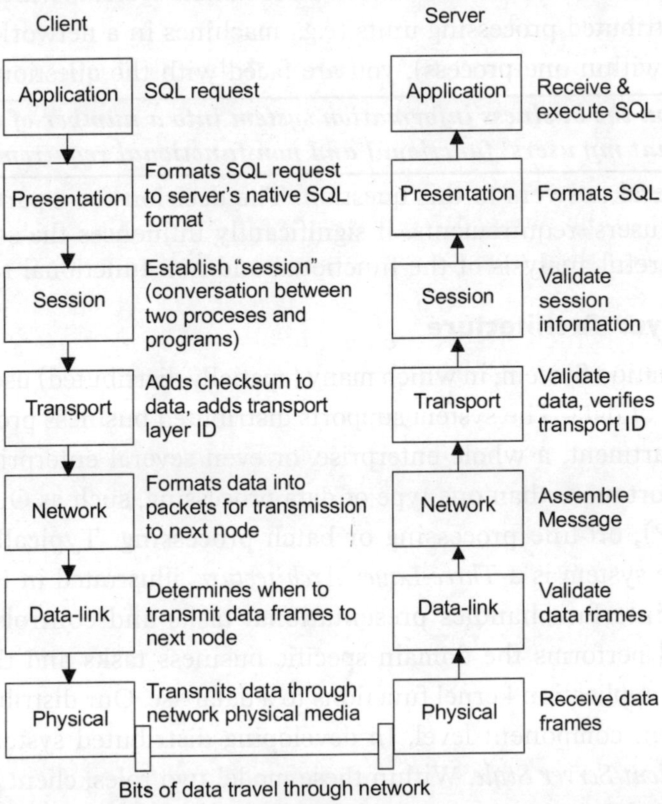

Fig.3.7: Flow of Information through the OSI Model

3.7 ARCHITECTURE FOR BUSINESS INFORMATION SYSTEM

3.7.1 Introduction

In this section, we will discuss several patterns for distributing business information systems that are structured according to a layered architecture. Each distribution pattern cuts the architecture into different client and server components. All the patterns discussed give an answer to the same question: How do I distribute a business information system? However, the consequences of applying the patterns are very different with regards to the forces influencing distributed systems design. Distribution brings a new design dimension into the architecture of information systems. It offers great opportunities for good systems design, but also complicates the development of a suitable architecture by introducing a lot of new design aspects and trap doors compared to a centralized system. While constructing the architecture for a business information system, which will be deployed across a set of distributed processing units (e.g., machines in a network, processes on one machine, threads within one process), you are faced with the question:

How do I partition the business information system into a number of client and server components, so that my users' functional and non-functional requirements are met?

There are several answers to this question. The decision for a particular distribution style is driven by users' requirements. It significantly influences the software design and requires a very careful analysis of the functional and non-functional requirements.

3.7.2 Three-Layer Architecture

A Business Information System, in which many (spatially distributed) users work in parallel on a large amount of data. The system supports distributed business processes, which may span a single department, a whole enterprise, or even several enterprises. Generally, the system must support more than one type of data processing, such as On-Line Transaction Processing (OLTP), off-line processing or batch processing. Typically, the application architecture of the system is a *Three-Layer Architecture*, illustrated in Fig. 3.8.

The user interface handles presentational tasks and controls the dialogue the application kernel performs the domain specific business tasks and the database access layer connects the application kernel functions to a database. Our distribution view focuses on this coarse-grain component level. In developing distributed system architecture we mainly use the *Client/Server Style.* Within these model two roles, client and server classify components of a distributed system. Clients and servers communicate via a simple request/response protocol.

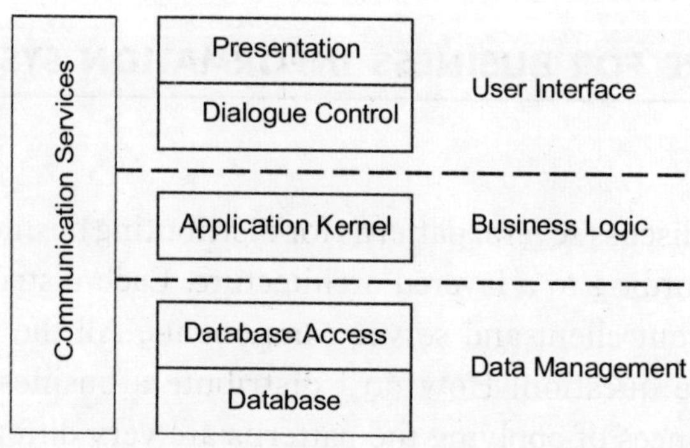

Fig.3.8: Three-Layer Architecture for Business Information System

3.7.3 General Forces

- *Business needs vs. construction complexity:* On one hand, allocating functionality and data to the places where it is actually needed supports distributed business processes very well, but on the other hand, distribution raises a system's complexity. Client server systems tend to be far more complex than conventional host software architectures. To name just a few sources of complexity: GUI, middleware, and heterogeneous operating system environments. It is clear that it often requires a lot of compromises to reduce the complexity to a level where it can be handled properly.

- *Processing style:* Different processing styles require different distribution decisions. Batch applications need processing power close to the data. Interactive processing should be close to input/output devices. Therefore, off-line and batch processing may conflict with transaction and on-line processing.
- *Distribution vs. performance:* We gain performance by distributed processing units executing tasks in parallel, placing data close to processing, and balancing workload between several servers. But raising the level of distribution increases the communication overhead, the danger of bottlenecks in the communication network, and complicates performance analysis and capacity planning. In centralized systems the effects are much more controllable and the knowledge and experience with the involved hardware and software allows reliable statements about the reachable performance of a configuration.
- *Distribution vs. security:* The requirement for secure communications and transactions is essential to many business domains. In a distributed environment the number of possible security holes increases because of the greater number of attack points. Therefore, a distributed environment might require new security architectures, policies and mechanisms.
- *Distribution vs. consistency:* Abandoning a global state can introduce consistency problems between states of distributed components. Relying on a single, centralized database system reduces consistency problems, but legacy systems or organizational structures (off-line processing) can force us to manage distributed data sources.
- *Software distribution cost:* The partitioning of system layers into client and server processes enables distribution of the processes within the network, but the more software we distribute the higher the distribution, configuration management, and installation cost. The lowest software distribution and installation cost will occur in a centralized system. This force can even impair functionality if the software distribution problem is so big that the capacities needed exceed the capacities of your network. The most important argument for so called diskless, Internet based network computers is exactly software distribution and configuration management cost.
- *Reusability vs. performance vs. complexity:* Placing functionality on a server enforces code reuse and reduces client code size, but data must be shipped to the server and the server must enable the handling of requests by multiple clients.

3.7.4 Distribution Pattern

To distribute an information system by assigning client and server roles to the components of the layered architecture we have the choice of several distribution styles. Figure 3.9 shows the styles, which build the pattern language. To take a glance at the pattern language we give an abstract for each pattern:

- *Distributed presentation:* This pattern partitions the system within the presentation component. One part of the presentation component is packaged as a distribution unit and is processed separately from the other part of the presentation, which can be packaged together with the other application layers. This pattern allows of an easy implementation and very thin clients. Host systems with 3270-terminals is a classical example for this approach. Network computers, Internet and intranet technology are modern environments where this pattern can be applied as well.
- *Remote user interface:* Instead of distributing presentation functionality the whole user interface becomes a unit of distribution and acts as a client of the application kernel on the server side.
- *Distributed application kernel:* The pattern splits the application kernel into two parts which are processed separately. This pattern becomes very challenging if transactions span process boundaries (distributed transaction processing).

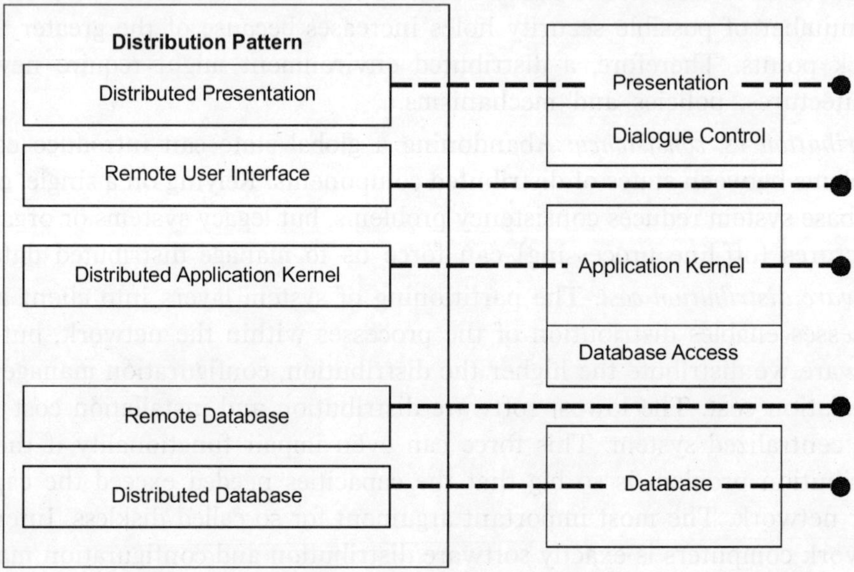

Fig.3.9: Pattern Resulting from Different Client/Server Cuts

- *Remote database:* The database is a major component of a business information system with special requirements on the execution environment. Sometimes, several applications work on the same database. This pattern locates the database component on a separate node within the system's network.

- *Distributed database:* The database is decomposed into separate database components, which interact by means of interprocess communication facilities. With a distributed database an application can integrate data from different database systems or data can be stored more closely to the location where it is processed.

3.8 EXISTING CLIENT/SERVER ARCHITECTURE

3.8.1 Mainframe-based Environment

In mainframe systems all the processing takes place on the mainframe and usually dumb terminals that are known as end user platform are used to display the data on screens.

Mainframes systems are highly centralized known to be integrated systems. Where dumb terminals do not have any autonomy. Mainframe systems have very limited data manipulation capabilities. From the application development point of view. Mainframe systems are over structured, time-consuming and create application backlogs. Various computer applications were implemented on *mainframe computers* (from IBM and others), with lots of attached (dumb, or semi-intelligent) terminals see the Fig. 3.10.

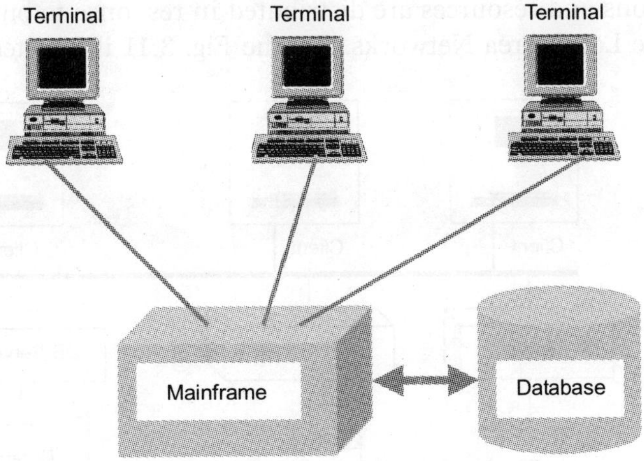

Fig.3:10: Mainframe-based Environment

There are some major problems with this approach:

- ⇨ Very inflexible.
- ⇨ Mainframe system are very inflexible.
- ⇨ Vendor lock-in was very expensive.
- ⇨ Centralized DP department was unable to keep up with the demand for new applications.

3.8.2 LAN-based Environment

LAN can be configured as a Client/Server LAN in which one or more stations called servers give services to other stations, called clients. The server version of network operating system is installed on the server or servers; the client version of the network operating system is installed on clients. A LAN may have a general server or several dedicated servers. A network may have several servers; each dedicated to a particular task for example database servers, print servers, and file servers, mail server. Each server in the Client/Server based LAN environment provides a set of shared user services to the clients. These servers enable many clients to share access to the same resources and enable the use of high performance computer systems to manage the resources.

A file server allows the client to access shared data stored on the disk connected to the file server. When a user needs data, it access the server, which then sends a copy, a print server allows different clients to share a printer. Each client can send data to be printed to the print server, which then spools and print them. In this environment, the file server station server runs a server file access program, a mail server station runs a server mail handling program, and a print server station a server print handling program, or a client print program.

Users, applications and resources are distributed in response to business requirements and linked by single Local Area Networks. See the Fig. 3.11 illustrated below:

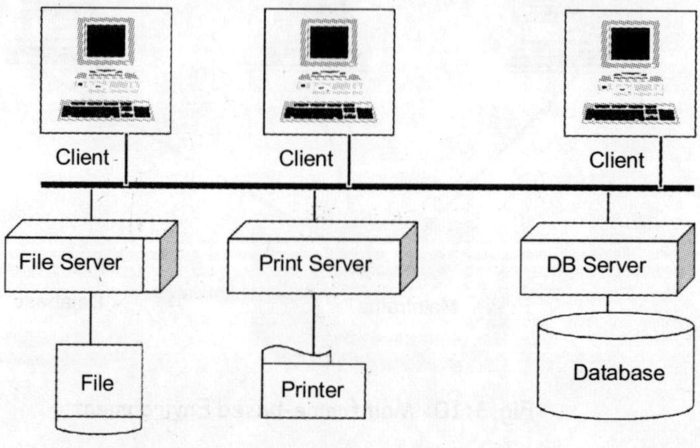

Fig.3.11: LAN Environment

3.8.3 Internet-based Environment

What the Internet brings to the table is a new platform, interface, and architectures. The Internet can employ existing Client/Server applications as true Internet applications, and integrate applications in the Web browser that would not normally work and play well together. The Internet also means that the vast amount of information becomes available from the same application environment and the interface. That's the value. See the Fig. 3.12 given below:

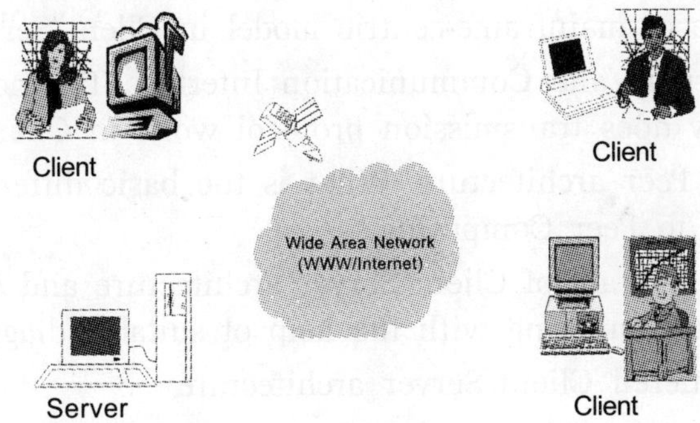

Fig.3.12: Internet-based Environment

The internet also puts fat client developers on a diet. Since most internet applications are driven from the Web server, the application processing is moving off the client and back onto the server. This means that maintenance and application deployment become much easier, and developers don't have to deal with the integration hassles of traditional Client/Server (such as loading assorted middleware and protocol stacks).

The web browsers are universal clients. A web browser is a minimalist client that interprets information it receives from a server, and displays it graphically to a user. The client is simply here to interpret the server's command and render the contents of an HTML page to the user. Web browsers-like those from Netscape and Spyglass – are primarily interpreters of HTML commands. The browser executes the HTML commands to properly display text and images on a specific GUI platform; it also navigates from one page to another using the embedded hypertext links. HTTP server produce platform independent content that clients can then request. A server does not know a PC client from a Mac client – all web clients are created equal in the eyes of their web server. Browsers are there to take care of all the platform-specific details.

At first, the Web was viewed as a method of publishing informaton in an attractive format that could be accessed from any computer on the internet. But the newest generation of the Web includes programmable clients, using such programming environments as Sun Microsystem's Java and Microsoft's ActiveX. With these programming environments, the Web has become a viable and compelling platform for developing Client/Server applications on the Internet, and also platform of choice for Client/Server computing. The World Wide Web (WWW) information system is an excellent example of client server "done right". A server system supplies multimedia documents (pages), and runs some application programs (HTML forms and CGI programs, for example) on behalf of the client. The client takes complete responsibility for displaying the hypertext document, and for the user's response to it. Whilst the majority of "real world" (i.e., commercial) applications of Client/ Server are in database applications.

EXERCISE 3

1. What is the role of mainframe-centric model in Client/Server computing?
2. Explain Connectivity and Communication Interface Technology in Client/Server application. How does transmission protocol work in Client/Server application?
3. Explain Peer to Peer architecture. What is the basic difference between Client/Server and Peer to Peer Computing?
4. Draw the block diagram of Client/Server architecture and explain the advantage of Client/Server computing with the help of suitable diagram.
5. Explain shared tiered Client/Server architecture.
6. How are connectivity and interoperability between Client/Server achieved? Explain.
7. Explain Client/Server architecture. What is the basic difference between Client/Server and peer to peer computing?
8. Explain the three-level architecture of database management system. Also explain the advantages and disadvantages of DBMS.
9. Draw the block diagram of Client/Server architecture and explain the advantage of Client/Server computing with the help of suitable example.
10. What are the various ways available to improve the performance of Client/Server computing?

4

Client/Server and Databases

4.1 INTRODUCTION

Storing Data and the Database

Server translates the ink/paper storage model into an electronic/magnetic media storage model, but the fundamental arrangement is the same. The basic building block (his computer equivalent of information-on-paper) is called data. Data is information in its simplest form, meaningless until related together in some fashion so as to become meaningful. Related data is stored on server's disk under a unique name, called file. Related file are gathered together into directories, and related directories are gathered together into larger and larger directories until all the required information is stored in a hierarchy of directories on the server's hard disk.

The server's "filing cabinet" is a database; it offers a number of advantages over the paper model. A particular file can be searched electronically, even if only remembering a tiny portion of the file contains.

A database, generally defined, is a flexible, hierarchical structure for storing raw data, which facilitates its organization into useful information. All data on computer is stored in one kind of database or another. A spreadsheet is a database, storing data in an arrangement of characters and formatting instructions. What a database does, then, is breakdown information into its most fundamental components and then create meaningful relationships between those components. We depend on databases of varying configurations and complexity for all our computerized information need.

The Fig. 4.1 illustrates the evolution of database technology from the first computer in late 1950's to the object-oriented database technologies.

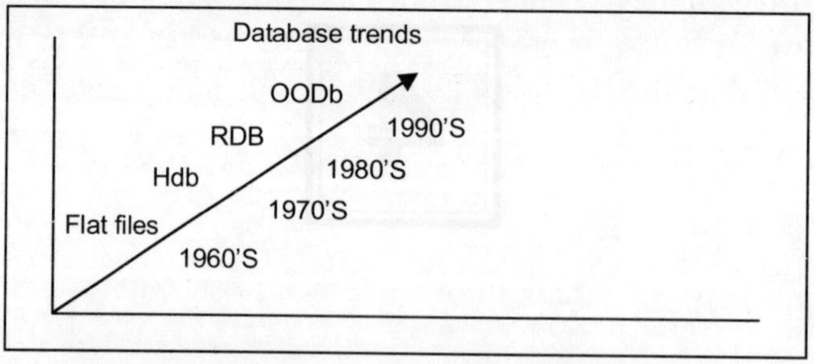

Fig.4.1: Evolution of Database Technologies

Using a database you can tag data, relating it to other data in several different ways, without having to replicate the data in different physical locations. This ability to access and organize data in a flexible manner without making physical copies of it (and thus preserving the integrity of the information at its most basic level) is what has lead to the increasing use of client/server technology as a widespread business information model.

Database System Architectures

Before proceeding to understand the Client/Server database it is quite essentials to have a brief introduction about the other available architecture of database systems.

Client/Server database system: The functionality is spilted between a server and multiple client systems, i.e., networking of computers allows some task to be executed on server system and some task to be executed on client system.

Distributed database system: Geographically or administratively distributed data spreads across multiple database systems.

Parallel database system: Parallel processing within computer system allows database system activities to be speeded up, allowing faster response to transaction; queries can be preceded in a way that exploits the parallelism offered by the underlying computer system.

Centralized database system: Centralized database systems are those run on a single system and do not interact with other computer systems. They are single user database systems (on a PC) and high performance database system (on high end server system).

4.2 CLIENT/SERVER IN RESPECT OF DATABASES

4.2.1 Client/Server Databases

Servers exist primarily to manage databases of information in various formats. Without the database, servers would be impractical as business tools. True, you could still use them to share resources and facilitate communication; but, in the absence of business database, a peer-to-peer network would be a more cost effective tool to handle these jobs. So the question of client server becomes a question of whether or not your business needs centralized database. Sharing and communications are built on top of that.

A Database Management System (DBMS) lies at the center of most Client/Server systems in use today. To function properly, the Client/Server DBMS must be able to:

- Provide transparent data access to multiple and heterogeneous clients, regardless of the hardware, software, and network platform used by the client application.
- Allow client request to the database server (using SQL requests) over the network.
- Process client data requests at the local server.
- Send only the SQL result to the clients over the network.

A Client/Server DBMS reduces network traffic because only the rows that match the query are returned. Therefore, the client computer resources are available to perform other system chores such as the management of the graphical user interface. Client/Server DBMS differ from the other DBMSs in term of where the processing take place and what data are sent over the network to the client computer. However, Client/Server DBMSs do not necessarily require distributed data.

Client/Server systems changes the way in which we approach data processing. Data may be stored in one site or in multiple sites. When the data are stored in multiple sites, Client/Server databases are closely related to distributed databases.

4.2.2 Client/Server Database Computing

Client/Server database computing evolved in response to the drawbacks of the mainframe (very expensive operating cost because they require specialized operational facilities demand expensive support, and do not use common computer components), and PC/file server computing environments (the drawback of PC-based computing is that all RDBMS processing is done on the local PC, when a query is made to the file server, the file server does not process the query, instead, it returns the data required to process the query, this can result in decreased performance and increased network bottlenecks). By combining the processing power of the mainframe and the flexibility and price of the PC, Client/Server database computing encompasses the best of both words.

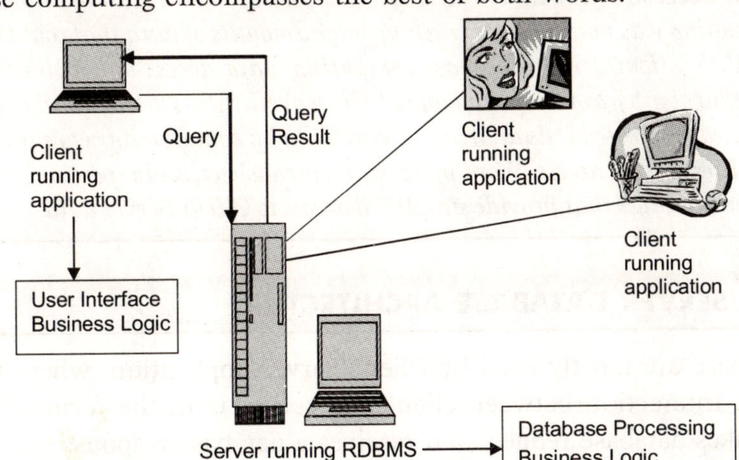

Fig. 4.2: Client/Server Database Computing

Client/Server database computing can be defined as the logical partition of the user interface, database management, and business; logic between the client computer and server computer. The network links each of these processes. The client computer, also called workstation, controls the user interface. The client is where text and images are displayed to the user and where the user inputs data. The user interface can be text based or graphical based. The server computer controls database management. The server is where data is stored, manipulated, and stored. In the Client/Server database environment, all database processing occurs on the server.

Business logic can be located on the server, on the client, or mixed between the two. This type of logic governs the processing of the application.

Client/Server database computing vs. Mainframe and PC/file server computing

Client/Server database computing is preferred in comparison to other database computing. Following are the reasons for its popularity:

Affordability: *Client/Server computing can be less expensive than mainframe computing. The underlying reason is simple: Client/Server computing is based on an open architecture, which allows more vendors to produce competing products, which drives the cost down. This is unlike mainframe-based systems, which typically use proprietary components available only through a single vendor. Also, Client/Server workstations and servers are often PC based. PC prices have fallen dramatically over the years, which has led to reduce Client/Server computing costs.*

Speed: *The separation of processing between the client and the server reduces the network bottlenecks, and allows a Client/Server database system to deliver mainframe performance while exceeding PC/file server performance.*

Adaptability: *The Client/Server database computing architecture is more open than the proprietary mainframe architecture. Therefore, it is possible to build an application by selecting an RDBMS from one vendor, hardware from another vendor. Customers can select components that best fit their needs.*

Simplified data access: *Client/Server database computing makes data available to the masses. Mainframe computing was notorious for tracking huge amounts of data that could be accessed only by developers. With Client/Server database computing, data access is not limited to those who understand procedural programming languages (which are difficult to learn and require specialized data access knowledge). Instead, data access is providing by common software products tools that hide the complexities of data access. Word processing, spreadsheet, and reporting software are just a few of the common packages that provide simplified access to Client/Server data.*

4.3 CLIENT/SERVER DATABASE ARCHITECTURE

Relational database are mostly used by Client/Server application, where the server is a database server. Interaction between client and server is in the form of transaction in which client makes database request and receives a database response.

In the architecture of such a system, server is responsible for maintaining the database, for that purpose a complex database management system software module is required.

Various types of applications that make use of the database can install on client machine. The "glue" that ties client and server together is software that enables the client to make request for access to the server's database, that is SQL (Structured Query Language), shown in the Fig. 4.3 given below:

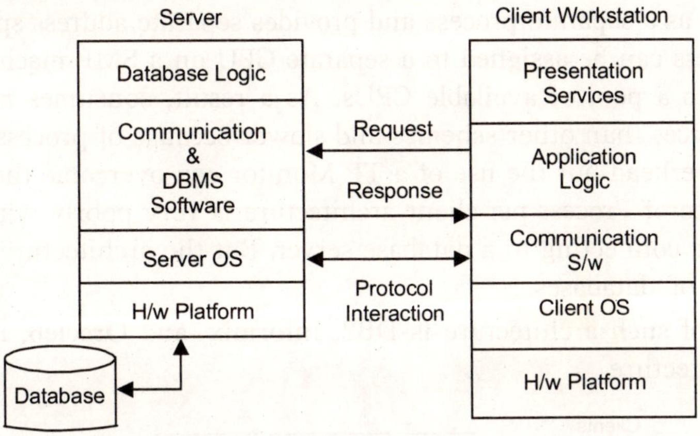

Fig.4.3: Client/Server Database Architecture

According to this architecture, all the application logic (software used for data analysis) is residing on the client side, while the server is concerned with managing the database. Importance of such architecture depends on the nature of application, where it is going to be implemented. And the main purpose is to provide on line access for record keeping. Suppose a database with million of records residing on the server, server is maintaining it. Some user wants to fetch a query that result few records only. Then it can be achieved by number of search criteria. An initial client query may yield a server response that satisfies the search criteria. The user then adds additional qualifiers and issues a new query. Returned records are once again filtered. Finally, client composes next request with additional qualifiers. The resulting search criteria yield desired match, and the record is returned to the client. Such Client/Server architecture is well-suited for such types of applications due to:

- Searching and sorting of large databases are a massive job; it requires large disk space, high speed CPU along with high speed Input/Output architecture. On the other hand, in case of single user workstations such a storage space and high power is not required and also it will be costlier.
- Tremendous traffic burden is placed on the network in order to move the million of records to the clients for searching, then it is not enough for the server to just be able to retrieve records on behalf of a client; the server needs to have database logic that enables it to perform searches on behalf of a client.

Various types of available Client/Server Database Architecture are discussed in detail; in the section given:

(*i*) Process-per-client architecture.
(*ii*) Multi-threaded architecture.
(*iii*) Hybrid architecture.

(*i*) **Process-per-client architecture:** As the name reveals itself server process considers each client as a separate process and provides separate address space for each user. Each process can be assigned to a separate CPU on a SMP machine, or can assign processes to a pool of available CPUs. As a result, consumes more memory and CPU resources than other schemes and slower because of process context switches and IPC overhead but the use of a TP Monitor can overcome these disadvantages. Performance of Process-per-client architecture is very poorly when large numbers of users are connecting to a database server. But the architecture provides the best protection of databases.

Examples of such architecture is DB2, Informix, and Oracle6, Fig. 4.4 illustrates such architecture.

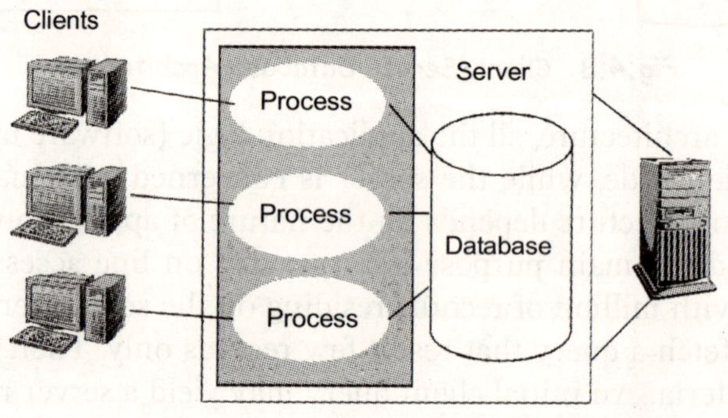

Fig.4.4: Process-per-client Architecture

(*ii*) **Multi-threaded architecture:** Architecture supports a large numbers of clients running a short transaction on the server database. Provide the best performance by running all user requests in a single address space. But do not perform well with large queries. Multi-threaded architecture conserves Memory and CPU cycles by avoiding frequent context switches. There are more chances of portability across the platforms.

But it suffers by some drawback first in case of any misbehaved user request can bring down the entire process, affecting all users and their requests and second long-duration tasks of user can hog resources, causing delays for other users. And the architecture is not as good at protection point of view. Some of the examples of such architecture are: Sybase, Microsoft SQL Server, and illustrated in Fig. 4.5.

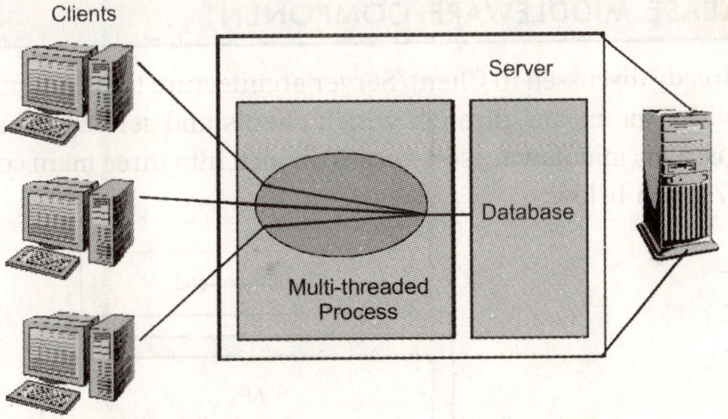

Fig.4.5: Multi-threaded Architecture

(iii) Hybrid architecture: Hybrid architecture provides a protected environment for running user requests without assigning a permanent process for each user. Also provides the best balance between server and clients. Hybrid architecture of Client/Server Database is basically comprised of three components:

- Multi-threaded network listener: Main task of this is to assign client connection to a dispatcher.
- Dispatcher processes: These processes are responsible for placing the messages on an internal message queue. And finally, send it back to client when response returned from the database.
- Reusable, shared, worker processes: Responsible for picking work off the message queue and execute that work and finally places the response on an output message queue.

Hybrid architecture of Client/Server database suffer from queue latencies, which have an adversely affect on other users. The hybrid architecture of Client/Server database is shown in Fig. 4.6 given below. Some of the examples of such architectures are Oracle7i and Oracle8i/9i.

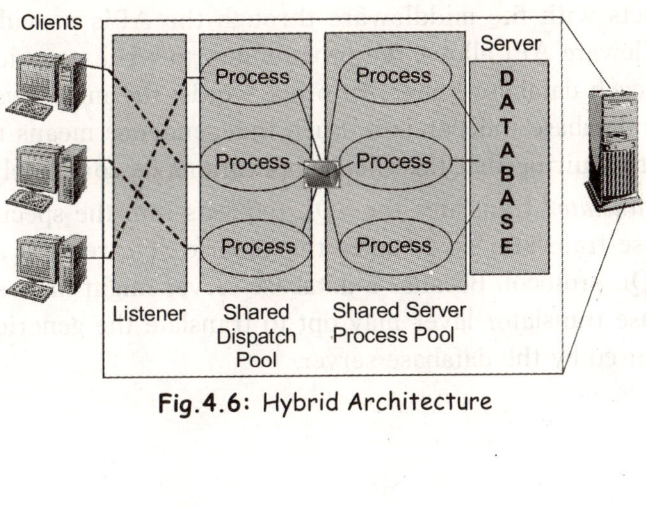

Fig.4.6: Hybrid Architecture

4.4 DATABASE MIDDLEWARE COMPONENT

As we have already discussed in Client/Server architecture that communication middleware software provides the means through which clients and servers communicate to perform specific actions. This middleware software is divided into three main components. As shown in the Fig. 4.7 given below:

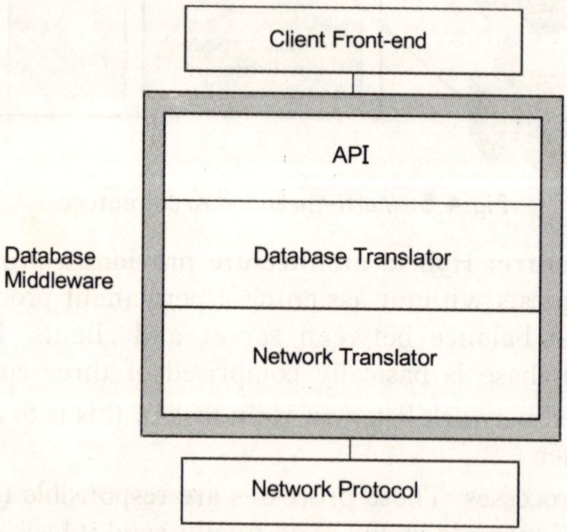

Fig.4.7: Database Middleware Components

- Application programming interface.
- Database translator.
- Network translator.

These components (or their functions) are generally distributed among several software layers that are interchangeable in a plug and play fashion.

The *application-programming interface* is public to the client application. The programmer interacts with the middleware through the APIs provided by middleware software. The middleware API allows the programmer to write generic SQL code instead of code specific to each database server. In other words, the middleware API allows the client process to be database independent. Such independence means that the server can be changed without requiring that the client applications be completely rewritten.

The *database translator* translates the SQL requests into the specific database server syntax. The database translator layer takes the generic SQL request and maps it to the database server's SQL protocol. Because a database server might have some non-standard features, the database translator layer may opt to translate the generic SQL request into the specific format used by the database server.

If the SQL request uses data from two different database servers, the database translator layer will take care of communicating with each server, retrieving the data using the common format expected by the client application.

The network translator manages the network communication protocols. Remember that database server can use any of the network protocols. If a client application taps into the two databases, one that uses TCP/IP and another that uses IPX/SPX, the network layer handles all the communications detail of each database transparently to the client application. Figure 4.8 illustrates the interaction between client and middleware database components.

Existence of these three middleware components reveals some benefits of using middleware software; according to that clients can:

- Access multiple (and quite different) databases
- Be database-server-independent
- Be network-protocol-independent

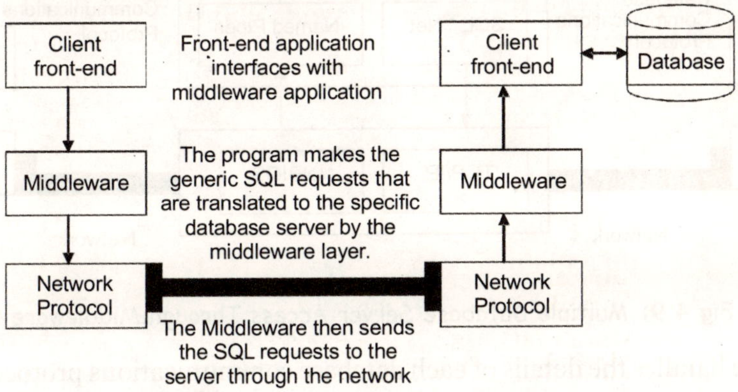

Fig.4.8: Interaction Between Client/Server Middleware Components

4.5 ACCESS TO MULTIPLE DATABASES

To understand how the three components of middleware database work together, lets us see how a client accesses two different databases servers. The Fig. 4.9 shows a client application request data from an oracle database server (Oracle Corporation) and a SQL Server database server (Microsoft Corporation). The Oracle database server uses SQL *Net as its communications protocol with the client; the SQL Server uses Named Pipes as the communications protocol. SQL *Net, a proprietary solution limited to Oracle database, is used by Oracle to send SQL request over a network. Named Pipes is a inter-process communication (IPC) protocol common to multitasking operating systems such as UNIX and OS/2, and it is used in SQL Server to manage both client and server communications across the network.

As per the Fig. 4.9, it is notable that the Oracle server runs under the UNIX operating system and uses TCP/IP as its network protocol. The SQL Server runs under the Windows NT operating system and uses NetBIOS as its network protocol. In this case, the client application uses a generic SQL query to access data in two tables: an Oracle table and a SQL Server table. The database translator layer of middleware software contains two modules, one for each database server type to be accessed.

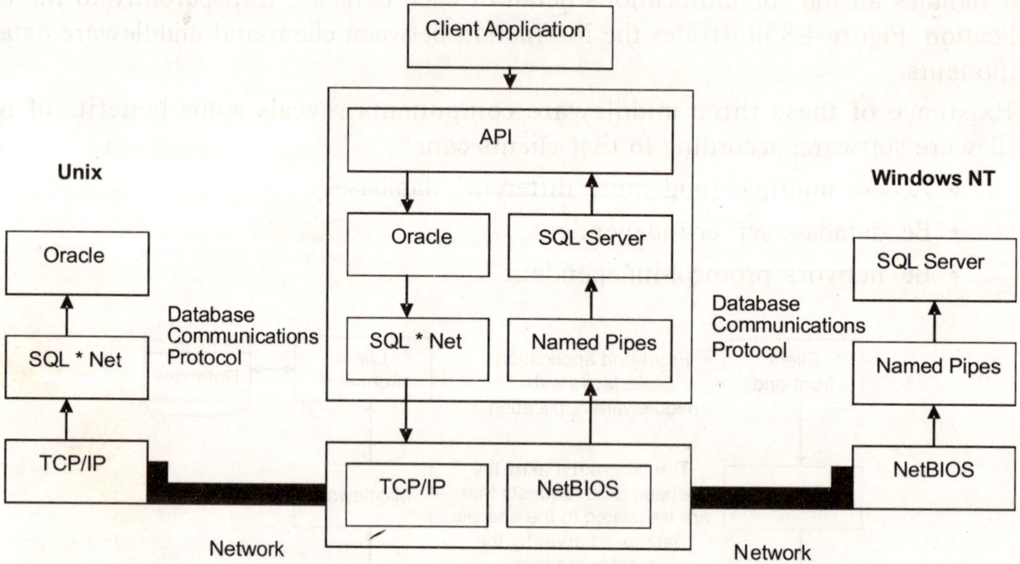

Fig.4.9: Multiple Database Server Access Through Middleware

Each module handles the details of each database communications protocol. The network translator layer takes care of using the correct network protocol to access each database. When the data from the query are returned, they are presented in a format common to the client application. The end user or programmer need not be aware of the details of data retrieval from the servers. Actually, the end user might not even know where the data reside or from what type of DBMS the data were retrieved.

4.6 DISTRIBUTED CLIENT/SERVER DATABASE SYSTEMS

Data Distribution

Distributed data and *distributed processing* are terms used widely in the word of Client/Server computing. The differences in these two can be easily understood by the two figures 4.10(a) and 4.10(b). Distributed data refers to the basic data stored in the server, which is distributed to different members of the work team. While distributed processing refers to the way different tasks are organized among members of the work team. If a set of information handling tasks is thought of as a single step-by-step process and is split among the members of the work-team so that they can handle the steps more efficiently, that process is distributed.

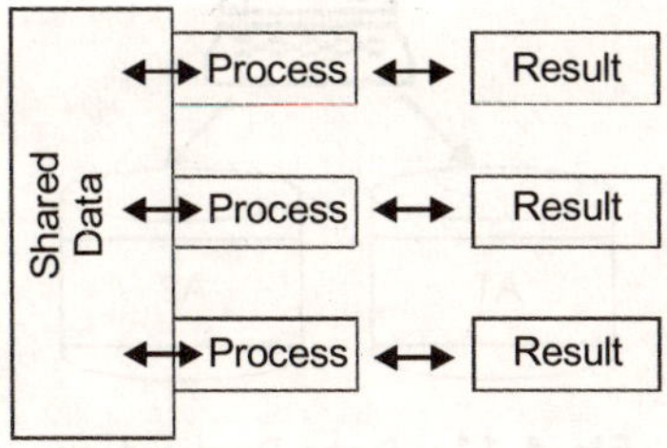

Fig.4.10(*a*): Distributed Data

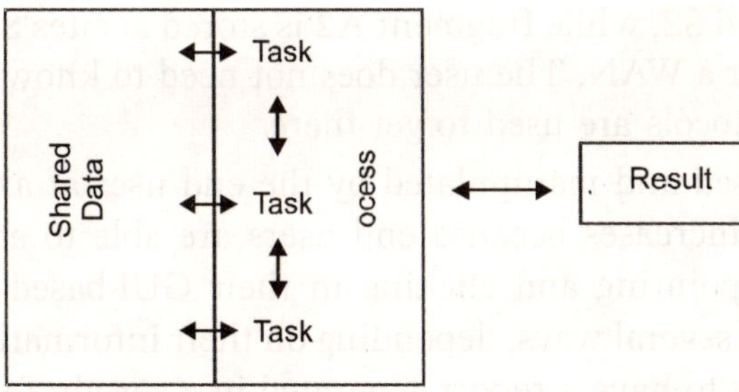

Fig.4.10(*b*): Distributed Processing

Here's an example: Imagine that a customer's ordering and payment information is stored in a central customer record on the server. This record is accessed by many departments in various locations throughout the company (accounting and shipping/receiving, to name two). Thus the data is an example of distributed data. In addition, because accounting and shipping/receiving work with the data in unique but related ways in order to accomplish a specific goal (updating the customer record), their activities are an example of distributed processing.

Distributed Client/Server database system must have some characteristics that are discussed in this section. The location of data is transparent to the user. The data can be located in the local PC, the department server, or in a mainframe across the country. The data can also be distributed among different locations and among different databases using the same or even the different data models.

The data in database can be partitioned in several ways. And the partitioned data may be allocated (process of data allocation describes where to locate the data, some data allocation strategies are: Centralized, partitioned, replicated) in several different ways, and the data may be replicated in several nodes see the Fig. 4.11.

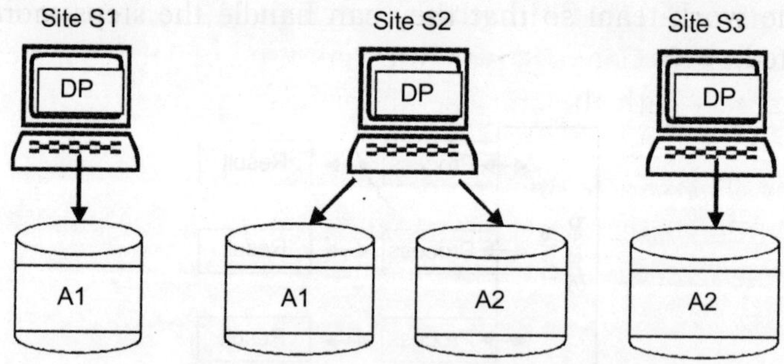

Fig.4.11: Data Replication

For example, suppose database A is divided into two fragments A1 and A2. Within a replicated distributed database, the scenario depicted in figure 4.11 is possible: fragment A1 is stored at sites S1 and S2, while fragment A2 is stored at sites S2 and S3. The network can be a LAN, a MAN, or a WAN. The user does not need to know the data location, how to get there, or what protocols are used to get there.

- Data can be accessed and manipulated by the end user at any time in many ways. Data accessibility increases because end users are able to access data directly and easily, usually by pointing and clicking in their GUI-based system. End user can manipulate data in several ways, depending on their information needs. For example, one user may want to have a report generated in a certain format, whereas another user may prefer to use graphical presentations. Powerful applications stored on the end user's side allow access and manipulation of data in a way that were never before available. The data request is processed on the server side; the data formatting and presentation are done on the client side.
- The processing of data (retrieval, storage, validation, formatting, presentation and so on) is distributed among multiple computers. For example, suppose that a distributed Client/Server system is used to access data from three DBMSs located at different sites. If a user requests a report, the client front-end will issue a SQL request to the DBMS server. The database server will take care of locating the data; retrieving it from the different locations, assembling it, and sending it back to the client. In this scenario, the processing of the data access and retrieval.

4.7 DISTRIBUTED DBMS

Client/Server database is commonly known for having distributed database capabilities. But is not necessarily able to fulfil the entire required Client/Server characteristics that are in need for particular system. Client/Server architecture refers to the way in which computers interact to form a system. The Client/Server architecture features a user of resources, or a client, and a provider of resources, or a server. The Client/Server architecture can be used to implement a DBMS in which the client is Transaction Processor and the server is the Data Processor. Client/Server interaction in a DDBMS are carefully scripted. The client (TP) interacts with the end use and sends a request to the server (DP). The server receives, schedules, and executes the request, selecting only those records that are needed by the client. The server then sends the data to the client only when the client requests the data. The database management system must be able to manage the distribution of data among multiple nodes. The DBMS must provide distributed database transparency features like:

- Distribution transparency.
- Transaction transparency.
- Failure transparency.
- Performance transparency.
- Heterogeneity transparency.

Number of relational DBMS, which are started as a centralized system with its components like user interface and application programs were moved to the client side. With standard language SQL, creates a logical dividing point between client and server. Hence, the query and transaction functionality remained at the server side. When DBMS access is required, the program establishes a connection to the DBMS; which is on the server side and once the connection is created, the client program can communicate with the DBMS.

Exactly how to divide the DBMS functionality between client and server has not yet been established. Different approaches have been proposed. One possibility is to include functionality of a centralized DBMS at the server level. A number of relational DBMS concepts have taken this approach, where an SQL server is provided to the clients. Each client must then formulate the appropriate SQL queries and provide the user interface and programming language interface functions. Since SQL is a relational standard, various SQL servers possibly provided by different vendors, can accept SQL commands. The client may also refer to a data dictionary that includes information on the distribution of data among the various SQL servers, as well as modules for decomposing a global query into a number of local queries that can be executed at the various sites. Interaction between client and server might proceed as follows during the processing of an SQL query:

- The client passes a user query and decomposes it into a number of independent site queries. Each site query is sent to the appropriate server site.
- Each server process the local query and sends the resulting relation to the client site.
- The client site combines the results of the subqueries to produce the result of the originally submitted query.

In this approach, the SQL server has also been called a transaction server or a Database Processor (DP) or a back-end machine, whereas the client has been called Application

Processor (AP) or a front-end machine. The interaction between client and server can be specified by the user at the client level or via a specialized DBMS client module that is part of DBMS package. For example, the user may know what data is stored in each server, break-down a query request into site subqueries manually, and submit individual subqueries to the various sites. The resulting tables may be combined explicitly by a further user query at the client level. The alternative is to have the client module undertake these actions automatically.

In a typical DBMS, it is customary to divide the software module into three levels:

L1: The server software is responsible for local data management at site, much like centralized DBMS software.

L2: The client software is responsible for most of the distributions; it access data distribution information from the DBMS catalog and process all request that requires access to more than one site. It also handles all user interfaces.

L3: The communication software (sometimes in conjunction with a distributed operating system) provides the communication primitives that are used by the client to transmit commands and data among the various sites as needed. This is not strictly part of the DBMS, but it provides essential communication primitives and services.

The client is responsible for generating a distributed execution plan for a multisite query or transaction and for supervising distributed execution by sending commands to servers. These commands include local queries and transaction to be executed, as well as commands to transmit data to other clients or servers. Hence, client software should be included at any site where multisite queries are submitted. Another function controlled by the client (or coordinator) is that of ensuring consistency of replicated copies of a data item by employing distributed (or global) concurrency control techniques. The client must also ensure the atomicity of global transaction by performing global recovery when certain sites fail. One possible function of the client is to hide the details of data distribution from the user; that is, it enables the user to write global queries and transactions as through the database were centralized, without having to specify the sites at which the data references in the query or transaction resides. This property is called distributed transparency. Some DDBMSs do not provide distribution transparency, instead requiring that users beware of the details of data distribution. In fact, there is some resemblance in between Client/Server and DDBMS. The Client/Server system distributes data processing among several sites, whether as the DDBMS distributes the data at different locations, involving some complimentary and overlapping functions. DDBMS use distributed processing to access data at multiple sites.

4.8 WEB/DATABASE SYSTEM FOR CLIENT/SERVER APPLICATIONS

Nowadays, almost all the MNC's providing information and performing all their activities online through internet or intranet. In this way, the information retrieval becomes quick and easier. It is obvious that all kinds of information the corporate world is providing through web pages. Also through links on home page they provides the facilities to enter into the corporate intranet, whether it is finance, human resource, sales, manufacturing or the marketing department. Departmental information as well as services can be accessed from web pages Even the web is powerful and flexible tool for supporting corporate requirements but they provides a limited capability for maintaining a large, change base of data. To get effectiveness on Intranet/Internet the organizations are connecting the web services to a database with its own database management systems.

Web-database integration has been illustrated in Fig. 4.12 shown below; a client machine that runs a web browser issues a request for information in the form of a URL (Uniform Resource Locator) reference. This reference triggers a program at the web server that issues the correct database command to a database server. The output returned to the web server is converted into a HTML format and returned to the web browser.

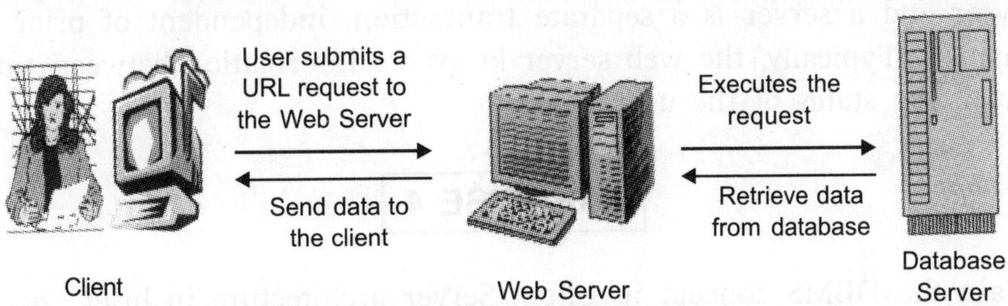

Fig.4.12: Web Database System Integration

4.8.1 Web/Database vs. Traditional Database

The section given below lists the advantages of a web/database system compared to a more traditional database approach.

- *Administration:* The only connection to the database server is the web server. The addition of a new type of database server does not require configuration of all the requisite drivers and interfaces at each type of client machine. Instead, it is only necessary for the web server to be able to convert between HTML and the database interface.
- *Deployment:* Browsers are already available across almost all platforms. Which relieves the developer of the need to implement graphical user interface across multiple customer machines and operating systems? In addition, developers can assume that customers already have and will be able to use browsers as soon as the internet web server is available. Avoiding deployment issues such as installation and synchronized activation.

- *Speed:* Large portion of the normal development cycle, such as development and client design, do not apply to web-based projects. In addition, the text based tags of HTML allow for rapid modification, making it easy to continually improve the look and feel of the application based on the ser feedback. By contrast, changing form or content of a typical graphical-based application can be a substantial task.
- *Information presentation:* Hypermedia base of the web enables the application developers to employ whatever information structure is best for given application, including the use of hierarchical formats in which progressive levels of detail are available to the user.

The section follows lists the disadvantages of a web/database system compared to a more traditional database approach.

- *Functionality*: Compared to the functionality available with a sophisticated graphical ser interface, a typical web browser interface is limited.
- *Operations*: The nature of the HTTP is such that each interaction between a browser and a server is a separate transaction, independent of prior or future exchanges. Typically, the web server keeps no information between transactions to track the states of the user.

EXERCISE 4

1. Explain the DBMS concept in Client/Server architecture in brief.
2. Is the structure of the data important to consider for processing environments? Discuss.
3. If the two servers process the same database, can it be called a Client/Server system? Explain with example.
4. One disadvantage of Client/Server system concerns control in a Database Management environment – explain the disadvantages with an example.
5. "Resource sharing architecture is not suitable for transaction processing in Client/ Server environment." Discuss.
6. Compare the object-oriented and relational database management system.
7. Discuss some types of database utilities, tools and their functions.
8. What are the responsibilities of the DBA and the database designers? Also discuss the capabilities that should be provided by a DBMS.

5

Client/Server Application Components

5.1 INTRODUCTION

A Client/Server application stand at a new threshold brought on by the exponential increase of low cost bandwidth on Wide Area Networks, for example, the Internet and CompuServe; and shows a new generation of network enabled, multi-threaded desktop operating systems, for example, OS/2 Warp Connect and Windows 95. This new threshold marks the beginning of a transition from Ethernet Client/Server to intergalactic Client/Server that will result in the irrelevance of proximity. The center of gravity is shifting from single server, two tiers; LAN based departmental Client/Server to a post scarcity form of Client/Server where every machine on the global information highway can be both a client and a server. When it comes to intergalactic Client/Server applications, the imagination is at the controls. The promise of high bandwidth at very low cost has conjured visions of an information highway that turns into the world's largest shopping mall. The predominant vision is that of an electronic bazaar of planetary proportions replete with boutiques, department stores, bookstores, brokerage services, banks, and travel agencies. Like a Club Med, the mall will issue its own electronic currency to facilitate round the clock shopping and business to business transactions. Electronic agents of all kinds will be roaming around the network looking for bargains and conducting negotiations with other agents. Billions of electronic business transactions will be generated on a daily basis. Massive amounts of multimedia data will also be generated, moved, and stored on the network.

5.2 TECHNOLOGIES FOR CLIENT/SERVER APPLICATION

Some key technologies are needed at the Client/Server application level to make all this happen, including:

- **Rich transaction processing:** In addition to supporting the venerable flat transaction, the new environment requires nested transactions that can span across multiple servers, long-lived transactions that execute over long periods of time as they travel from server to server, and queued transactions that can be used in secure business-to-business dealings. Most nodes on the network should be able to participate in a secured transaction; super server nodes will handle the massive transaction loads.
- **Roaming agents:** The new environment will be populated with electronic agents of all types. Consumers will have personal agents that look after their interests; businesses will deploy agents to sell their wares on the network; and sniffer agents will be sitting on the network, at all times, collecting information to do system management or simply looking for trends. Agent technology includes cross-platform scripting engines, workflow, and Java-like mobile code environments that allow agents to live on any machine on the network.
- **Rich data management:** This includes active multimedia compound documents that you can move, store, view, and edit in-place anywhere on the network. Again, most nodes on the network should provide compound document technology — for example, OLE or OpenDoc – for doing mobile document management. Of course, this environment must also be able to support existing record-based structured data including SQL databases.
- **Intelligent self-managing entities:** With the introduction of new multi-threaded, high-volume, network-ready desktop operating systems; we anticipate a world where millions of machines can be both clients and servers. However, we can't afford to ship a system administrator with every $99 operating system. To avoid doing this, we need distributed software that knows how to manage and configure itself and protect itself against threats.
- **Intelligent middleware:** The distributed environment must provide the semblance of a single-system-image across potentially millions of hybrid Client/Server machines. The middleware must create this Houdini-sized illusion by making all servers on the global network appear to behave like a single computer system. Users and programs should be able to dynamically join and leave the network, and then discover each other. You should be able to use the same naming conventions to locate any resource on the network.

5.3 SERVICE OF A CLIENT/SERVER APPLICATION

In this section, the discussion is about most widely used five types of Client/Server applications. In no way is this meant to cover all Client/Server applications available today. The truth, there is no agreement within the computer industry as to what constitutes Client/Server and therefore, what one expect or vendor may claim to be Client/Server may not necessarily fit the definition of others.

In general, Client/Server is a system. It is not just hardware or software. It is not necessarily a program that comes in a box to be installed onto your computer's hard drive (although many software manufacturers are seeing the potential market for Client/Server products, and therefore are anxious to develop and sell such programs). Client/Server is a conglomeration of computer equipment, infrastructure, and software programs working together to accomplish computing tasks which enable their users to be more efficient and productive. Client/Server applications can be distinguished by the nature of the service or type of solutions they provide. Among them five common types of solutions are as given below.

- File sharing.
- Database centered systems.
- Groupware.
- Transactional processing.
- Distributed objects.

- **File sharing:** File sharing is Client/Server in its most primitive form. It is the earliest form of computing over a network. Some purists would deny that file sharing is Client/Server technology. In file sharing, a client computer simply sends a request for a file or records to a file server. The server, in turn, searches its database and fills the request. Usually, in a file sharing environment, the users of the information have little need for control over the data or rarely have to make modifications to the files or records. File sharing is ideal for organizations that have shared repositories of documents, images, large data objects, read-only files, etc.
- **Database centered systems:** The most common use of Client/Server technology is to provide access to a commonly shared database to users (clients) on a network. This differs from simple file sharing in that a database centered system not only allows clients to request data and data-related services, but it also enables them to modify the information on file in the database. In such systems, the database server not only houses the database itself; it helps to manage the data by providing secured access and access by multiple users at the same time. Database-centered systems utilize SQL, a simple computer language which enables data request and fulfillment messages to be understood by both clients and servers. Database-centered Client/Server applications generally fall into one of two categories:
  (*i*) Decision-Support Systems (DSS) or
  (*ii*) Online Transaction Processing (OLTP).

Both provide data on request but differ in the kinds of information needs they fulfill.

(*i*) **Decision-support systems (DSS):** Decision-Support Systems (DSS) are used when clients on the system frequently do analysis of the data or use the data to create reports and other documents. DSS provides a "snapshot" of data at a particular point in time. Typically, DSS might be utilized for a library catalog, WWW pages, or patient records in a doctor's office.

(ii) Online transaction processing: Online Transaction Processing (OLTP) provides current, up-to-the-minute information reflecting changes and continuous updates. Users of an OLTP system typically require mission-critical applications that perform data access functions and other transactions with a one to two seconds response time.

Airline reservations systems, point-of-sale tracking systems (i.e., "cash registers" in large department stores or super markets), and a stockbroker's workstation are OLTP applications.

Structured Query Language (SQL): SQL, pronounced "sequel", stands for Structured Query Language. It is a simple set of commands which allows users to control sets of data. Originally developed by IBM, it is now the predominant database language of mainframes, minicomputers, and LAN servers. It tells the server what data the client is looking for, retrieves it, and then figures out how to get it back to the client.

SQL has become the industry standard for creating shared databases having received the "stamp of approval" from the ISO and ANSI. That's important since prior to this, there was no one commonly agreed upon way to create Client/Server database applications. With standardization, SQL has become more universal which makes it easier to set up Client/Server database systems in multi-platform/multi-NOS environments.

* **Groupware**

Groupware brings together five basic technologies multimedia document management, workflow, scheduling, conferencing, and electronic mail, in order to facilitate work activities. One author defines groupware as "software that supports creation, flow, and tracking of non-structured information in direct support of collaborative group activity." Groupware removes control over documents from the server and distributes it over a network, thus enabling collaboration on specific tasks and projects. The collaborative activity is virtually concurrent meaning that clients on the network, wherever they may be, can contribute, produce, and modify documents, and in the end, using the management and tracking features, synchronizes everything and produces a collective group product.

Multimedia Document Managements (MMDM)

With groupware, clients can have access to documents and images as needed. Multimedia document management (MMDM) allows them to take those documents and modify them. The modifications can take place in real time with several clients making changes and modifications simultaneously, or they can be modified, stored on the server for review or future action by other clients. MMDM is, in essence, an electronic filing cabinet that holds documents in the form of text, images, graphics, voice clips, video, and other media.

Workflow

Workflow refers to technologies which automatically route events (work) from one program to the next in a Client/Server groupware environment. It determines what needs to be done to complete a task or project, then merges, transforms, and routes the work item through the collaborative process.

Workflow is especially applicable to routine tasks such as processing insurance claims or income tax return preparation.

Scheduling (or Calendaring)

Scheduling or calendaring is native to groupware technology. It electronically schedules things like meetings and creates shared calendars and "to do" lists for all users on client workstations. It can work with the workflow function to monitor progress on a project (i.e., monitoring the project completion timeline), schedule a meeting or conference among key persons if needed, and notify them by automatic e-mail.

Conferencing

Conferencing is another native groupware application. This allows users at different client workstations to hold "electronic meetings." These meetings can be either "real time" or "anytime." In real time conferencing clients are interacting simultaneously. With "anytime" conferencing, documents and messages are posted to bulletin boards and clients can add their "two cents" in the form of comments, messages, or modifications.

Electronic Mail (E-mail)

E-mail is an essential element of groupware technology. It facilitates communication among clients on a network. In a groupware environment, the e-mail can be integrated with the multimedia document management, workflow, scheduling/calendaring, and conferencing features.

- **Transactional Processing**

To create truly effective Client/Server solutions, the various components within the system (the application software, the network operating system, utilities, and other programs) need to work together in unison. If infrastructure and software which enable Client/Server computing are musicians in a symphony, transaction processing would be the conductor.

- **Distributed Objects**

A distributed object is a vague term used to describe the technologies which allow clients and servers from different technologies from different environments and platforms to work seamlessly together. Its goal is to provide users with single-image, easy-to-use, virtually transparent applications.

Distributed object technology is still in its infancy and has yet to fulfill its promise of making Client/Server into the flexible, robust, intelligent, and self-managing systems that most users want and expect. Distributed objects technology has great "potential" but at this point in time, it remains just that potential.

5.4 CATEGORIES OF CLIENT/SERVER APPLICATIONS

There are variety of ways to divide the processing between client and server. But the exact distribution of data and application programming depends on the nature of the database, the type of application supported, the availability of interoperable vendor equipment, and the usage patterns within an organization. Depending on the database applications various classes of Client/Server Application has been characterized.

(*i*) Host-based processing.
(*ii*) Server-based processing.
(*iii*) Client-based processing.
(*iv*) Cooperative processing.

(*i*) Host-based processing: Virtually all the processing is done on a central host, often user interface is via a dumb terminal. It is mainly mainframe environment, not true Client/Server computing. In such a processing's workstations have very limited role as shown in Fig. 5.1 given below:

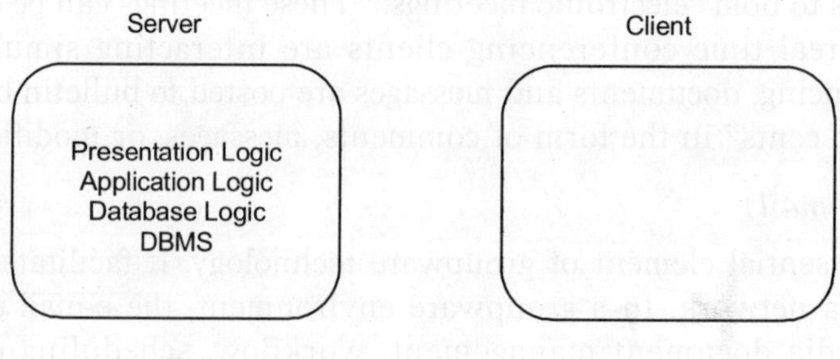

Fig.5.1: Host-base Processing

(*ii*) Server-based processing: All the processing is done on the server, and server is responsible for providing graphical user interface. A considerable fraction of the load is on the server, so this is also called *fat server* model shown in Fig. 5.2 given below:

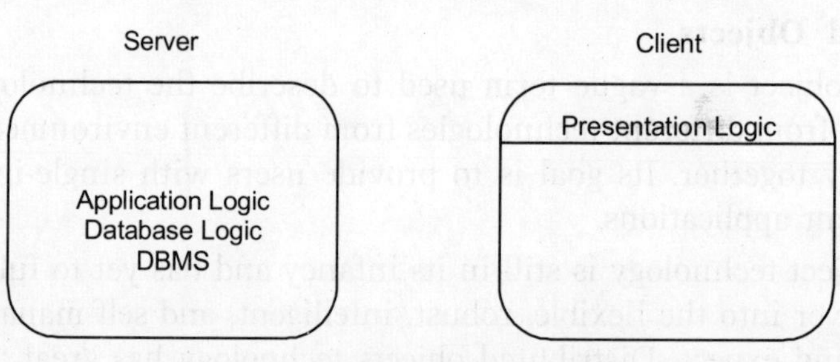

Fig.5.2: Server-base Processing

(*iii*) Client-based processing: Virtually all application processing may be done at the client, with the exception of data validation routines and other database logic functions that are best performed at the server. Some of the sophisticated database logic functions residing on the client side. This architecture is the most common Client/Server approach in current use. It enables the user to employ applications tailored to local need shown in Fig 5.3 given below:

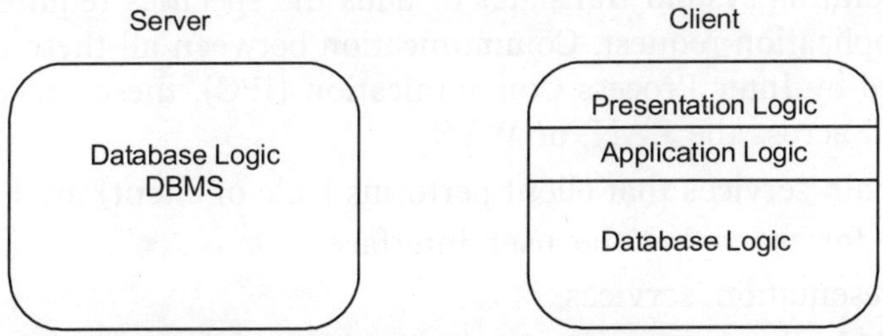

Fig. 5.3: *Client-base Processing*

(*iv*) Cooperative processing: Taking the advantage of the strengths of both client and server machine and of the distribution of data, the application processing is performed in an optimized fashion. Such a configuration of Client/Server approach is more complex to set up and maintain. But in the long run, this configuration may offer greater user productivity gain and greater network efficiency than others Client/Server approaches. A considerable fraction of the load is on the client, so this is also called *fat client* model. In case of some application development tools this model is very popular shown in Fig. 5.4 given below:

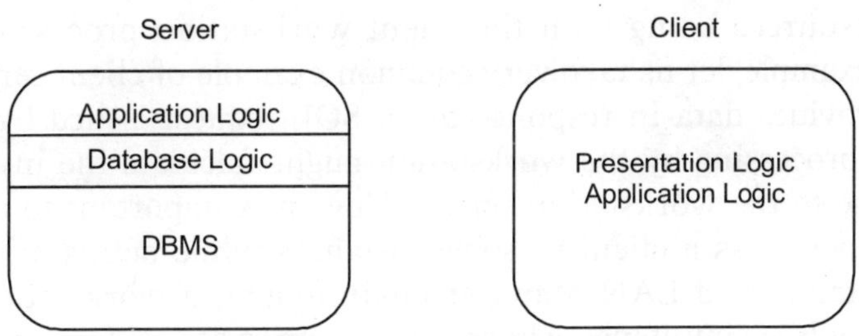

Fig. 5.4: *Cooperative Processing*

5.5 CLIENT SERVICES

Any workstation that is used by a single user is a client, it has been noticed during last decade the workstations are improving their performance surprisingly. Having same cost you can purchase CPU that can perform more than 50 times, main memory approximately

30 times and Hard Disk up to 40 times. These are considered as power factor of computer, hence, as a result, more sophisticated applications can be run from the workstations. To run various applications workstation uses the available operating systems like DOS, Windows (98, 2000, NT) and UNIX or Linux, Mac, OS/2. In case of, network environment (LAN, WAN) workstations also avails the services provided by the network operating systems. Client workstations request services from the attached server. Whether this server is in fact the same processor or a network processor, the application format of the request is the same. Network operating system translates or adds the specifics required by the targeted requester to the application request. Communication between all these running processes are better described by Inter Process Communication (IPC), these processes might be on the same computer, across the LAN, or WAN.

Some of the main services that client performs (role of client) are listed below:

- Responsible for managing the user interface.
- Provides presentation services.
- Accepts and checks the syntax of user inputs. User input and final output, if any, are presented at the client workstation.
- Acts as a consumer of services provided by one or more server processors.
- Processes application logic.
- The role of the client process can be further extended at the client by adding logic that is not implemented in the host server application. Local editing, automatic data entry, help capabilities, and other logic processes can be added in front of the existing host server application.
- Generates database request and transmits to server.
- Passes response back to server.

But in client server model one thing is very obvious that the services are provided by combination of resources using both the client workstation processor and the server processor. For an example, let us take very common example of client server application, a database server provides data in response to an SQL request issued by the workstation application. Local processing by the workstation might calculate the invoice amount and format the response to the workstation screen. Now, it is important to understand that a workstation can operate as a client in some instances while acting as a server in other instances. For example, in a LAN Manager environment, a workstation might act as a client for one user while simultaneously acting as a print server for many users. In other words we can say "the client workstation can be both client and server when all information and logic pertinent to a request is resident and operates within the client workstation."

Apart from these services discussed above some of the other important services that are directly or indirectly attached with the client services are given below:

(*a*) Inter process communication.
(*b*) Remote services.
(*c*) Window services.

(*d*) Dynamic data exchange.
(*e*) Object linking and embedding.
(*f*) Common object request broker architecture (CORBA).
(*g*) Print/Fax services.
(*h*) Database services.

5.5.1 Inter Process Communication

The communication between two processes take place via buffer. The alternative way of communication is the process of the interprocess communication. The simple mechanism of this is synchronizing their action and without sharing the same address space. This play an important role in the distribute processing environment.

While signals, pipes and names pipes are ways by which processes can communicate. The more redefined method of inter process communication are message queues, semaphores and shared memory. There are four types of mechanisms, involved for such a communications:-

(*i*) Message passing.
(*ii*) Direct communication.
(*iii*) Indirect communication.
(*iv*) Remote procedures call.

(*i*) **Message passing:** This mechanism allows process to communicate without restoring the shared data, for example in micro kernel, message is passed to communicate in which services acts as an ordinary user where these services act outside the kernel. At least, there are two processes involved in an IPC. See the Fig. 5.5 given below:

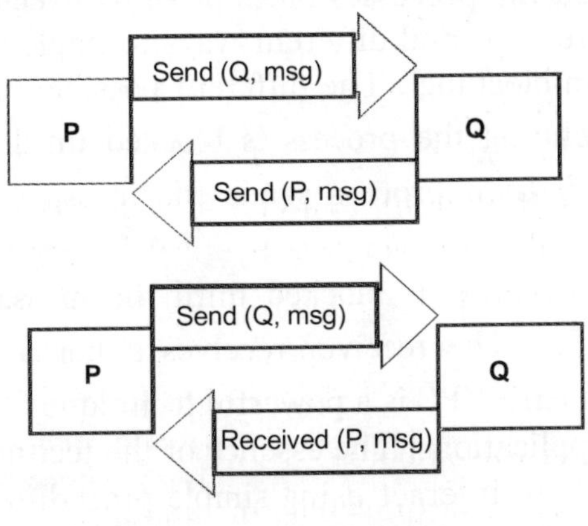

Fig.5.5: Message Passing

- Sending process for sending the message.
- Receiving process for receiving the message.

Messages sent by the processes are of two types, fixed and variable. For the communication to be taking place, a link is to be set in between the two processes.

(ii) Direct communication: In this mechanism of communication processes have to specify the name of sender and recipient process name. This type of communication has the following features:

- A link is established in between the sender and receiver along with full known information of their names and addresses.
- One link must be established in between the processes.
- There is symmetry in between the communication of the processes.

(iii) Indirect communication: In indirect communication, messages are sending to the mail box and then they are retrieved from mailbox, see the Fig 5.6 given below:

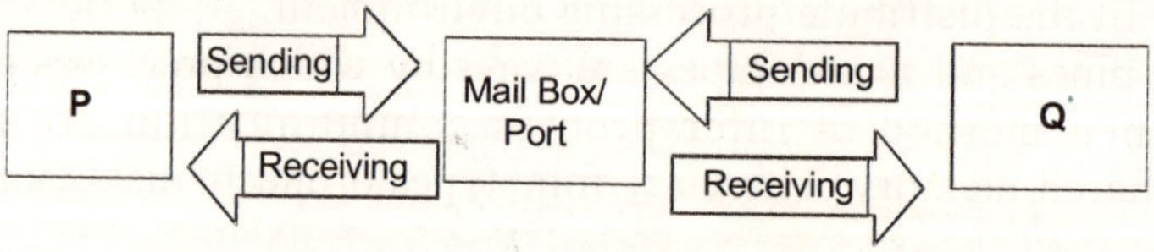

Fig. 5.6: Indirect Communication

The role of the mailbox is quite similar to the role of the postman. The indirect communication can also communicate with other processes via one or more mailbox. The following features are associated with indirect communication:

- A link is established between a pair of process, if they share a mailbox.
- A link is established between more than one processes.
- Different number of links can be established in between the two communicating processes.

Communication between the processes takes place by executing calls to the send and receive primitive. Now there is several different ways to implement these primitives, they can be "blocking" and "non-blocking". The different possible combinations are:

- *Blocking send*: Sending the process is blocked until the message is received.
- *Non-blocking send*: In it process sends the message and then it resumes the operation.
- *Blocking receive:* Receiver is blocked until the message is available.
- *Non-blocking receive:* The receiver receives either a valid message or a null.

(iv) Remote procedures call: RPC is a powerful technique for constructing distributed, client-server based applications. The essence of the technology is to allow programs on different machines to interact using simple procedure call or return semantics, just as if the two programs were on the same machine. It is based on extending the notion of conventional or local procedure calling, so that the called procedure need not exist in the same address space as the calling procedure. The two processes may be on the same system, or they may be on different systems with a network connecting them. That is, the procedure call is used for access to remote services.

In client-server based applications a binding is formed when two applications have made a logical connection and are prepared to exchange commands and data. This client server binding specifies how the relationship between a remote procedure and the calling program will be established. By using RPC, programmers of distributed applications avoid the details of the interface with the network. The transport independence of RPC isolates the application from the physical and logical elements of the data communications mechanism and allows the application to use a variety of transports.

How RPC Works: An RPC mechanism is analogous to a function call. Like a function call, when an RPC is made, the calling arguments are passed to the remote procedure and the caller waits for a response to be returned from the remote procedure. Figure 5.7 illustrates the general architecture of remote procedure call mechanism that takes place during an RPC call between two networked systems. The client makes a procedure call that sends a request to the server and waits. The thread is blocked from processing until either a reply is received, or it times out. When the request arrives, the server calls a dispatch routine that performs the requested service, and sends the reply to the client. After the RPC call is completed, the client program continues. RPC specifically supports network applications.

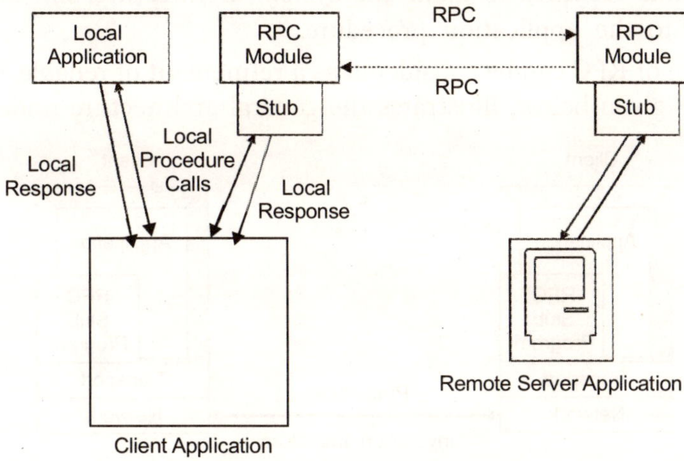

Fig. 5.7: RPC Mechanism

A remote procedure is uniquely identified by the triple: (program number, version number, procedure number), the program number identifies a group of related remote procedures, each of which has a unique procedure number. A program may consist of one or more versions. Each version consists of a collection of procedures which are available to be called remotely. Version numbers enable multiple versions of an RPC protocol to be available simultaneously. Each version contains a number of procedures that can be called remotely. Each procedure has a procedure number. Procedure may or may not be transparent to the user that the intention is to invoke a remote procedure on the same machine.

A stub procedure is added in the callers users address space (or dynamically linked to it at call time). This stub procedure creates a message that identifies the procedure being called and includes the parameters. Stub procedure provides a perfectly local procedure call abstraction by concealing from PROM programs the interface to the underlying RPC system.

RPC provides method for communication between processes residing over a distributed system. Procedure call is used for access to remote services. Basic concepts about this technique is that allowing programs residing on different machines to interact using simple procedures in a similar way like two programs running on the same machine. That is programmers feels an isolation from the network intricacies and got easy access to network functions by using RPC systems services.

RPCs, are APIs, layered on top of a network IPC mechanism, allows users to communicate users directly with each others. They allows individual processing components of an application to run other nodes in the network. Distributed file systems, system management, security and application programming depend on the capabilities of the underlying RPC mechanisms. Server access control and use of a directory service are common needs that can be met with RPCs. RPCs also manage the network interface and handle security and directory services. Tools of RPC comprises of:

- A language and a compiler to produce portable source code.
- Some run time facilities to make the system architecture and network protocols transparent to the application procedure.

The mechanism of RPC can be considered as a refinement of reliable, blocking message passing. Figure 5.8 given below, illustrates the general architecture understanding.

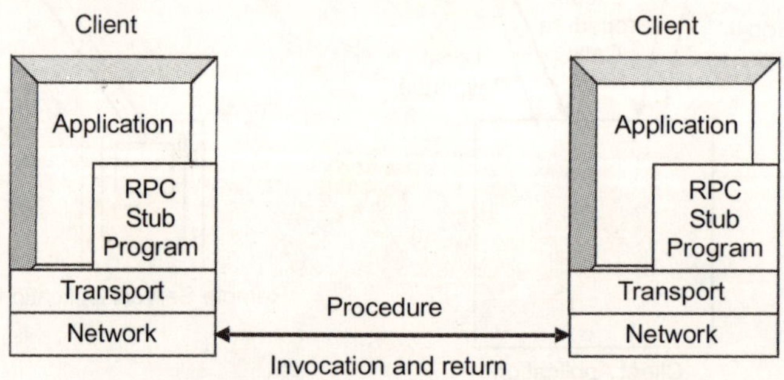

Fig. 5.8: *General Architecture*

Here, the structure of RPC allows a client to invoke a procedure on the remote host locally, which is done with the help of "stub" which is provided by the client. Thus, when the client invokes the remote procedure RPC calls the appropriate stub, passes the parameters to it, which are then provided, to remote procedure. This stub locates the port on the server and **marshalling** involves packaging the parameter into a form, which may be transmitted over network. The stub then transmits a message to server using message passing. Now the message sent by the host is received at the client side with the help of similar type of stub.

Limitation of RPC: There are number of limitations associated with RPC given below.

1. RPC requires synchronous connections. If an application uses an RPC to link to a server that is busy that time then application will have to wait for the data rather than switching to other task.
2. Local procedure call fails under the circumstances where RPC can be duplicated under and executed more than one, which is due to unreliable communication.
3. The communication in between the client and server is done with help of the standard procedure calls; therefore some binding must take place during the link load and execution, such that the process is replaced by the address. The RPC binds the same thing to the client and server. A general problem that exists is that there is no shared memory in between them so how they can come to know about the address of the other system.
4. The binding information may be predetermined in the form of the port address, at the compile time, a RPC call, that has a fix port number is associated with it. Once a program is compiled, it then cannot change its port number.
5. Binding can be done dynamically by rendezvous mechanism. Typically an operating system provides rendezvous demon requesting the port address of RPC, it needed to execute. The port address is then returned and the RPC call may be sent to the port until the process terminates.

5.5.2 Remote Services

In client server model applications can be invoked directly from the client to execute remotely on a server. The workstation is responsible to provide various remote services. Among them some services like remote login, remote command execution, remote backup services, remote tape drive access and remote boot services, and remote data access are important. Software available with Network Operating System is responsible to run on the client workstation to initiate all these remote services. Client server technology supports full-powered workstations with the capability for GUI applications consistent with the desktop implementation. Remote command execution is when a process on a host cause a program to be executed on another host, usually the invoking process wants to pass data to the remote program, and capture its output also. From a client workstation backup services may be invoked remotely. Some of the business functions such as downloading data from a host or checking a list of stock prices might also be invoked locally to run remotely. To run the application, some of the workstation clients (like X-terminals) do not have the local storage facility. In such scenario, client provides appropriate software's that are burned into E-PROM (Erasable Programmable Read-Only Memory) to start the initial program load (IPL)that is known as Boot Process. If E-PROM is inbuilt with X-terminals to hold the Basic Input/Output System services. Then partial operating system will be able to load the remote software's that provides the remaining services and applications functions to the client workstation. This is known as remote boot service provided by client workstation and X-terminals.

Remote data access is one of the ISO multi-site transaction processing and communication protocol used for heterogeneous data access. Using RDA technology, any client running an application will be able to access more than one database residing at the different servers.

5.5.3 Window Services

In client server application, operating system at the client workstation provides some windows services, these services are capable of to move, view, activate, hide, or size a particular window. This is very helpful in implementation of several applications because a client workstation may have several windows open on-screen at a time. And also, all these applications interact with message services provided to notify the user of events that occur on a server. Application programs running on workstations have been written with no windowing sensitivity. These application programs are written under virtual screen assumptions, that virtual screens are generally dissimilar to the actual available physical screens. Now with the help of interface software client application places data into virtual screen, and then the windows services handles manipulation and placement of application windows. Thus, pursuing that way application development has been enhanced tremendously due to developers less involvement in managing or building the windowing services. The client user is fully in grip of his desktop and can give priority to the most important tasks at hand simply by positioning the window of interest to the workstation.

The NOS provides some software's on the client workstation which is able to manage the creation of pop-up windows that display alerts generated from remote servers. Print complete, E-mail receipt, Fax available, and application termination are examples of alerts that might generate a pop-up window to notify the client user.

5.5.4 Dynamic Data Exchange (DDE)

DDE is usually described as a conversation between two applications, a client application and a server application. As we know that the client program is on that requests (receives) the information, and the server is the one that response (supplies) it. DDE is a feature of some operating systems (like Windows 98, OS/2) presentation manager that enable users to pass data between applications to application. For an example, if an application wants to connect a Microsoft Excel spreadsheet with Microsoft Word for windows report in such a way that changes to the spreadsheet are reflected automatically in the report, in that case Microsoft Word for windows is the client and Microsoft Excel is the server. A DDE conversation always concerns a particular topic and a particular item. The topic and item spell out the nature of the information that the client is requesting from the server. For an example, if the Word for Windows document is to receive data automatically from a range named IBM in a Microsoft Excel worksheet, named STOCKS.XLS then STOCKS.XLS is the topic and IBM is the item. With most of the programs, a simplest way to set up a DDE link is to copy a block of data from the server application to the clipboard, activate the client application, move the insertion point to the location in the receiving document where you want the information to go, and then use a Paste Link command. With most server programs, some times it requires to save data in a disk file before to paste it into a client programs. Using Paste Link is the easiest way to establish a DDE link, but it's not the only way. Some programs that act as DDE clients have commands that allow you to set up a DDE connection without first putting the source data on the clipboard. Many DDE supporting applications also have macro language that you can use to establish DDE links. This is true with MS Excel, Word, Powerpoint, dynacomm, and many other advanced windows applications. A DDE link may be automatic or manual. An automatic link is refreshed whenever the source data changes, provided both the client and server applications are running. A manual link is refreshed only when you issue a command in the client application.

5.5.5 Object Linking and Embedding (OLE)

Object Linking and Embedding two services collectively called as a single one, carried out with simple edit menu procedures. OLE is a software package accesses data created from another through the use of a *viewer* or *launcher*. These viewers and launchers must be custom built for every application. With the viewer, users can see data from one software package while they are running another package. Launchers invoke the software package that created the data and thus provide the full functionality of the launched software. To link with OLE copy data from OLE supporting program to the Clipboard. Then use the paste link command in another OLE supporting program. To embed, follow the same procedure but use Paste instead of Paste Link. Both programs must support OLE, the program that supplies the data must support OLE as a server application, and the one that receives the data must support as a client application. Some program may support OLE in one mode or the other, (it means either as a server or as client only). For an example, Paintbrush can act only as a server. Write and Card file can act only as OLE clients. Some other programs are also available which support OLE in both modes. Most of the Windows applications support OLE, and also the Microsoft has released its OLE 2.0 Software Development Kit (SDK). The toolkit greatly simplifies OLE integration into third-party, developed applications. Organizations wanting to create a consistent desktop are beginning to use the OLE SDK as part of custom applications. OLE 2.0 extends OLE capabilities to enable a group of data to be defined as an object and saved into a database. This object can then be dragged and dropped into other applications and edited without the need to switch back to the application which created it. This provides a more seamless interface for the user. In OLE 2.0, the active window menu and toolbar change to that of 1-2-3. The user deals only with the object, with no need to be aware of the multiple software being loaded. Generally, the OLE is known as an extension to DDE that enables objects to be created with the object components software aware (a reference to the object or one of its components automatically launches the appropriate software to manipulate the data). Both the techniques (OLE and DDE) require the user to be aware of the difference between data sources. DDE and OLE provide a substantial advantage; any DDE-or OLE-enabled application can use any software that supports these data interchange APIs. An e-mail application will be able to attach any number of components into the mail object without the need to provide custom viewers or launchers. But here, linking with OLE offers one big advantage over linking with DDE; that is the ability to launch the server program directly forms the client document. Client need not to remember from where the data came from. And if the server renames or relocates a document it requires repairing or abandoning any links in client documents. Most OLE client's applications include commands to assist such an application with this.

5.5.6 Common Object Request Broker Architecture (CORBA)

CORBA an object oriented architecture that provides an mechanism that allows various clients to share/call the object (applications) over a mixed networks. More specifically CORBA is a process of moving objects over network proving cross platform for data transfer. A client that needs a service sends a request to an object request broker (which acts as a directory) of all the remote services available on the network, illustrated in Fig. 5.9 given below:

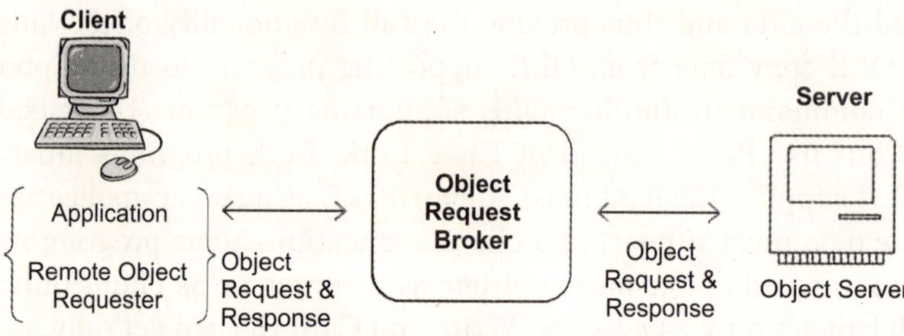

Fig. 5.9: Object Request Broker

The broker calls the appropriate object and passes along any relevant data. Then the remote object services the request and replies to the broker, which returns the response to the client. The object communication may rely on an underlying message or RPC structure or be developed directly on top of object-oriented capability in the operating system. The architecture of CORBA application is similar to the client server architecture by maintaining the notion of client and servers. In CORBA, a component can act as both a client and server. A component is considered as a server if it contains CORBA objects whose services are accessible form some other CORBA object. Likewise, a component is considered as a client if it access services from some other CORBA objects. Here a component can simultaneously provides and use various services and so any component can be considered as a client or as a server depending on the nature of the application running currently. When considering a single remote method invocation, however the role of client and server can be temporarily reversed because a CORBA object can participate in multiple interactions simultaneously.

Furthermore, any component that provides an implementation for an object is considered as a server, at least where that object is concerned. If a component creates an object and provides other components with visibility to that object (i.e., allows other components to obtain references to that object), that components acts as server for that object; any requests made on that object by other components will be processed by the components that creates the object. Thus, a CORBA server means the components execute methods for a particular object on behalf of other components (Clients). An application component can provide services to other application components while accessing services from other components. In that scenario, the components is acting as a client of one component and as a server to the other components i.e., two components can simultaneously act as client and server to each other, illustrated in Fig. 5.10, shown below. CORBA concepts and its role in Client/Server architecture is discussed in more detail in Chapter 9.

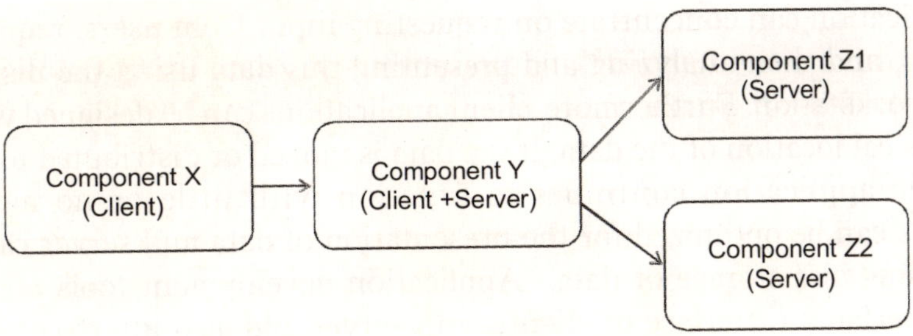

Fig. 5.10: Acting as a Client and a Server

5.5.7 Print/Fax Services

Client generates print/fax requests to the printer/fax machine without knowing whether they are free or busy. In that task network operating system helps the client to generate the requests. These requests are redirected by the NOS redirector software and managed by the print/fax server queue manager. The users at the client workstation can view the status of the print/fax queues at any time. And also some of the print/fax servers acknowledge the client workstation when the print/fax request is completed.

5.5.8 Database Services

Client/Server model provides integration of data and services allow clients to be isolated from inherent complexities such as communication protocols. The simplicity of client server architecture allows clients to make request that are routed to the database server (These requests are made in the form of transactions). In other words, client application submit database request to the server using SQL statements. Once received the server processes the SQL statement and the request are returned to the client application. That is illustrated in Fig. 5.11.

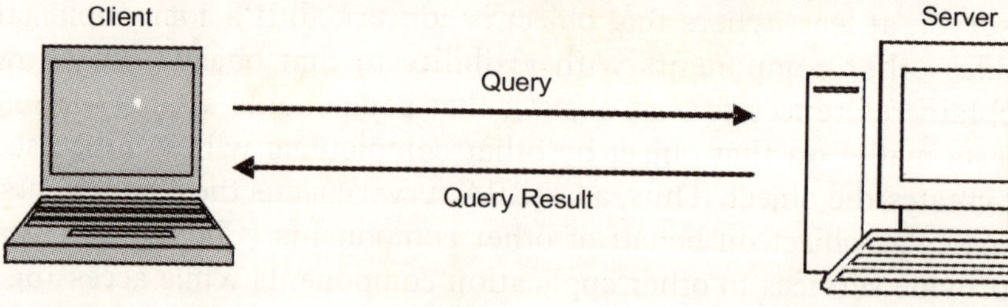

Fig. 5.11: Execution of SQL

Hence, most of the database requests are made using the SQL syntax. Now, the SQL's have became the industry standard language supported by many vendors. Because the language uses a standard form, the same application may be run on multiple platforms. Client application can concentrate on requesting input from users, requesting desired data from server, and then analyzing and presenting this data using the display capabilities of the client workstation. Furthermore, client applications can be designed with no dependence on the physical location of the data. If the data is moved or distributed to the other database servers, the application continues to function with little or no modification. Client applications can be optimized for the presentation of data and server can be optimized for the processing and storage of data. Application development tools are used to construct the user interfaces (interface of clients with server and also interface of front-end user to the back-end server); they provide graphical tools that can be used to construct interfaces without any programming. Examples of such tools are Visual Basic, Borland Delphi, Magic, and Power Builder. Some application programs (spreadsheet and statistical-analysis packages) uses the client server interface directly to access data from back-end server.

5.6 SERVER SERVICES

The server is responsible for controlling and providing shared access to available server resources. Remote workgroups have needed to share these resources when they are connected with server station through a well-managed network. The applications on a server must be isolated from each other so that an error in one application cannot damage another application. Furthermore, the server is responsible for managing the server-requester interface so that an individual client request response is synchronized and directed back only to the client requester. This implies both security when authorizing access to a service and integrity of the response to the request. For a Client/Server applications servers performs well when they are configured with an operating system that supports shared memory, application isolation, and preemptive multitasking (an operating system with preemptive multitasking enables a higher priority task to preempt or take control of the processor from a currently executing, lower priority task). These preemptive multitasking ensures that no single task can take overall the resources of the server and prevent other tasks from providing service. There must be a means of defining the relative priority of the tasks on the server. These are specific requirements to the Client/Server implementation.

One of the prime server characteristic is that it must support for multiple simultaneous client request for service. So that, the server must provide shared memory services and multitasking support. In that respect, the following server platform provides best processors for client server implementation are IBM System/370, DEC VAX , Intel and RISC (Reduced Instruction Set Computers like Sun SPARC, IBM/Motorola PowerPC, HP PA RISC, SGI MIPS, and DEC Alpha). Some of the main operations that server perform are listed below:

- Accepts and processes database requests from client.
- Checks authorization.
- Ensure that integrity constraints are not violated.
- Performs query/update processing and transmits response to client.
- Maintains system catalog.
- Provide concurrent database access.
- Provides recovery control.

Apart from these services discussed above some of the other important services that are directly or indirectly attached with the server services in a network operating system environment are given below:

(*i*) Application services.
(*ii*) File services.
(*iii*) Database services.
(*iv*) Print/fax/image services.
(*v*) Communications services.
(*vi*) Security systems services.
(*vii*) Network management services.
(*viii*) Server operating system services.

(*i*) **Application services:** Application servers provide business services to support the operation of the client workstation. In the Client/Server model these services can be provided for entire partial business functions that are invoked by IPC (Inter Process Communication) or RPCs request for service. A collection of application servers may work in concert to provide an entire business function. For an example, in a inventory control system the stock information may be managed by one application server, sales information are maintained by another application server, and purchase information are maintained by a third application server. On larger and more complicated systems, server responsibility may be distributed among several different types of servers. All these servers are running at different operating systems on various hardware platforms and may use different database servers. The client application invokes these services without consideration of the technology or geographic location of the various servers.

(ii) **File services:** A file server can store any type of data, and so on simpler systems, may be the only server necessary. Space for storage is allocated, and free space is managed by the file server. Catalog functions are also provided by the file server to support file naming and directory structure.

File services are responsible to handle access to the virtual directories and files located on the client workstation and to the server's permanent storage. Redirection software provides these services which are installed as part of client workstation operating system. Finally, all clients' workstation requests are mapped into the virtual pool of resources and redirected as necessary to the appropriate local or remote server. The file services provide this support at the remote server processor. File server manages databases, software's, shared data, and backups that are stored on tape, disk, and optical storage devices. In order to minimize the installation and maintenance effort of software, software should be loaded directly from the server for execution on the client workstations. New versions of any application software can be updated on the server and made immediately available to all users.

(iii) **Database services:** Early database servers were actually file servers with a different interface. Products such as dBASE, Clipper, FoxPro, and Paradox execute the database engine primarily on the client machine and use the file services provided by the file server for record access and free space management. These are new and more powerful implementations of the original flat-file models with extracted indexes for direct record access. Currency control is managed by the application program, which issues lock requests and lock checks, and by the database server, which creates a lock table that is interrogated whenever a record access lock check is generated. Because access is at the record level, all records satisfying the primary key must be returned to the client workstation for filtering. There are no facilities to execute procedural code at the server, to execute joins, or to filter rows prior to returning them to the workstation. This lack of capability dramatically increases the likelihood of records being locked when several clients are accessing the same database and increases network traffic when many unnecessary rows are returned to the workstation only to be rejected.

The lack of server execution logic prevents these products from providing automatic partial update backout and recovery after an application, system, or hardware failure. For this reason, systems that operate in this environment require an experienced system support programmer to assist in the recovery after a failure. When the applications are very straight forward and require only a single row to be updated in each interaction, this recovery issue does not arise. However, many Client/Server applications are required to update more than a single row as part of one logical unit of work.

Client/Server database engines such as Sybase, IBM's Database Manager, Ingres, Oracle, and Informix provide support at the server to execute SQL requests issued from the client workstation. The file services are still used for space allocation and basic directory services, but all other services are provided directly by the database server. Relational database management systems are the current technology for data management. Figure 4.1 charts the evolution of database technology from the first computers in the late 1950s to the object-oriented database technologies that are becoming prevalent in the mid-1990s.The following DBMS features must be included in the database engine:

- Performance optimization tools.
- Dynamic transaction backout.
- Roll back from, roll forward to last backup.
- Audit file recovery.
- Automatic error detection and recovery.
- File reclamation and repair tools.
- Support for mirrored databases.
- Capability to split database between physical disk drives.
- Remote distributed database management features.
- Maintenance of accurate and duplicate audit files on any LAN node.

In the Client/Server implementation, database processing should offload to the server. Therefore, the database engine should accept SQL requests from the client and execute them totally on the server, returning only the answer set to the client requestor. The database engine should provide support for stored procedures or triggers that run on the server.

The Client/Server model implies that there will be multiple concurrent user access. The database engine must be able to manage this access without requiring every developer to write well-behaved applications. The following features must be part of the database engine:

- Locking mechanisms to guarantee data integrity.
- Deadlock detection and prevention.
- Multithreaded application processing
- User access to multiple databases on multiple servers.

(iv) **Print/fax/image services:** High-quality printers, workstation-generated faxes, and plotters are natural candidates for support from a shared server. The server can accept input from many clients, queue it according to the priority of the request and handle it when the device is available. Many organizations realize substantial savings by enabling users to generate fax output from their workstations and queue it at a fax server for transmission when the communication costs are lower. Incoming faxes can be queued at the server and transmitted to the appropriate client either on receipt or on request. In concert with workflow management techniques, images can be captured and distributed to the appropriate client

workstation from the image server. In the Client/Server model, work queues are maintained at the server by a supervisor in concert with default algorithms that determine how to distribute the queued work.

Incoming paper mail can be converted to image form in the mail room and sent to the appropriate client through the LAN rather than through interoffice mail. Centralized capture and distribution enable images to be centrally indexed. This index can be maintained by the database services for all authorized users to query. In this way, images are captured once and are available for distribution immediately to all authorized users. Well-defined standards for electronic document management will allow this technology to become fully integrated into the desktop work environment. There are dramatic opportunities for cost savings and improvements in efficiency, if this technology is properly implemented and used. Chapter 9 discusses in more detail the issues of electronic document management.

(v) **Communications services:** Client/server applications require LAN and WAN communication services. Basic LAN services are integral to the NOS. WAN services are provided by various communications server products. Chapter 5 provides a complete discussion of connectivity issues in the Client/Server model.

(vi) **Security systems services:** Client/server applications require similar security services to those provided by host environments. Every user should be required to log in with a user ID and password. If passwords might become visible to unauthorized users, the security server should insist that passwords be changed regularly. The enterprise on the desk implies that a single logon ID and logon sequence is used to gain the authority once to access all information and process for the user has a need and right of access. Because data may be stored in a less physically secure area, the option should exist to store data in an encrypted form. A combination of the user ID and password should be required to decrypt the data.

New options, such as floppy less workstation with integrated Data Encryption Standard (DES) coprocessors, are available from vendors such as Beaver Computer Company. These products automatically encrypt or decrypt data written or read to disk or a communication line. The encryption and decryption are done using the DES algorithm and the user password. This ensures that no unauthorized user can access stored data or communications data. This type of security is particularly useful for laptop computers participating in Client/Server applications, because laptops do not operate in surroundings with the same physical security of an office. To be able to access the system from a laptop without properly utilizing an ID number and password would be courting disaster.

5.7 CLIENT/SERVER APPLICATION: CONNECTIVITY

The communication middleware software provides the means through which clients and servers communicate to perform specific actions. It also provides specialized services to the client process that insulate the front-end applications programmer from the internal working of the database server and network protocols. In the past, applications programmers had to write code that would directly interface with specific database language (generally a version of SQL) and the specific network protocol used by the database server. For example, when writing a front-end application to access an IBM OS/2 database manager database, the programmer had to write SQL and Net BIOS (Network Protocol) command in the application. The Net BIOS command would allow the client process to establish a session with the database server, send specific control information, send the request, and so on. If the same application is to be use with a different database and network, the application's routines must be rewritten for the new database and network protocols. Clearly such a condition is undesirable, and this is where middleware comes in handy. Here definition of middleware is based on the intended goals and main functions of this new software category. In chapter three communication middleware is also discussed, further role and mechanism of middleware is discussed in this section.

5.7.1 Role and Mechanism of Middleware

Role of middleware component can be exactly understand by the way in which Client/ Server computing being used , we know that there are number of approaches are there like host-based processing, server based processing, cooperative processing and client based processing. And all these depend on application functionality being used in Client/Server architecture. A Middleware component resides on both Client/Server machine enabling an application or user at a client to access a variety of services provided by server.

In other words, we can say middleware provides basis for logical view of Client/Server architecture. Morever, middleware enables the realization of the promises of distributed Client/ Server computing concepts. See the Fig. 5.12 (*a*) and (*b*) that depicts the role and logical view of middleware in Client/Server architecture. The entire system of the architecture represents a view of a set of applications and resources available to clients. Any client need not be concerned with the location of data or indeed the location of the application.

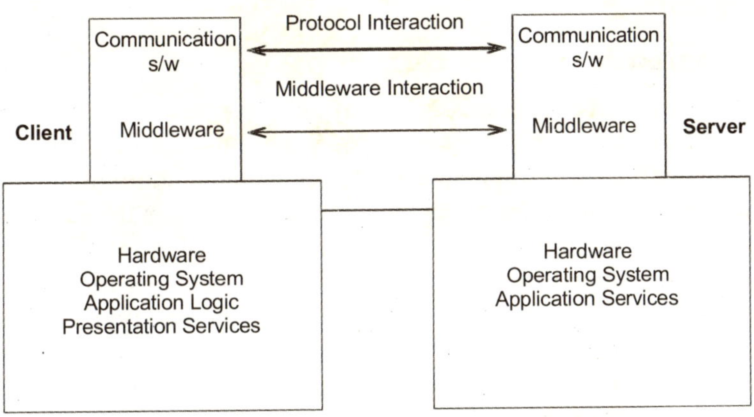

Fig. 5.12(a): Middleware Role in Client/Server Architecture

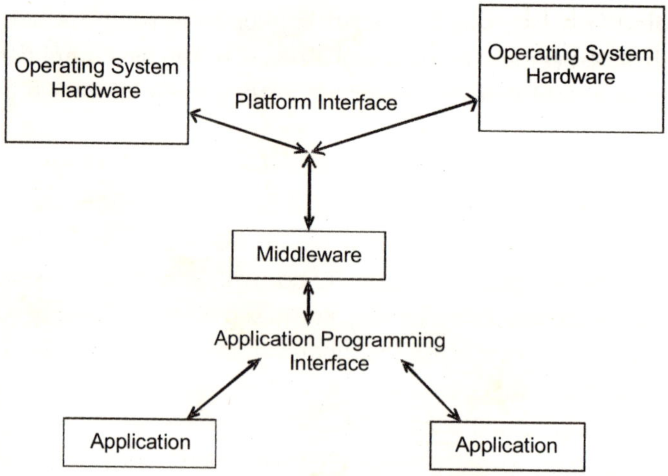

Fig. 5.12(*b*): Middleware Role in Client/Server Architecture

All applications operate over a uniform application programming interface. The middleware is responsible for routing client requests to the appropriate server. Also middleware used to overcome operating system as well as network incompatibility. This middleware running on each network component ensures that all network users have transparent access to applications and resources of any networks.

5.8 CLIENT/SERVER APPLICATION: LAYERED ARCHITECTURE

An essential factor in the success of a client/server environment is the way in which the user interacts with the system as a whole. Thus the design of the user interface to the client machine is critical. In most client/server systems, there is heavy emphasis on providing a graphical user interface that is easy to use, easy to learn, yet powerful and flexible. Section follow covers the design issues of client/server architecture. And also designing issues associated with layered application architecture with their interfaces in the three-layered application architecture.

5.8.1 Design Approach

In client/server architecture as a design approach, the functional components of an application are partitioned in a manner that allows them to be spread and executed across different computing platforms, and share access to one or more common repositories. Client/server architecture is therefore a design approach that distributes the functional processing of an application across two or more different processing platforms. The phrase 'client/server' reflects the role played by an application's functions as they interact with one another. One or more of these functions is to provide a service, typically in the form of a database server that is commonly used by other functions across the application(s). In this regard, it is important to discuss the concept of 'layered application architecture'.

Application design architecture plays a crucial role in aiding development of robust applications. Figure. 5.13 given below shows the three layers of any fairly large business application. The most detailed layer is the database layer, the centre of an application. The next higher layer is the business rule layer. Finally, the highest level of abstraction is the document layer. This is the layer visible to users of the application.

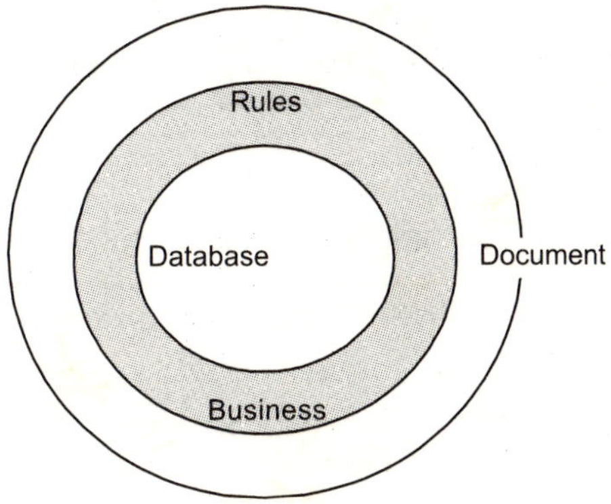

Fig. 5.13: Three-layered Application Architecture

Designing a client/server application offers challenges not normally faced by developers of mainframe-oriented multiuser applications. To realize full benefits of client/server architecture, developers need to incorporate a greater potential for functionality and data distribution in the fundamental design of their applications.

A client/server application operates across multiple platforms, i.e. a server platform for the database, and a client platform for the application. At this minimum level of utilization, the design of client/server does not differ much from its mainframe counterpart, and the physical issues faced by developers on both the platforms are primarily those of packaging. But to take full advantage of client/server paradigm, developers need to address issues of functional distribution for their applications, not just across client and server platform but also across all nodes of the network. Issues surrounding functional distribution constitute the single biggest difference between physical designs of multiuser and client/server application.

5.8.2 Interface in Three **Layers**

The key to use a three-layered application architecture is to understand the interfaces used in all its three layers. Figure 5.14 illustrates these interfaces. They are:

- Graphical user interface.
- Process request interface.
- Transaction and query manager interface.

An interface enables a component in one layer to communicate with a component in another layer; it also enables a component to interact with another component in the same layer. In Fig. 5.14 communication between components in the same layer is indicated by a semicircular arrow. Moreover, we can say that this describes a collection of mutually cooperating components that make request to each other, both within and across layers, with its components working together thus, and processing various requests—wherever they comes from; a business application comes to life.

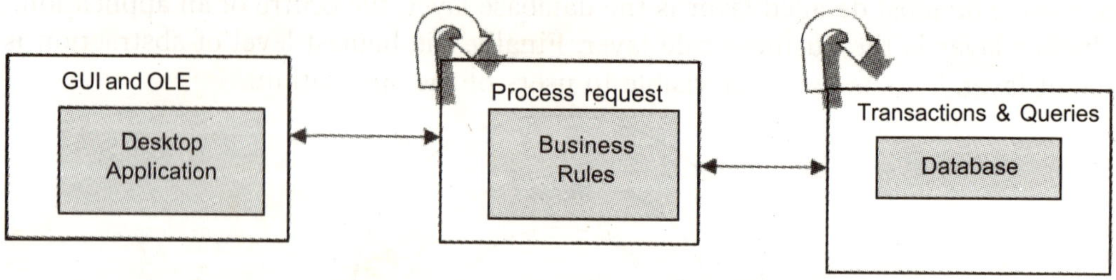

Fig. 5.14: Interface in a Three-layered Application Architecture

Cooperating components in a layered application design provide the following:

- A framework for building highly flexible applications that can be changed easily to meet the changing needs of business.
- A high level of software reuse.
- Easier development of large, complex applications that can sustain high throughput levels in both decision support and transaction environments.
- Easier development of distributed applications that support centrally and self-managed teams.

EXERCISE 5

1. In Client/Server computing, explain the following with example in detail
   (*a*) Dynamic Data Exchange
   (*b*) RPC, Remote Procedure Call
   (*c*) Remote Boot Service
   (*d*) Diskless Computer
   (*e*) Object-linking and embedding
2. Explain the role of client in Client/Server computing and also explain the various services provide by client.
3. Explain the server functionality, in detail, for Client/Server computing.
4. What is Interring Process Communication (IPC) and what are services provided by IPC? Also explain various protocol used for IPC.
5. What was the primary motivation behind the development of the RPC facility? How does a RPC facility make the job of distributed applications programmers simpler?
6. Explain basic Interprocess Communication Mechanism. Explain Port Management and Message Passing in IPC.
7. What are the main similarities and differences between the RPC model and the ordinary procedure call model?
8. Why do most RPC system support call by value semantics for parameter passing?
9. Explain the difference between the terms service and server.
10. Explain the role of server in Client/Server computing and also explain the various services provided by server.

6

System Development

6.1 HARDWARE REQUIREMENTS

6.1.1 PC Level Processing Units

UNIX Workstations

The user running Client/Server applications form DOS or Windows typically run only a single business process at a time. And also UNIX has locked the familiar personal productivity tools such as word processors, e-mail, spreadsheet, presentation graphics and database management system, but recently few personal productivity applications were in place, user needs have increased with providing reliability with multitasking. Many Unix implementation with application execution offers the best of all words for the desktop user reliability and functionality. Nowadays Unix supports many of the most familiar personal computer applications like WordPerfect, DBASE IV, Lotus 1-2-3. Unix has become the workstation of choice for Client/Server environment on the basis of cost performance rather than functionality.

X-Window System

The X-Window System is an open, cross-platform, Client/Server system for managing a windowed graphical user interface in a distributed network. In X-Window, the Client/ Server relationship is reversed from the usual. Remote computers contain applications that make client requests for display management services in each PC or workstation. X-Window is primarily used in networks of interconnected mainframes, minicomputers, and workstations. It is also used on the X-terminal, which is essentially a workstation with display management capabilities but without its own applications. (The X-terminal can be seen as a predecessor of the network PC or thin client computer).

X-Window System (commonly X11 or X) is a windowing system for bitmap displays. It provides the standard toolkit and protocol to build graphical user interfaces on Unix, Unix-like operating systems, and OpenVMS; and almost all modern operating systems support it. X provides the basic framework for a GUI environment to do drawing and moving windows on the screen and interacting with a mouse and keyboard. X does not mandate the user interface, individual client programs handle this. As such, the visual styling of X-based environments varies greatly; different programs may present radically different interfaces. X provides network transparency in which the machine where application programs (the *client* applications) run can differ from the user's local machine (the display *server*).

X-Terminal

An X-terminal is typically a diskless terminal especially designed to provide a low-cost user interface for applications that run in a network X-server as part of a distributed X-Window System. Typically, X-terminals are connected to a server running a UNIX-based operating system in a mainframe, minicomputer, or workstation. A terminal specially designed to run an X-server which allows users to display the output of programs running on another computer using the X-protocol over a network.

The X-terminal concept is essentially like tel-neting into a machine and then running some application there. All the working is done on the machine that you are connecting to but the display is shown on your machine. That just gives you access to console mode text applications, whereas an X-terminal setup will give you access to the entire range of GUI applications. All applications will be run on the server but the display will be exported to your computer. The machine that you setup as the X-terminal just serves as a display. This setup works very well with diskless workstations and older computers. An X-terminal is a great way to expand the computing presence in a home or office.

An X-terminal consists of a piece of dedicated hardware running an X-server as a thin client. This architecture became popular for building inexpensive terminal parks for many users to simultaneously use the same large server. X-terminals can explore the network (the local broadcast domain) using the X-Display Manager Control Protocol to generate a list of available hosts that they can run clients from. The initial host needs to run an X-display manager. Dedicated (hardware) X-terminals have become less common; a PC with an X-server typically provides the same functionality at a lower cost.

X-Server

An X-server is a server of connections to X-terminal in a distributed network that uses the X-Window System. From the terminal user's point-of-view, the X-server may seem like a server of applications in multiple windows. Actually, the applications in the remote computer with the X-server are making client request for the services of a windows manager that runs in each terminal. X-servers (as part of the X-Window System) typically are installed in a UNIX-based operating system in a mainframe, minicomputer, or workstation.

The X-server is the software that handles all the interactions between the GUI and hardware used. Windows equivalent would be the graphics card driver. But X is a lot more than that. Here it becomes a server with whom clients get connected. Clients would be the various GUI applications like GNOME, KDE etc. communicating through network protocols. This architecture allows a lot of flexibility. The clients can be run on any machine but the display can be routed to another machine. The X-server provides the following services.

- *Window services:* Clients ask the server to create or destroy windows, to change their attributes, to request information about them, etc.
- *Input handling:* Keyboard and mouse input are detected by the server and sent to clients.
- *Graphic operations:* Clients ask the server to draw pixels, lines, strings, etc. The client can ask information about fonts (size, etc.) and can ask transfer of graphic content.
- *Resource management:* The X-resource manager provides a content addressable database for clients. Clients can be implemented so they are customizable on a system and user basis.

The X-Client/Server model and network transparency

In X-Client/Server model, an *X-server* communicates with various *client* programs. The server accepts requests for graphical output (windows) and sends back user input (from keyboard, mouse, or touchscreen). The server may function as any one of the following:

- an application displaying to a window of another display system.
- a system program controlling the video output of a PC.
- a dedicated piece of hardware.

This Client/Server terminology the user's terminal as the "server", the remote applications as the "clients" often confuses new X users, because the terms appear reversed. But X takes the perspective of the program, rather than the end-user or the hardware. The local X display provides display services to programs, so it is acting as a server; the remote program uses these services, thus it acts as a client.

In above example, the X-server takes input from a keyboard and mouse and displays to a screen. A web browser and a terminal emulator run on the user's workstation, and a system updater runs on a remote server but is controlled from the user's machine. Note that the remote application runs just as it would locally.

The communication protocol between server and client operates network-transparently. The client and server may run on the same machine or on different ones, possibly with different architectures and operating systems, but they run the same in either case. A client and server can even communicate securely over the Internet by tunneling the connection over an encrypted connection. To start a remote client program displaying to a local server, the user will typically open a terminal window and telnet or ssh to the remote machine, tell it to display to the user's machine (*e.g.*, export DISPLAY = *[user's machine]*:0 on a remote machine running bash), then start the client. The client will then connect to the local server and the remote application will display to the local screen and accept input from the local input devices. Alternately, the local machine may run a small helper program to connect to a remote machine and start the desired client application there. Practical examples of remote clients include:

- administering a remote machine graphically.
- running a computationally-intensive simulation on a remote Unix machine and displaying the results on a local Windows desktop machine.
- running graphical software on several machines at once, controlled by a single display, keyboard and mouse.

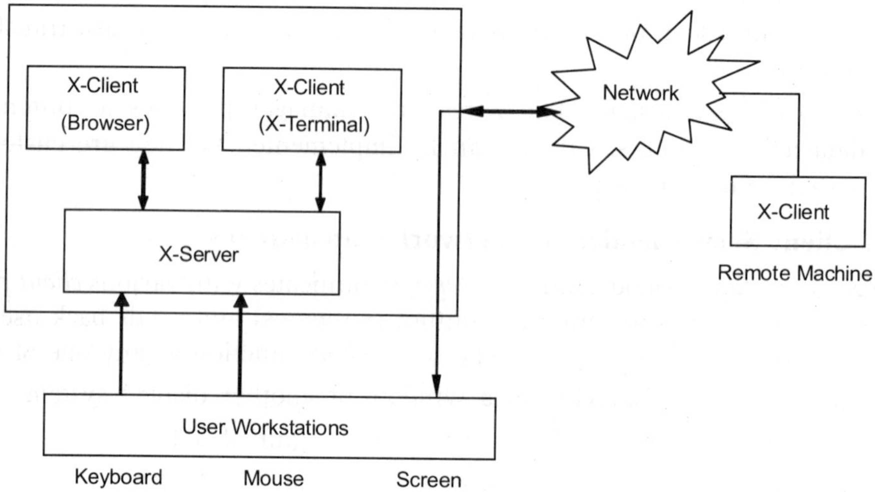

Fig. 6.1: X-Client-Server Model

Light Pen

Light Pen is an input device that utilizes a light-sensitive detector to select objects on a display screen. It is similar to a mouse, except that with a light pen you can move the pointer and select objects on the display screen by directly pointing to the objects with the pen. A light pen is pointing device that can be used to select an option by simply pointing at it, drawing figures directly on the screen. It has a photo-detector at its tip. This detector can detect changes in brightness of the screen. When the pen is pointed at a particular spot on the screen, it records change in brightness instantly and inform the computer about this. The computer can find out the exact spot with this information. Thus, the computer can identify where you are pointing on the screen.

Light pen is useful for menu-based applications. Instead of moving the mouse around or using a keyboard, the user can select an option by pointing at it. A light pen is also useful for drawing graphics in CAD.

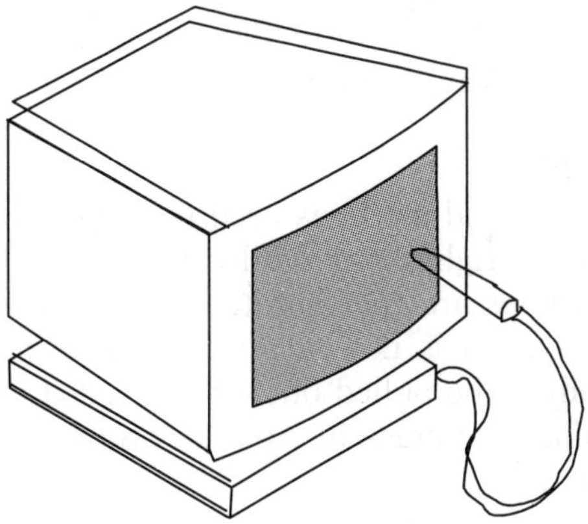

Fig. 6.2: Light Pen

Digital Pen

A digital pen writes on paper like any normal pen. The difference is that it captures everything you write. The digital pens include a tiny camera, some memory, a CPU and a communications unit. The paper is also special in that it needs to have an almost invisible dot pattern printed on it. You could use your laser to print this or get a specialist stationery printer to do it. Many paper products from 3M yellow sticky notes to black n' red notebooks are already available with the pattern pre-printed on them. The pen senses the pattern and this is how it knows where on the page you are writing. Most importantly using the digital pen is as easy as a normal pen with the quite significant benefit that a digital record is simultaneously created as you write.

They are available with desktop software applications integrating the pen with Microsoft Word and Outlook as well as a searchable notebook application. The pen is able to sent what you have written to a computer for storage and processing, or as an e-mail or fax. Applications range from: removing the need to re-key forms, to automatically storing and indexing pages written in a notebook. You can even send faxes and emails by simply writing them with a pen. Example of digital pens is Logitech io2 or a Nokia SU-1B pen.

Notebook Computers

If the portable computers are classified, they are of three types: laptops, notebooks and palmtops. Notebook computers are about the size of a notebook (approx. 21* 29.7 cm) and weight about 3 to 4 kg. Notebooks also offer the same power as a desktop PC. Notebooks have been designed to overcome the disadvantage of laptops that is they are bulky. Notebook/Portable computers are productivity-enhancement tools that allow busy execution to carry their office work with them. They are smaller in size. Several innovative techniques are being used to reduce size. Like VDU is compact, light, and usesless power, LCD (liquid crystal display that are light and consume very little power are used. Further numbers of keys on keyboard are reduced and also they are made to perform multiple functions. The size of hard disk is reduced is of 2.5" in diameter but capable of storing large quantities of data with weight only 300 gms. Examples of notebooks are Conture 3/20 from Compaq, and AcerAnyWhere from Zenith Computers.

6.1.2 Storage Devices

Storage refers to the media and methods used to keep information available for later use. Some things will be needed right away while other won't be needed for extended periods of time. So different methods are appropriate for different uses. Auxiliary Storage that is Secondary Storage holds what is not currently being processed. This is the stuff that is "filed away", but is ready to be pulled out when needed. It is non-volatile, meaning that turning the power off does not erase it. Auxiliary Storage is used for:

- Input—data and programs.
- Output—saving the results of processing.

So, Auxiliary Storage is where you put last year's tax info, addresses for old customers, programs you may or may not ever use, data you entered yesterday - everything that is not being used right now.

- Magnetic tape.
- Magnetic disks.
- Optical disks.
- Other storage devices—flash drives.

Magnetic Tape

Magnetic tape is a secondary storage device, generally used for backup purposes. They are permanent and not volatile by nature. The speed of access can be quite slow, however, when the tape is long and what you want is not near the start. So this method is used primarily for major backups of large amounts of data. Method used to store data on magnetic tape is similar to that of VCR tape. The magnetic tape is made up of mylar (plastic material) coated only on one side of the tape with magnetic material (Iron oxide). There are various types of magnetic tapes are available. But each different tape storage system has its own requirements as to the size, the container type, and the magnetic characteristics of the tape. Older systems designed for networks use reel-to-reel tapes. Newer systems use cassettes. Some of these are even smaller than an audio cassette but hold more data that the huge reels. Even if they look alike, the magnetic characteristics of tapes can vary. It is important to use the tape that is right for the system. Just as floppy disks and hard disks have several different formats, so do magnetic tapes. The format method will determine the some important characteristics like

Density: Higher density means more data on shorter tape that is measured as bpi (bits per inch that ranges from 800 bpi up to 6250 bpi.

Block: The tape is divided into logical blocks, as a floppy is divided into tracks and sectors. One file could take up many logical blocks, but must take up one whole block at least. So smaller blocks would result in more room for data.

Gap: Two kinds of blank spots, called gaps, are set on the tape. Interblock gap, which separates logical blocks. Interrecord gap, which is wider and separates records. Notice the two size lines cutting across the tape in the Fig. 6.3 below. Smaller gaps would allow more data to be stored on the same size tape.

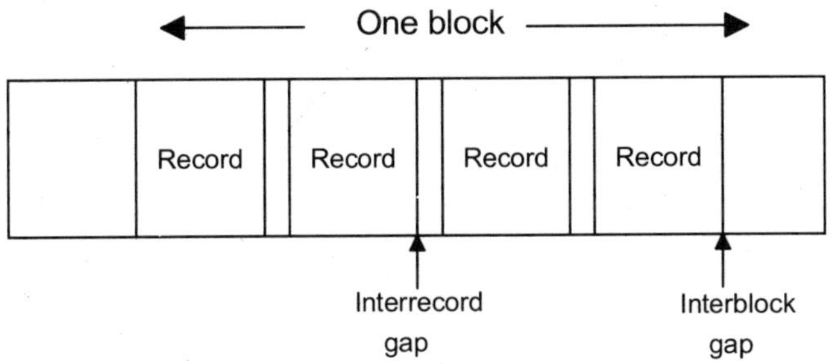

Fig. 6.3: Magnetic Tape

Magnetic Disks

There are various types of auxiliary storage; all of them involve some type of magnetic disk. These come in various sizes and materials, as we shall see. This method uses magnetism to store the data on a magnetic surface. The advantages associated with such type of storage media is they are of high storage capacity, reliable and provides direct access to the data. A drive spins the disk very quickly underneath a *read/write head*, which does what its name says. It reads data from a disk and writes data to a disk.

There are various types of auxiliary storage; all of them involve some type of magnetic disk. These come in various sizes and materials. This method uses magnetism to store the data on a magnetic surface. The advantages associated with such type of storage media is they are of high storage capacity, reliable and provides direct access to the data. A drive spins the disk very quickly underneath a *read/write head*, which does what its name says. It reads data from a disk and writes data to a disk. The available magnetic disks are Diskette/ Floppy disk and Hard disk.

All the magnetic disks are similarly formatted, or divided into areas that are tracks sectors and cylinders. The formatting process sets up a method of assigning addresses to the different areas. It also sets up an area for keeping the list of addresses. Without formatting there would be no way to know what data went with what. It would be like a library where the pages were not in books, but were scattered around on the shelves and tables and floors.

All the magnetic disks contain a track that is a circular ring on one side of the disk. Each track has a number. A disk sector is a wedge-shape piece of the disk. Each sector is numbered. Generally on a 5¼″ disk there are 40 tracks with 9 sectors each and on a 3½″ disk there are 80 tracks with 9 sectors each. Further a track sector is the area of intersection of a track and a sector. A cluster is a set of track sectors, ranging from 2 to 32 or more, depending on the formatting scheme in use.

The most common formatting scheme for PCs sets the number of track sectors in a cluster based on the capacity of the disk. A 1.2 giga hard drive will have clusters twice as large as a 500 MB hard drive. One cluster is the minimum space used by any read or write. So there is often a lot of slack space, unused space, in the cluster beyond the data stored there. The only way to reduce the amount of slack space is to reduce the size of a cluster by changing the method of formatting. You could have more tracks on the disk, or else more sectors on a track, or you could reduce the number of track sectors in a cluster.

A cylinder is a set of matched tracks on a double-sided floppy, a track from the top surface and the same number of track from the bottom surface of the disk make up a cylinder. The concept is not particularly useful for floppies. On a hard disk, a cylinder is made of all the tracks of the same number from all the metal disks that make up the "hard disk." If all these are putted together on the top of each others. It will looks like a tin can with no top or bottom forming a cylinder.

What happens when a disk is formatted?

Whether all data is erased? Surfaces are checked for physical and magnetic defects. A root directory is created to list where things are on the disk.

The capacity of a magnetic disk depends on several factors.

Optical Disk

The disk is made up of a resin (such as polycarbonate) coated with a highly reflective material (Aluminium and also silicon, silver, or gold in double-layered DVDs). The data is stored on a layer inside the polycarbonate. A metal layer reflects the laser light back to a sensor. Information is written to read from an optical disk using laser beam. Only one surface of an optical disk is used to store data. The coating will change when a high intensity laser beam is focused on it. The high intensity laser beam forms a tiny pit along a trace to represent 1 for reading the data laser beam of less intensity is employed (normally it is 25mW for writing and 5mW for reading). Optical disks are inexpensive and have long life up to 100 years. The data layer is physically molded into the polycarbonate. Pits (depressions) and lands (surfaces) form the digital data. A metal coating (usually aluminium) reflects the laser light back to the sensor. Oxygen can seep into the disk, especially in high temperatures and high humidity. This corrodes the aluminium, making it too dull to reflect the laser correctly. There are three types of optical disk are available:

- Compact Disk Read Only Memory (CD-ROM)
- Write Once Read Many (WORM)
- Erasable Optical Disk
- Digital Video Device (DVD)

All these optical disk are of similar characteristics like formed layers, organization of data in a spiral groove on starting form the center of the disk and finally nature of stored data is digital. 1's and 0's are formed by how the disk absorbs or reflects light from a tiny laser. An option for backup storage of changing data is **rewritable disks,** CD-RW, DVD-

RW, DVD + RW, and DVD + RAM. The data layer for these disks uses a phase-changing metal alloy film. This film can be melted by the laser's heat to level out the marks made by the laser and then lasered again to record new data. In theory you can erase and write on these disks as many as 1000 times, for CD-RW, and even 100,000 times for the DVD-RW types.

In case of WORM, the user can write data on WORM and read the written data as many times desired. Its tracks are concentric circles. Each track is divided into a number of sectors. Its disk controller is somewhat more expensive than that required for reading. The advantages of WORM are its high capacity, longer life and better reliability.

The Erasable optical disk is read/write optical memory. The disk contents can be erased and new data can be rewritten to it. It is also used as secondary memory of computer. The tracks are concentric circle. The coating of an erasable optical disk is done by a magnetic material, which does not lost its magnetic properties at the room temperature. The reading and writing operations are performed using magneto-optical system. In which a laser beam is employed together with a magnetic field to read/write operations.

Working mechanism of Optical disks in case of CD vs. DVD

As it has been discussed above that an optical disc is made mainly of polycarbonate (a plastic) see the Fig. 6.4 given below. The data is stored on a layer inside the polycarbonate. A metal layer reflects the laser light back to a sensor. And to read the data on a disk, laser light shines through the polycarbonate and hits the data layer. How the laser light is reflected or absorbed is read as a 1 or a 0 by the computer.

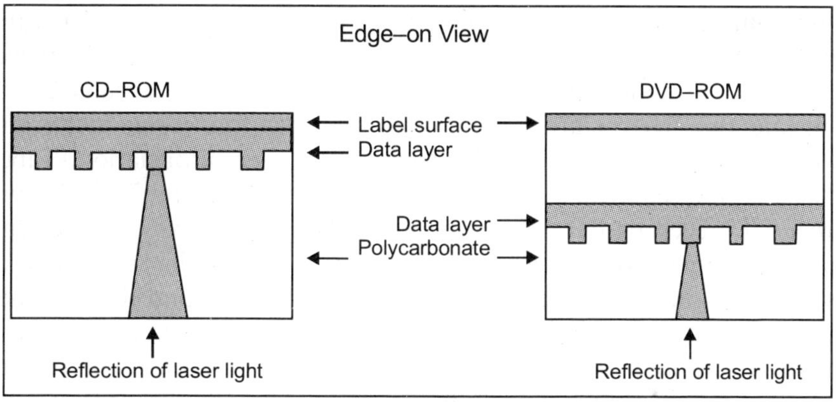

Fig. 6.4: Optical Disks (CD vs. DVD)

In a CD, the data layer is near the top of the disk, the label side. In a DVD the data layer is in the middle of the disk. A DVD can actually have data in two layers. It can access the data from 1 side or from both sides. This is how a double-sided, double-layered DVD can hold 4 times the data that a single-sided, single-layered DVD can. The CDs and DVDs that are commercially produced are of the Write Once Read Many (WORM) variety. They can't be changed once they are created.

Other Storage Devices—Flash Drives

Pen Drives

Also known as USB Flash Drive, USB Thumb Drive, Flash Drives. A thumb drive is portable memory storage. It is rewritable and holds its memory without a power supply, unlike RAM. Thumb drives will fit into any USB port on a computer. They will also "hot swap," which means a user can plug the drive into a computer and will not have to restart it to access the thumb drive. The drives are small, about the size of a human thumb hence, their name and are very stable memory storage devices. The thumb drive is available in storage sizes of up to 8 gigabytes (starting from 128MB, 256MB, 512MB, 1GB, 2GB, 4GB, 8GB). They are stable, versatile, durable and portable data storage devices. As such they are ideal for almost any computer user who wants safe, long-term storage for a low price. USB flash drives may have different design, different capacity and different price and some USB flash drives feature add-on functions such as MP3 players. But they do share some other characteristics:

USB flash drives are lightweight. Most USB flash drives are as light as a car key.

USB flash drives are small. Can be kept in your or attached with key chain.

USB flash drives carry large capacity of data, up to 8GB USB flash drives.

USB flash drives are helpful to store personal information without saving them in computer hard drive in case of sharing of a computer with other peoples at work place.

Tape Drives

A device, like a tape recorder, that reads data from and writes it onto a tape. Tape drives have data capacities of anywhere from a few hundred kilobytes to several gigabytes of information without having to spend large sums of money on disks. Their transfer speeds also vary considerably. Fast tape drives can transfer as much as 20MB (megabytes) per second. Tape Drives software is generally easy to use and can usually be ran without supervision. While Tape Drives are cost efficient and easy to use one major disadvantage. Tape Drives have the speed which they backup and recover information. Tape drives are a sequential access device, which means to read any data on the Tape Drive; the Tape Drive must read all preceding data. Tape drives are available in various design and shape like 8mm tape drive similar to what are used in camcorder with the transfer rate up to 6M/ Sec. Other is DLT (Digital Linear Tape) drive that is a robust and durable medium. The DLT segments the tape into parallel horizontal tracks and records data by streaming the tape across a single stationary head. Some other examples are DAT (Digital Audio Tape), QIC Standard. The disadvantage of tape drives is that they are *sequential-access* devices, which means that to read any particular block of data, it requires to read all the preceding blocks. This makes them much too slow for general-purpose storage operations. However, they are the least expensive media for making backups.

Zip Drives

Zip disks are high capacity(up to 100MB), removable, magnetic disks. ZIP disks are similar to floppy disks, except that they are much faster, and have a much greater capacity.

While floppy disks typically hold 1.44 megabytes, ZIP disks are available in two sizes, namely 100 megabytes and 250 megabytes. ZIP drives should not be confused with the super-floppy, a 120 megabyte floppy drive which also handles traditional 1.44 megabyte floppies. ZIP drives are available as internal or external units, using one of three interfaces:

- Small Computer Standard Interface (SCSI): Interface is the fastest, most sophisticated, most expandable, and most expensive interface. The SCSI interface is used by all types of computers from PC's to RISC workstations to minicomputers, to connect all types of peripherals such as disk drives, tape drives, scanners, and so on. SCSI ZIP drives may be internal or external, assuming your host adapter has an external connector.
- Integrated Drive Electronics (IDE): Interface is a low-cost disk drive interface used by many desktop PC's. Most IDE devices are strictly internal.
- The parallel port interface is popular for portable external devices such as external ZIP drives and scanners, because virtually every computer has a standard parallel port (usually used for printers). This makes things easy for people to transfer data between multiple computers by toting around their ZIP drive.

Zip disks can be used to store, backup, and move basic office application files, digital music, presentations, digital photos, digital video, etc. On the other hand, in spite of Iomega's claims that this drives "meet high capacity storage needs" for PC users, these products belong to the mobile storage rather than to the back-up category.

6.1.3 Network Protection Devices

System and network security is the term used to describe the methods and tools employed to prevent unauthorized and malicious access or modification of data on a system or during data transmission over network. Network security is not just for big corporations and government organizations only. The new breed of viruses, worms, and deceptive software that can infect computer or allow malicious hackers to unauthorized use of computers from any type of network interconnects. A bigger question arises what to protect on the network? The protection involves the following:

- Intrusion prevention.
- Intrusion detection.
- Web filtering.
- E-mail security.
- Security management.
- Integrated security appliance.
- Vulnerability assessment.

Network protection devices are used to preemptively protect computer network from viruses, worms and other Internet attacks. Intrusion detection and prevention, firewalls, vulnerability assessment, integrated security appliances, web filtering, mail security and a centralized management system, all work to maximize your network uptime and minimize the need for active administrator involvement.

Firewall used for all these provides only one entry point to your network. And if the modems are allowed to answer incoming calls, can provide an easy means for an attacker to sneak around the firewall. Just as castles weren't built with moats only in the front, then network needs to be protected at all of its entry points.

Secure Modems; Dial-Back Systems: If modem access is to be provided, this should be guarded carefully. The *terminal server*, or network device that provides dial-up access to your network needs to be actively administered, and its logs need to be examined for strange behaviour. Its password need to be strong. Accounts that are not actively used should be disabled. In short, it is the easiest way to get into your network from remote: guard it carefully. There are some remote access systems that have the feature of a two-part procedure to establish a connection. The first part is the remote user dialing into the system, and providing the correct user-Id and password. The system will then drop the connection, and call the authenticated user back at a known telephone number. Once the remote user's system answers that call, the connection is established, and the user is on the network. This works well for folks working at home, but can be problematic for users wishing to dial in from hotel rooms and such when on business trips. Other possibilities include one-time password schemes, where the user enters his user-Id, and is presented with a "challenge," a string of between six and eight numbers.

Crypto-Capable Routers: A feature that is being built into some routers is the ability to session encryption between specified routers. Because traffic travelling across the Internet can be seen by people in the middle, who have the resources (and time) to snoop around, these are advantageous for providing connectivity between two sites, such that there can be secure routes.

Virtual Private Networks

Given the ubiquity of the Internet, and the considerable expense in private leased lines, many organizations have been building *VPNs* (Virtual Private Networks). Traditionally, for an organization to provide connectivity between a main office and a satellite one, an expensive data line had to be leased in order to provide direct connectivity between the two offices. Now, a solution that is often more economical is to provide both offices connectivity to the Internet. Then, using the Internet as the medium, the two offices can communicate. The danger in doing this, of course, is that there is no privacy on this channel, and it's difficult to provide the other office access to "internal" resources without providing those resources to everyone on the Internet. VPNs provide the ability for two offices to communicate with each other in such a way that it looks like they're directly connected over a private leased line. The session between them, although going over the Internet, is private (because the link is encrypted), and the link is convenient, because each can see each other's internal resources without showing them off to the entire world.

Wireless Network Protection

In case of wireless network, it requires to take an additional security steps when wireless access point is set up first. Wireless networks are protected by something called Wired Equivalent Privacy (WEP) encryption. There are two steps to enabling WEP:

Step-1 is the configuring the wireless access point: The wireless access point is the device that is probably connected to cable or DSL modem. Instructions for configuration will vary slightly for wireless access points from different manufacturers.

Step-2 is the configuring the wireless network adapter: The wireless network adapter is either plugged into computer, or that is built-in to computer. In case of an older wireless network adapter, it requires check with the manufacturer to find out which WEP key lengths it supports.

6.1.4 Surge Protectors

A surge is defined as a voltage increase that lasts for as little as three nanoseconds (one nanosecond is one billionth of a second), and significant damage can be done in that miniscule amount of time, if the voltage surge is strong enough. A spike, which lasts for only one or two nanoseconds, can also do its share of damage, especially when several spikes occur repeatedly over an extended period. Voltage surges and spikes occur for a number of reasons. Perhaps the most common is the sudden jump in voltage that occurs when high-power appliances such as refrigerators and air conditioners first start up. The appliances need quite a bit of electrical energy to activate compressors, and that sudden and sharp increase in flow through the lines will be felt by the electronics. A surge protector is necessary to protect electronics against "dirty" electricity. Electrical power has a standard voltage for most residential uses of 120 volts to 240 volts, and it remains relatively steady. But when that power makes a sharp and brief jump for any of a variety of reasons, the resulting sudden alteration in voltage can seriously damage delicate circuits.

Electricity is your computer's lifeblood. Power anomalies and surges also pose a big threat to computer equipment. But the power line that supplies your computer with electricity also carries the seeds of your computer's destruction. Surges that are brief pulses of high voltage they sneak down the power line and, in an instant, can destroy the circuits inside computer. The way to protect your computer from lightning and power surges is to use a good surge protector. A power strip, which is a simple strip of outlets, is not necessarily a surge protector. A surge protector may look like a power strip, but it has built-in protection against power surges. Surge protectors are simple to install, maintenance free and have become much more affordable. Surge protection units are available that offer four to six protected outlets in one protection "center," which makes it easy and convenient to protect not only the computer but the printer, fax, external modem, scanner and other home office components. Many of these units also offer surge protection for one or more phone lines. A good surge protector should offer four features.

- The surge protector should cover lightning strikes. Some do not.

- The surge protector should offer insurance to cover the loss of properly attached equipment.
- For a regular modem, get a surge protector with an R-11 telephone jack where it can be hooked up with telephone line.
- With a cable modem, use a surge protector which will also accommodate the television/Internet cable.

The performance of surge protectors is rated three ways that are clamping voltage, response time and energy absorption. The first, clamping voltage, tells what level of voltage surge has to occur before the surge protector activates and diverts the excess voltage to ground. With this rating, the lower the voltage number is the better the surge protector will perform. It takes less of a surge to activate. For good protection, especially for computers, a protector with a clamping voltage of less than 400 volts will be preferred. Response time is the amount of time it takes for the surge protector to respond to the surge. Obviously, a fast response time is important, so look for a unit that will respond in one nanosecond or less. Surge protectors are not made to last forever, so the third rating, energy absorption, indicates how much energy the unit will absorb before it fails. For this rating, look for a unit rated at 300 joules or better, up to around 600 joules for even better performance.

A surge protection strip or center is also well-suited for home entertainment components like TV, VCR, stereo, etc. While not as delicate as computers, providing good surge protection will certainly help extend the useful life of any of these components. Entertainment center surge protectors may also contain protection for a phone line and a cable TV line, and typically cost a little less than the ones designed for computer protection. Example of some most commonly used surge protectors are ISP3 Inline Surge Protector with audible alarm, ISP 4 (Inline Surge Protector), ISP 5-perfect protection, ISP6 (Inline Surge Protector) 'cloverleaf'.

UPS (Uninterruptible Power Supply)

A UPS (Uninterruptible Power Supply) is basically a battery back-up system to maintain power in the event of a power outage for computer. UPS provides power for a short time (usually 10 or 15 minutes) to the computer or other critical hardware when its primary power source is unavailable. A UPS keeps a computer running for several minutes after a power outage, enabling you to save data that is in RAM and shutdown the computer gracefully. Power spikes, sags, and outages can not only cause lose of unsaved work and precious data, they can also damage valuable hardware and network infrastructure.

It acts as a surge suppressor, filtering line noise and providing protection against spikes. But, in the event of a power outage it keeps your computer up and running, sounding an alarm and allowing you to close any running programs and shutdown your computer safely. There are various common power problems that UPS units are used to correct. They are as follows:

Power failure: Total loss of utility power, causes electrical equipment to stop working.

Voltage sag: Transient (short term) under-voltage that causes flickering of lights.

Voltage spike: Transient (short term) over-voltage i.e., spike or peak that causes wear or acute damage to electronic equipment.

Under-voltage (brownout): Low line voltage for an extended period of time that causes overheating in motors.

Over-voltage: Increased voltage for an extended period of time that causes light bulbs to fail.

Line noise: Distortions superimposed on the power waveform that causes electro-magnetic interference.

Frequency variation: Deviation from the nominal frequency (50 or 60 Hz) that causes motors to increase or decrease speed and line-driven clocks and timing devices to gain or lose time.

Switching transient: Instantaneous undervoltage (notch) in the range of nanoseconds. May cause erratic behaviour in some equipment, memory loss, data error, data loss and component stress.

Harmonic distortion: Multiples of power frequency superimposed on the power waveform that causes excess heating in wiring and fuses.

There are two basic types of UPS systems available in the market one is on-line UPS systems. And other one is off-line UPS systems (also known as standby power systems. An on-line UPS always powers the load from its own internal energy supply, which is in turn continuously charged by the input power. An SPS monitors the power line and switches to battery power as soon as it detects a problem. The switch to battery, however, can require several milliseconds, during which time the computer is not receiving any power. Standby Power Systems are sometimes called Line-interactive UPSs. An on-line UPS avoids these momentary power lapses by constantly providing power from its own inverter, even when the power line is functioning properly. In general, on-line UPSs are much more expensive than SPSs. In a standby (off-line) system the load is powered directly by the input power and the backup power circuitry is only invoked when the utility power fails.

Most UPS below 1 kVA are of the standby variety which are cheaper, though inferior to on-line systems which have no delay between a power failure and backup power being supplied. A true 'uninterruptible' system is a double-conversion system. In a double-conversion system alternating current (AC) comes from the power grid, goes to the battery (direct current or DC), then is converted back to AC power. Most systems sold for the general market, however, are of the "standby" type where the output power only draws from the battery, if the AC power fails or weakens. For large power units, Dynamic Uninterruptible Power Supply are sometimes used. A synchronous motor/alternator is connected on the mains via a choke. Energy is stored in a flywheel. When the mains fails, an Eddy-current regulation maintains the power on the load. DUPS are sometimes combined or integrated with a diesel-genset. In recent years, Fuel cell UPS have been developed that uses hydrogen and a fuel cell as a power source potentially providing long run times in a small space. A fuel cell replaces the batteries as energy storage used in all UPS design.

6.1.5 RAID Technology

RAID is also known as redundant array of independent disks or often incorrectly known as redundant array of inexpensive disks. RAID is a system of using multiple hard drives for sharing or replicating data among the drives. Depending on the version chosen, the benefit of RAID is one or more of increased data integrity, fault-tolerance, throughput or capacity compared to single drives. In its original implementations its key advantage is the ability to combine multiple low-cost devices using older technology into an array that offeres greater capacity, reliability, or speed, or a combination of these things, than affordably available in a single device using the newest technology.

At the very simplest level, RAID combines multiple hard drives into one single logical unit. Thus, instead of seeing several different hard drives, the operating system sees only one. RAID is typically used on server computers, and is usually implemented with identically-sized disk drives. With decreases in hard drive prices and wider availability of RAID options built into motherboard chipsets. RAID is also being found and offered as an option in more advanced end user computers. This is especially true in computers dedicated to storage-intensive tasks, such as video and audio editing.

The RAID specification suggests a number of prototype "RAID levels", or combinations of disks. Each had theoretical advantages and disadvantages. Over the years, different implementations of the RAID concept have appeared. Most differ substantially from the original idealized RAID levels, but the numbered names have remained. The very definition of RAID has been argued over the years. The use of the term *redundant* leads many to split hairs over whether RAID 0 is a "real" RAID type. Similarly, the change from *inexpensive* to *independent* confuses many as to the intended purpose of RAID. There are even some single-disk implementations of the RAID concept. For the purpose of this article, we will say that any system which employs the basic RAID concepts to recombine physical disk space for purposes of reliability, capacity, or performance is a RAID system. There are number of different RAID levels:

Level 0—RAID (Striped Disk Array without fault tolerance)

Level 1—RAID (Mirroring and Duplexing)

Level 2—RAID (Error-Correcting Coding)

Level 3—RAID (Bit-Interleaved Parity)

Level 4—RAID (Dedicated Parity Drive)

Level 5—RAID (Block Interleaved Distributed Parity)

Level 6—RAID (Independent Data Disks with Double Parity)

Nested RAID levels: Many storage controllers allow RAID levels to be nested. That is, one RAID can use another as its basic element, instead of using physical disks.

Hardware and Software of RAID

RAID can be implemented either in dedicated hardware or custom software running on standard hardware. Additionally, there are hybrid RAIDs that are partly software and partly hardware-based solutions. With a software implementation, the operating system manages the disks of the array through the normal drive controllers like IDE (Integrated Drive Electronics)/ATA (Advanced Technology Attachment), SCSI (Small Computer System Interface) and Fibre Channel or any other. With present CPU speeds, software RAID can be faster than hardware RAID, though at the cost of using CPU power which might be best used for other tasks. One major exception is where the hardware implementation of RAID incorporates a battery backed-up write cache and an application, like a database server. In this case, the hardware RAID implementation flushes the write cache to a secure storage to preserve data at a known point if there is a crash. The hardware approach is faster and limited instead by RAM speeds, the amount of cache and how fast it can flush the cache to disk. For this reason, battery-backed caching disk controllers are often recommended for high transaction rate database servers. In the same situation, the software solution is limited to no more flushes than the number of rotations or seeks per second of the drives. Another disadvantage of a pure software RAID is that, depending on the disk that fails and the boot arrangements in use, the computer may not be able to be rebooted until the array has been rebuilt.

A hardware implementation of RAID requires (at a minimum) a special-purpose RAID controller. On a desktop system, this may be a PCI (Peripheral Component Interconnect) expansion card, or might be a capability built in to the motherboard. In larger RAIDs, the controller and disks are usually housed in an external multi-bay enclosure. The disks may be IDE, ATA, SATA, SCSI, Fibre Channel, or any combination thereof. The controller links to the host computer(s) with one or more high-speed SCSI, Fibre Channel or ISCSI (Internet SCSI) connections, either directly, or through a fabric, or is accessed as network attached storage. This controller handles the management of the disks, and performs parity {In computing and telecommunication, a parity bit is a binary digit that takes on the value zero or one to satisfy a constraint on the overall parity of a binary number. The *parity scheme* in use must be specified as even or odd (also called *even parity* and *odd parity*, respectively). Parity is even if there are an even number of '1' bits, and odd otherwise} calculations (needed for many RAID levels). This option tends to provide better performance, and makes operating system support easier. Hardware implementations also typically support hot swapping, allowing failed drives to be replaced while the system is running. In rare cases hardware controllers have become faulty, which can result in data loss. Because of this drawback, software RAID is a slightly more reliable and safer option.

Hybrid RAIDs have become very popular with the introduction of very cheap *hardware RAID controllers*. The hardware is just a normal disk controller that has no RAID features, but there is a boot-time set-up application that allows users to set up RAIDs that are controlled via the BIOS(Basic input output systems) . When any modern operating systems are used, they will need specialized RAID drivers that will make the array look like a single block device. Since these controllers actually do all the calculations in software, not hardware, they are often called "fakeraids". Unlike software RAID, these "fakeraids" typically cannot span multiple controllers.

Both hardware and software versions may support the use of a *hot spare* (A hot spare is a disk or group of disk used to automatically or manually, depending on the Hot spare policy, replace a failing disk in a RAID), a preinstalled drive which is used to immediately (and almost always automatically) replace a failed drive. This cuts down the time period in which a second failure can take out the array. Some software RAID systems allow building arrays from partitions instead of whole disks. Unlike Matrix RAID they are not limited to just RAID 0 and RAID 1 and not all partitions have to be RAID.

Reliability Factors of RAID

There are some important factors affecting the relaibility of RAID configuration like failure rate of disk, mean time of data loss and mean time of recovery.

Failure rate: A failure rate is the average frequency with which something fails. Failure rate can be defined as " The total number of failures within an item population, divided by the total time expended by that population, during a particular measurement interval under stated conditions. (MacDiarmid, et al.)" The meantime to failure of a given RAID may be lower or higher than those of its constituent hard drives, depending on what type of RAID is employed.

Mean Time to Data Loss (MTTDL): In this context, the meantime to elapse before a loss of user data in a given array, usually measured in hours.

Mean Time to Recovery (MTTR): Meantime to recovery is the average time that a device will take to recover from a non-terminal failure. Examples of such devices range from self-resetting fuses (where the MTTR would be very short, probably seconds), up to whole systems which have to be replaced. In arrays that include redundancy for reliability, this is the time following a failure to restore an array to its normal failure-tolerant mode of operation. This includes time to replace a failed disk mechanism as well as time to rebuild the array (i.e., to replicate data for redundancy).

6.1.6 Server Specific Jargon

In the client/server environment servers are also computers like other workstations with some configurational differences where processing speed is measured megahertz (MHz), hard disk capacity measured in gigabytes (GB), data transfer rates measured in milliseconds (MS); apart from these, there are some server specific jargon that are useful to know like EDC Memory, Memory Cache, Rack Mounting, Power Protection, RAID and Symmetrical Multiprocessing.

EDC Memory

Error Detection and Correction (EDC) such type of memory is configured at the hardware level with special circuitry that verifies RAM output and resends output whenever the memory errors occur. This type of memory is used to boost overall reliability of servers and tending to become standard equipment.

Memory Cache

Memory cache sets aside a portion of the server RAM to store the most frequently used network instructions so that these instructions can be accessed as soon as possible. While the server is in operation cache storage is being constantly updated. While network processing, less frequently accessed instructions are pushed out of cache, replaced by instructions that are accessed more frequently. The larger the size of the memory cache, the more instructions the server can keep on hand for fast access.

Rack Mounting

A rack mount server usually refers to multiple servers stacked on top of one another in a single cabinet to save space. In case of very large client/server a system that requires more than a single file server rack mount can be used, where the system is complex and highly centralized.

Power Protection

Power supply is a unit that distributes electricity within the server. A RDS redundant power supply is a backup power supply that takes over in the event that the main power supply fails. This feature is different from an UPS (uninterruptible power supply) an external device that provides continuous electrical power to the server, usually for a short time, in the event of an electrical power failure. Details of UPS has already discussed in Section 6.1.4, i.e. surge protectors, RDS keeps the network running indefinitely, as long as electricity is being fed to it on other hand UPS keeps the network running just long enough after a power failure to store and protect data before shuting down. A line conditioner that is another form of power protectors can be used to monitor the electrical current and compensates for extreme fluctuations (i.e. *spikes,* burst of too much voltage or *brownouts,* sudden drop in voltage).

Symmetrical Multiprocessing

Symmetrical Multiprocessing (SMP) technology is used to integrate the power of more than one central processor into a single file server, along with necessary additional hardware and software to divide processing chores between them. There is a drastic effect on the server speed by using multiple processors, although it is not as simple as doubling speed with two processors or tripling speed with three. SMP involves additional processing overhead to manage the distribution of processing among those multiple processors. In case of big client/server systems where a large scale networks is involved the features of SMP are used.

6.2 SOFTWARE REQUIREMENTS

6.2.1 Client OS

The client always provides presentation services, all the user Input and Output are presented at client workstation. Software to support specific functions like field edits, context-sensitive help, navigation, training, personal data storage, and manipulation frequently get executes on the client workstation. All these functions use the GUI and windowing functionality. Additional business logic for calculations, selection, and analysis can reside on the client workstation. A client workstation uses a local operating system to host both basic services and the network operating system interfaces. This operating system may be the same or different from that of the server. Numbers of OS are installed depending upon the application and user requirement running on Client/Server environment. There are various OS are in use as a client platform like DOS, Windows 3.1, OS/2, UNIX, Windows NT (New Technology), AIX and Mc systems 7. The client workstation frequently provides personal productivity functions, such as word processing, which use only the hardware and software resident right on the workstation. When the client workstation is connected to a LAN, it has access to the services provided by the network operating system (NOS) in addition to those provided by the client workstation. The workstation may load software and save word-processed documents from a server and therefore use the file server functions provided through the NOS. It also can print to a remote printer through the NOS. The client workstation may be used as a terminal to access applications resident on a host minicomputer or mainframe processor. This enables the single workstation to replace the terminal, as well as provide client workstation functionality.

6.2.2 Server OS

Servers provide the platform for application, database, and communication services also the server provides and controls shared access to server resources. Applications on a server must be isolated from each other so that an error in one cannot damage another. Preemptive multitasking ensures that no single task can take overall the resources of the server and prevent other tasks from providing service. There must be a means of defining the relative priority of the tasks on the server. These requirements are specific to the Client/Server implementation and not to the file server implementation. Because file servers execute only the single task of file service, they can operate in a more limited operating environment without the need for application isolation and preemptive multitasking.

The server is a multiuser computer. There is no special hardware requirement that turns a computer into a server. The hardware platform should be selected based on application demands and economics. There is no pre-eminent hardware technology for the server. The primary characteristic of the server is its support for multiple simultaneous client requests for service. Therefore, the server must provide multitasking support and shared memory services. Servers for Client/Server applications work best when they are configured with an operating system that supports shared memory, application isolation, and preemptive multitasking. High-end Intel, RISC (including Sun SPARC, IBM/Motorola PowerPC, HP PA RISC, SGI MIPS, and DEC Alpha), IBM System/370, and DEC VAX processors are all candidates for the server platform. The server is responsible for managing the server-requester interface so that an individual client request response is synchronized and directed back only to the client requester. This implies both security when authorizing access to a service and integrity of the response to the request. Some of the operating system dominating the server word nowadays are NetWare, Windows NT, OS/2, MVS, VMS, and UNIX.

NetWare

In 2003, Novell announced the successor product to NetWare (Open Enterprise Server OES). Later on completes the separation of the services traditionally associated with NetWare like directory services, file, and printer from the platform underlying the delivery of those services. OES is essentially a set of applications (eDirectory, NetWare Core Protocol services, iPrint, etc.) that can run a top either a Linux or a NetWare kernel platform. Also known as self-contained operating system so does not requires separate operating system to run.

OS/2

The last released version was 4.0 in 1996. Early versions found their way into embedded systems and still, as of mid-2003, run inside many of the world's automated teller machines. Like Unix, OS/2 was built to be preemptively multitasking and would not run on a machine without an MMU (early versions simulated an MMU using the 286's memory segmentation). Unlike Unix, OS/2 was never built to be a multiuser system. Process-spawning was relatively cheap, but IPC was difficult and brittle. Networking was initially focused on LAN protocols, but a TCP/IP stack was added in later versions. There were no programs analogous to Unix service daemons, so OS/2 never handled multi-function networking very well. OS/2 had both a CLI and GUI. Most of the positive legendary around OS/2 was about the Workplace Shell (WPS), the OS/2 desktop. The combination of Novell with an OS/2 database and application servers can provide the necessary environment for a production-quality Client/Server implementation.

Windows NT

Windows NT (New Technology) is Microsoft's operating system released in september 1993, for high-end personal and server use. Microsoft staked its unique position with a server operating system. Microsoft's previous development of OS/2 with IBM did not create the single standard UNIX alternative that was hoped for. NT provides the preemptive multitasking services required for a functional server. It provides excellent support for Windows clients and incorporates the necessary storage protection services required for a reliable server operating system.

NT has file attributes in some of its file system types. They are used in a restricted way, to implement access-control lists on some file systems, and do not affect development style very much. It also has a record-type distinction, between text and binary files, that produces occasional annoyances (both NT and OS/2 inherited this misfeature from DOS).

NT systems on the Internet are notoriously vulnerable to worms, viruses, defacements, and cracks of all kinds. There are many reasons for this, some more fundamental than others. The most fundamental is that NT's internal boundaries are extremely porous. Because Windows does not handle library versioning properly, it suffers from a chronic configuration problem called "DLL hell", in which installing new programs can randomly upgrade (or even downgrade!) the libraries on which existing programs depend. This applies to the vendor-supplied system libraries as well as to application-specific ones: it is not uncommon for an application to ship with specific versions of system libraries, and break silently when it does not have them. On the bright side, NT provides sufficient facilities to host Cygwin, which is a compatibility layer implementing Unix at both the utilities and the API level, with remarkably few compromises. Cygwin permits C programs to make use of both the Unix and the native APIs, and is the first thing many Unix hackers install on such Windows systems as they are compelled by circumstances to make use of. The intended audience for the NT operating systems is primarily nontechnical end users, implying a very low tolerance for interface complexity. It is used in both client and server roles. Early in its history Microsoft relied on third-party development to supply applications. They originally published full documentation for the Windows APIs, and kept the price of development tools low. But over time, and as competitors collapsed, Microsoft's strategy shifted to favor in-house development, they began hiding APIs from the outside world, and development tools grew more expensive.

MVS

MVS (Multiple Virtual Storage) is IBM's flagship operating system for its mainframe computers as a platform for large applications. MVS is the only one OS that could be considered older than Unix. It is also the least influenced by Unix concepts and technology, and represents the strongest design contrast with Unix. The unifying idea of MVS is that all work is batch; the system is designed to make the most efficient possible use of the machine for batch processing of huge amounts of data, with minimal concessions to interaction with human users. MVS uses the machine MMU; processes have separate address spaces. Interprocess communication is supported only through shared memory. There are facilities for threading (which MVS calls "subtasking"), but they are lightly used, mainly because the facility is only easily accessible from programs written in assembler. Instead, the typical batch application is a short series of heavyweight program invocations glued together by JCL (Job Control Language) which provides scripting, though in a notoriously difficult and inflexible way. Programs in a job communicate through temporary files; filters and the like are nearly impossible to do in a usable manner. The intended role of MVS has always been in the back office. Like VMS and Unix itself, MVS predates the server/client distinction. Interface complexity for back-office users is not only tolerated but expected, in the name of making the computer spend fewer expensive resources on interfaces and more on the work it's there to get done.

VMS

OpenVMS is a multi-user, multiprocessing virtual memory-based operating system (OS) designed for use in time sharing, batch processing, real time (process priorities can be set higher than OS kernel jobs) and transaction processing. It offers high system availability through clustering, or the ability to distribute the system over multiple physical machines. This allows the system to be "disaster-tolerant" against natural disasters that may disable individual data-processing facilities. VMS also includes a process priority system that allows for real-time process to run unhindered, while user processes get temporary priority "boosts" if necessary Open VMS commercialized many features that are now considered standard requirements for any high-end server operating system. OpenVMS commercialized many features that are now considered standard requirements for any high-end server operating system. These include Integrated computer networking, a distributed file system , Integrated database features and layered databases including relational database, Support for multiple computer programming languages, Hardware partitioning of multiprocessors, High level of security. Enterprise class environments typically select and use OpenVMS for various purposes including as a mail server, network services, manufacturing or transportation control and monitoring, critical applications and databases, and particularly environments where system uptime and data access is critical.

UNIX

Unix operating system developed in 1969 by a group of AT&T employees at Bell Labs including Ken Thompson, Dennis Ritchie and Douglas McIlroy. During the late 1970s and early 1980s, Unix's influence in academic circles led to large-scale adoption of Unix by commercial startups, the most notable of which is Sun Microsystems. Today, in addition to certified Unix systems, Unix-like operating systems such as Linux and BSD derivatives are commonly encountered. Sometimes, "traditional Unix" may be used to describe a Unix or an operating system that has the characteristics of either Version 7 Unix or UNIX System V.

Unix operating systems are widely used in both servers and workstations. The Unix environment and the Client/Server program model were essential elements in the development of the Internet and the reshaping of computing as centered in networks rather than in individual computers. Unix was designed to be portable, multi-tasking and multi-user in a time-sharing configuration. Unix systems are characterized by various concepts like the use of plain text for storing data, a hierarchical file system, treating devices and certain types of inter-process communication (IPC) as files and the use of a large number of small programs that can be strung together through a command line interpreter using pipes, as opposed to using a single monolithic program that includes all of the same functionality. Unix operating system consists of many of these utilities along with the master control program, the kernel. The kernel provides services to start and stop programs, handle the file system and other common "low level" tasks that most programs share, and, perhaps most importantly, schedules access to hardware to avoid conflicts if two programs try to access the same resource or device simultaneously. To mediate such access, the kernel was given special rights on the system, leading to the division between *user-space* and *kernel-space.*

6.2.3 Network OS

A Network Operating System (NOS) is a systen software that controls a network and its message (e.g., packet) traffic and queues, controls access by multiple users to network resources such as files, and provides for certain administrative functions, including security. Also includes special functions for connecting computers and devices into a local-area network (LAN) or Inter-networking. A Network Operating System (NOS) is an operating system that has been specifically written to keep networks running at optimal performance with a native structure for use in a network environment. Some of the important features of Network Operating System includes:

- Provide file, print, web services, back-up and replication services.
- Provide basic operating system features such as support for processors, protocols, automatic hardware detection and support multi-processing of applications.
- Security features such as authentication, authorization, logon restrictions and access control.
- Provide name and directory services.
- User management and support for logon and logoff, remote access, system management, administration and auditing tools with graphic interfaces.
- Support Internetworking such as routing and WAN ports.

Some of the components that an NOS usually has built in that a normal operating system might not have are built in NIC (network interface card) support, file sharing, server log on, drive mapping, and native protocol support. Most operating systems can support all of these components with add-on either by the original manufacture of the operating system or from a third party vendor. Some of the operating system dominating the networking OS are Novell NetWare, LAN Manager, IBM LAN Server, Banyan VINES etc.

Novell NetWare

NetWare is a network operating system developed by Novell, Inc. The latest version of NetWare is v6.5 Support Pack 7, which is identical to OES 2, NetWare Kernel. It initially used cooperative multitasking to run various services on a PC, and the network protocols were based on the archetypal Xerox XNS stack. NetWare has been superseded by Open Enterprise Server (OES). With Novell NetWare, disk space was shared in the form of NetWare volumes, comparable to DOS volumes. Clients running MS-DOS would run a special Terminate and Stay Resident (TSR) program that allowed them to *map* a local drive letter to a NetWare volume. Clients had to log in to a server in order to be allowed to map volumes, and access could be restricted according to the login name. Similarly, they could connect to the shared printers on the dedicated server, and print as if the printer was connected locally.

Novell had introduced limited TCP/IP support in NetWare v3.x (circa 1992) and v4.x (circa 1995), consisting mainly of FTP services and UNIX-style LPR/LPD printing (available in NetWare v3.x), and a Novell-developed webserver (in NetWare v4.x). Native TCP/IP support for the client file and print services normally associated with NetWare was introduced in NetWare v5.0. Most network protocols in use at the time NetWare was developed didn't trust the network to deliver messages. A typical client file read would work something like this:

- Client sends read request to server.
- Server acknowledges request.
- Client acknowledges acknowledgement.
- Server sends requested data to client.
- Client acknowledges data.
- Server acknowledges acknowledgement.

In contrast, NCP was based on the idea that networks worked perfectly most of the time, so the reply to a request served as the acknowledgement. Here is an example of a client read request using this model:

- Client sends read request to server.
- Server sends requested data to client.

All requests contained a sequence number, so if the client didn't receive a response within an appropriate amount of time it would re-send the request with the same sequence number. If the server had already processed the request it would re-send the cached response, if it had not yet had time to process the request it would send a 'positive acknowledgement' which meant, "I received your request but I haven't gotten to it yet so don't bug me." The bottom line to this 'trust the network' approach was a 2/3 reduction in network traffic and the associated latency. In 4.x and earlier versions, NetWare did not support preemption, virtual memory, graphical user interfaces etc. Processes and services running under the NetWare OS were expected to be cooperative, that is to process a request and return control to the OS in a timely fashion. On the down side, this trust of application processes to manage themselves could lead to a misbehaving application bringing down the server.

LAN Manager

LAN Manager is a network operating system developed by Microsoft developed in cooperation with 3Com (Computers, Communication and Compatibility) that runs as a server application under OS/2. It supports DOS, Windows and OS/2 clients. LAN Manager provides client support for DOS, Windows, Windows NT, OS/2, and Mac System 7. Server support extends to NetWare, AppleTalk, UNIX, Windows NT, and OS/2. Client workstations can access data from both NetWare and LAN Manager Servers at the same time. LAN Manager supports NetBIOS and Named Pipes LAN communications between clients and OS/2 servers. Redirection services are provided to map files and printers from remote workstations for client use. LAN Manager was superseded by Windows NT Server, and many parts of LAN Manager are used in Windows NT and 2000.

IBM LAN Server

A network operating system developed by IBM that runs as a server application under OS/2 and supports DOS, Windows and OS/2 clients. Originally based on LAN Manager when OS/2 was jointly developed by IBM and Microsoft, starting with LAN Server 3.0, it runs only under IBM's version of OS/2. Short term LAN Server refers to the IBM OS/2 LAN Server product. There were also LAN Server products for other operating systems, notably AIX (now called Fast Connect) and OS/400. LAN server is a file server in a network. LAN Server provides disk mirroring, CID capability and Network Transport Services/2 (NTS/2) for concurrent access to NetWare servers. Options are LAN Server for the Macintosh for Mac client access and System Performance/2 (SP/2), a series of network management utilities. LAN Server, are the standard products for use in Client/Server implementations using OS/2 as the server operating system. LAN Manager/X is the standard product for Client/Server implementations using UNIX System V as the server operating system.

Banyan VINES

Banyan VINES (Virtual Integrated Network Service) is developed during 1980. Banyan VINES is a computer network operating system and set of computer network protocols, it used to talk to client machines on the network. In other words Banyan VINES is a network operating system with a UNIX kernel that allows clients operating systems such as DOS, OS/2, Windows, and those for Macintosh systems to share information and resources with each other and with host computing systems. VINES provide full UNIX NFS (Network File System) support in its core services and the Transmission Control Protocol/Internet Protocol (TCP/IP) for transport, it also includes Banyan's StreetTalk Directory Services, one of the first viable directory services to appear in a network operating system.

VINES ran on a low-level protocol known as VIP (VINES Internetwork Protocol) essentially identical to the lower layers of XNS), addresses consisted of a 32-bit address and a 16-bit subnet, which mapped onto the 48-bit Ethernet address in order to route to machines. This meant that, like other XNS-based systems, VINES could only support a two-level internet. However, a set of routing algorithms set VINES apart from other XNS systems at this level. The key differentiator, ARP (Address Resolution Protocol), allowed VINES clients to automatically set up their own network addresses. When a client first booted up it broadcast a request on the subnet asking for servers, which would respond with suggested addresses. The client would use the first to respond, although the servers could hand off better routing instructions to the client if the network changed. The overall concept very much resembled AppleTalk's AARP system, with the exception that VINES required at least one server, whereas AARP functioned completely headlessly. Like AARP, VINES required an inherently chatty network, sending updates about the status of clients to other servers on the internetwork. At the topmost layer, VINES provided the standard file and print services, as well as the unique StreetTalk, likely the first truly practical globally consistent name service for an entire internetwork. Using a globally distributed, partially replicated database, StreetTalk could meld multiple widely separated networks into a single network that allowed seamless resource sharing. It accomplished this through its rigidly hierarchical naming scheme; entries in the directory always had the form *item@group@organization*. This applied to user accounts as well as to resources like printers and file servers. VINES client software ran on most PC-based operating systems, including MS-DOS and earlier versions of Microsoft Windows. It was fairly light weight on the client, and hence remained in use during the later half of the 1990s, when many machines not up to the task of running other networking stacks then in widespread use. This occurred on the server side as well, as VINES generally offered good performance even from mediocre hardware.

6.3 COMMUNICATION INTERFACE TECHNOLOGY

For the data communication to be taking place on a network, four basic elements are involved there:

Sender: the device that creates and transmits the data.

Message: the data to be sent. It could be a spreadsheet, database, or document, converted to digital form.

Medium: the physical material that connects the devices and carries the data from the sender to the receiver. The medium may consist of an electrical wire or airwaves.

Receiver: the destination device for the data.

To communicate with other devices, a sending device must know and follow the rules for sending data to receiving devices on the network. These rules for communication between devices are called *protocols*. Numerous standards have been developed to provide common foundations for data transmission. The International Standards Organization (ISO) has divided the required communication functions into seven levels to form the Open Systems Interconnections (OSI) model. Each layer in the OSI model specifies a group of functions and associated protocols used at that level in the source device to communicate with the corresponding level in the destination device.

Connectivity and interoperability between the client and the server are achieved through a combination of physical cables and devices and software that implements communication protocols. To communicate on a network the following components are required:

- A network interface card (NIC) or network adapter.
- Software driver.
- Communication protocol stack.

Computer networks may be implemented using a variety of protocol stack architectures, computer buses or combinations of media and protocol layers, incorporating one or more of among the LAN Cabling, WAN, Ethernet, IEEE NIC, Token Ring, Ethernet and FDDI.

6.3.1 Network Interface Card

The physical connection from the computer to the network is made by putting a network interface card (NIC) inside the computer and connecting it to the shared cable. A network interface card is a device that physically connects each computer to a network. This card controls the flow of information between the network and the computer. The circuit board needed to provide network access to a computer or other device, such as a printer. Network interface cards, or NICs, mediate between the computer and the physical media, such as cabling, over which transmissions travel. NIC is an adapter card that is installed in the controller that allows it to connect to a network (for example, Ethernet and Token Ring etc. The card contains both the hardware to accommodate the cables and the software to use the network's protocols. The NIC is also called a network adapter card.

6.3.2 LAN Cabling

LAN is data communication network, which connects many computers or client workstations and permits exchange of data and information among them within a localized area (2 to 5 Km). Where all connected devices share transmission media (cable) and also each connection device can work either stand alone or in the network. Each device connected in the network can communicate with any other device with a very high data transmission rate that is of 1Mbps to 100Mbps. Due to rapid change in technology, design and commercial applications for the LANs the number of approaches has emerged like High speed wireless LAN fast Ethernet. At the result, in many applications the volume of data handled over the LAN has been increased. For example in case of centralized server farms there is need for higher speed LAN. There is a need for client system to be able to draw huge amount of data from multiple centralized servers.

6.3.3 WAN

WAN (Wide area network) is a data communications network that covers a large geographical area such as cities, states or countries. WAN technologies generally function at the lower three layers of the OSI reference model, the physical layer, the data-link layer, and the network layer. WAN consists of a number of interconnected switching nodes via telephone line, satellite or microwaves links. A transmission form any one device is routed through internal nodes to the specific destination device. In WAN two computing device are not connected directly, a network of 'switching nodes' provides a transfer path and the process of transferring data block from one node to another is called data switching. Further this switching technique utilizes the routing technology for data transfer. Whereas the routing is responsible for searching a path between source and destination nodes. Earlier WAN have been implemented using circuit or packet switching technology, but now frame relay, ATM and wireless networks are dominating the technology.

WANs use numerous types of devices that are specific to WAN environments. WAN switches, access servers, bridge, gateway, repeater, brouter, modems, CSU/DSUs and ISDN terminal adapters. Other devices found in WAN environments that are used in WAN implementations include routers, ATM switches, and multiplexers.

6.3.4 ATM

Asynchronous Transfer Mode (ATM) is a connection-oriented technology, in which a logical connection is established between the two end points before the actual data exchange begins. ATM has proved very successful in the WAN scenario and numerous telecommunication providers have implemented ATM in their wide-area network cores ATM is a cell relay, packet switching network and data link layer protocol which encodes data traffic into small (53 bytes; 48 bytes of data and 5 bytes of header information) fixed-sized cells. ATM provides data link layer services that run over Layer 1 links. This differs from other technologies based on packet-switched networks (such as the Internet Protocol or Ethernet), in which variable sized *packets* (known as *frames* when referencing layer 2) are used. The motivation for the use of small data *cells* was the reduction of jitter (delay variance, in this case) in the multiplexing of data streams; reduction of this (and also end-to-end round-trip delays) is particularly important when carrying voice traffic. An ATM network is designed to be able to transfer many different types of traffic simultaneously, including real time flows such as video, voice and bursty TCP flows. ATM services are categorised into mainly two categories one is Real-Time Services and other one is Non-real-Time Services which are used by an end system to identify the type of service required. RTS concerns the delay and the variability of delay, referred to as jitter, that the application can tolerate. Real time applications typically involve a flow of information to a user that is intended to reduce that flow at a source. Constant Bit Rate services are the simplest real time services. CBR are used by the applications that requires a fixed data rate that is continuously available during the connections lifetime and a relatively tight upper bound on transfer delay. CBR applications are used mostly in video conferencing, interaction audio and audio/video retrieval and distribution. Real time variable bit rate (rtVB) are another real-time services that allows the network more flexibility than CBR. The network is able to statistically multiplex a number of connections over the same dedicated capacity and still provide the required service to each connection.

6.3.5 Ethernet

Ethernet is a family of frame-based computer networking technologies for Local Area Networks (LANs) that is also based on the idea of computers communicating over a shared coaxial cable acting as a broadcast transmission medium. The name comes from the physical concept of the ether. It defines a number of wiring and signaling standards for the physical layer, through means of network access. The communication methods used shows some similarities to radio systems, although there are fundamental differences, such as the fact that it is much easier to detect collisions in a cable broadcast system than a radio broadcast. The coaxial cable was replaced with point-to-point links connected by hubs and/or switches to reduce installation costs, increase reliability, and enable point-to-point management and troubleshooting. StarLAN was the first step in the evolution of Ethernet from a coaxial cable bus to a hub-managed, twisted-pair network.

Eathernet is most widely used LAN technology to get connected PCs and workstations more than 84% world wide due to its protocol that has following characteristics:

- Is easy to understand, implement, manage, and maintain.
- Allows low-cost network implementations.
- Provides extensive topological flexibility for network installation.
- Guarantees successful interconnection and operation of standards.
- Compliant products, regardless of manufacturer.

Ethernet LANs consist of network nodes and interconnecting media. The network nodes fall into two major classes:

- Data Terminal Equipment (DTE)—Devices that are either the source or the destination of data frames. DTEs are typically devices such as PCs, workstations, file servers, or print servers that, as a group, are all often referred to as end stations.
- Data Communication Equipment (DCE)—Intermediate network devices that receive and forward frames across the network. DCEs may be either stand alone devices such as repeaters, network switches, and routers, or communications interface units such as interface cards and modems.

6.3.6 Token Ring

Token-Ring was developed and promoted by IBM in the early 1980s and standardized as IEEE 802.5. Physically, a token ring network is wired as a star, with 'hubs' and arms out to each station and the loop going out-and-back through each. Stations on a token ring LAN are logically organized in a ring topology with data being transmitted sequentially from one ring station to the next with a control token circulating around the ring controlling access. Token ring is a local area network protocol which resides at the Data Link Layer (DLL) of the OSI model. It uses a special three-byte frame called a token that travels around the ring. Token ring frames travel completely around the loop.

Token-passing networks move a small frame, called a token, around the network. Possession of the token grants the right to transmit. If a node receiving the token has no information to send, it passes the token to the next end station. Each station can hold the token for a maximum period of time. If a station possessing the token does have information to transmit, it seizes the token, alters 1 bit of the token (which turns the token into a start-of-frame sequence), appends the information that it wants to transmit, and sends this information to the next station on the ring. While the information frame is circling the ring, no token is on the network (unless the ring supports early token release), which means that other stations wanting to transmit must wait. Therefore, collisions cannot occur in Token Ring networks. Token ring networks had significantly superior performance and reliability compared to early shared-media implementations of Ethernet (IEEE 802.3), and were widely adopted as a higher-performance alternative to the shared-media Ethernet.

6.3.7 FDDI

FDDI (Fiber Distributed Data Interface), as a product of American National Standards Institute X3T9.5 (now X3T12), conforms to the Open Systems Interconnection (OSI) model of functional layering of LANs using other protocols.

FDDI provides a standard for data transmission in a local area network that can extend in range up to 200 kilometers. In addition to covering large geographical areas, FDDI local area networks can support thousands of users. As a standard underlying medium, it uses optical fiber (though it can use copper cable, in which case one can refer to CDDI). A FDDI network contains two token rings (dual-ring architecture) with traffic on each ring flowing in opposite directions (called counter-rotating). The dual rings consist of a primary and a secondary ring. During normal operation, the primary ring is used for data transmission, and the secondary ring remains idle. Secondary ring also provides possible backup in case the primary ring fails. The primary ring offers up to 100 Mbit/s capacity. When a network has no requirement for the secondary ring to do backup, it can also carry data, extending capacity to 200 Mbit/s. The single ring can extend the maximum distance; a dual ring can extend 100 km. FDDI has a larger maximum-frame size than standard 100 Mbit/s ethernet, allowing better throughput. The primary purpose of the dual rings is to provide superior reliability and robustness.

6.3.8 TCP/IP

The Internet protocol suite is the set of communications protocols that implement the protocol stack on which the Internet and most commercial networks run. It has also been referred to as the TCP/IP protocol suite, which is named after two of the most important protocols in it: the Transmission Control Protocol (TCP) and the Internet Protocol (IP). TCP/IP is referred as protocol suite because it contains many different protocols and therefore many different ways for computers to talk to each other. TCP/IP is not the only protocol suite, although TCP/IP has gained wide acceptance and is commonly used. TCP/IP also defines conventions by connecting different networks, and routing traffic through routers, bridges, and other types of connections. The TCP/IP suite is result of a Defence Advanced Research Projects Agency (DARPA) research project about network connectivity, and its availability has made it the most commonly installed network software.

6.3.9 SNMP

The Simple Network Management Protocol (SNMP) forms part of the internet protocol suite as defined by the Internet Engineering Task Force (IETF). SNMP is used in network management systems to monitor network-attached devices for conditions that warrant administrative attention. It consists of a set of standards for network management, including an Application Layer protocol, a database schema, and a set of data objects.

SNMP exposes management data in the form of variables on the managed systems, which describe the system configuration. These variables can then be queried (and sometimes set) by managing applications. In typical SNMP usage, there are a number of systems to be managed, and one or more systems managing them. A software component called an *agent* runs on each managed system and reports information via SNMP to the managing systems. An SNMP-managed network consists of three basic key components:

- Managed devices
- Agents
- Network-Management Systems (NMSs)

A managed device is a network node that contains an SNMP agent and that resides on a managed network. Managed devices collect and store management information and make this information available to NMSs using SNMP. Managed devices, sometimes called network elements, can be any type of device including, but not limited to, routers and access servers, switches and bridges, hubs, IP telephones, computer hosts, or printers.

An agent is a network-management software module that resides in a managed device. An agent has local knowledge of management information and translates that information into a form compatible with SNMP.

An NMS executes applications that monitor and control managed devices. NMSs provide the bulk of the processing and memory resources required for network management. One or more NMSs may exist on any managed network.

6.3.10 NFS

Network File System (NFS) is a network file system protocol originally developed by Sun Microsystems in 1984, allowing a user on a client computer to access files over a network as easily as if the network devices were attached to its local disks. NFS, like many other protocols, builds on the Open Network Computing Remote Procedure Call (ONC RPC) system. Assuming a Unix-style scenario in which one machine (the client) requires access data, stored on another machine (the NFS server).

The server implements NFS daemon processes (running by default as NFSD) in order to make its data generically available to clients. The server administrator determines what to make available, exporting the names and parameters of directories (typically using the/etc./exports configuration file and the exports command).

The server security-administration ensures that it can recognize and approve validated clients. The server network configuration ensures that appropriate clients can negotiate with it through any firewall system. The client machine requests access to exported data, typically by issuing a mount command. If all goes well, users on the client machine can then view and interact with mounted file systems on the server within the parameters permitted.

6.3.11 SMTP

Simple Mail Transfer Protocol (SMTP) is the standard for e-mail transmissions across the Internet developed during 1970's. SMTP is a relatively simple, text-based protocol, in which one or more recipients of a message are specified (and in most cases verified to exist) and then the message text is transferred. It is a Client/Server protocol, whereby a client transmits an e-mail message to a server. Either an end-user's e-mail client, a.k.a. MUA (Mail User Agent), or a relaying server's MTA (Mail Transfer Agents) can act as an *SMTP client.* An email client knows the *outgoing mail* SMTP server from its configuration. A relaying server typically determines which SMTP server to connect to by looking up the MX (Mail eXchange) DNS record for each recipient's domain name (the part of the e-mail address to the right of the at (@) sign). Conformant MTAs (not all) fall back to a simple A record in the case of no MX. Some current mail transfer agents will also use SRV records, a more general form of MX, though these are not widely adopted. (Relaying servers can also be configured to use a smart host. SMTP is a "push" protocol that does not allow one to "pull" messages from a remote server on demand. To do this a mail client must use POP3 or IMAP. Another SMTP server can trigger a delivery in SMTP using ETRN.

An e-mail client requires the name or the IP address of an SMTP server as part of its configuration. The server will deliver messages on behalf of the user. This setting allows for various policies and network designs. End users connected to the Internet can use the services of an e-mail provider that is not necessarily the same as their connection provider. Network topology, or the location of a client within a network or outside of a network, is no longer a limiting factor for e-mail submission or delivery. Modern SMTP servers typically use a client's credentials (authentication) rather than a client's location (IP address), to determine whether it is eligible to relay e-mail.

One of the limitations of the original SMTP is that it has no facility for authentication of senders. Therefore, the SMTP-AUTH extension was defined. However, the impracticalities of widespread SMTP-AUTH implementation and management means that E-mail spamming is not and cannot be addressed by it.

EXERCISE 6

1. In a typical Client/Server under Network environment, explain the following in details:
   (*a*) What are the Server requirements?
   (*b*) What are the H/W requirements?
   (*c*) What are the Client requirements?
   (*d*) What are the Network requirements?
   (*e*) What do you mean by a thin client network?
   (*f*) List some advantages of Thin Client Network system.
2. Microsoft Windows NT Server provides various network services to support specific requirements of the users on the network. All network services impact the capacity of a network. Some of the services are:

(*a*) Net Logon
(*b*) Computer Browser
(*c*) DHCP
(*d*) Internet Explorer
(*e*) Workstation
(*f*) Server

Explain the above part in brief in a Client/Server environment.

3. In Client/Server architecture in a network environment, explain the following phenomena examples:–
(*a*) UPS
(*b*) Surge Protector
(*c*) Optical Disk
(*d*) CDDI
4. Explain the functions and features of Network Operating System.
5. Explain the working principal of following:
(*a*) CDROM
(*b*) WORM
(*c*) Mirror disk
(*d*) Tape optical disk
(*e*) UNIX Workstation
(*f*) Notebooks
6. In design a network operating system; discuss the relative advantages and disadvantages of using a single server and multiple servers for implementing a service.
7. Write short notes on the following:
(*a*) X-Terminals
(*b*) RAID Array Disk
(*c*) FDDI
(*d*) Power Protection Devices
(*e*) Network Interface Cards
(*f*) Network Operating System
(*g*) Fax Print Services
8. Explain how microkernels can be used to organize an operating system in a Client/Server fashion.
9. What are different client hardware and software for end users? Explain them.

7

Training and Testing

7.1 INTRODUCTION

In addition to being an important factor in the successful implementation of a Client/Server system, training makes employees aware of security concerns. It also educates employees for needed behavioural changes to comply with internal controls. Additionally, it provides employees with the basic knowledge to operate well in a new system environment.

User training for a Client/Server system is complicated by the interface of multiple front-end systems with servers. The user-friendly design provides users with a variety of options for their applications. As front-end applications vary, so do the training and technical support needs. Training of programming and support personnel is also complicated because the underlying system is more complex than traditional systems.

To teach the fundamental technologies involved in a modern Client/Server system in an easy manner, so that one can understand the business requirements, design issues, scalability and security issues in an enterprise system. Teaching style is explanation of concepts, supported by hands on examples. Apart from this required training, it needs training for system administrator, database administrator training, end user training. Existing training delivery vehicles are being revolutionized using new information and telecommunication systems. Classroom delivery can now take place in a synchronous mode across the entire planet. Trainees can participate in learning activities at any time and location using Internet and satellite technologies. These vehicles are breaking the boundaries of space and time, offering unlimited learning possibilities to organizations and those who work for them.

The effectiveness of training in Client/Server computer application development depends on the combination of instructor-led and team-based learning methods. Ten persons familiar with the course content generated 90 statements and each subsequently, completed a similarity sort of the statements. The concept map showed eleven clusters ranging from contextual supports and general methodology on the top and left, to more specific Client/Server concepts on the right and bottom. The cluster describing the actual coding and testing of Client/Server applications are very important for training. The Fig. 7.1 given below shows the concept map for training in Client/Server computer application development.

One consistent pattern that emerged is that the highest achievement tended to be evidenced in clusters most related to the way the course was taught, a combination of instructor-led and team-based learning. The clusters related to communication, teaming and coaching consistently placed in the top five across all administrations. One implication may be that the training methods used may have been more salient than the content.

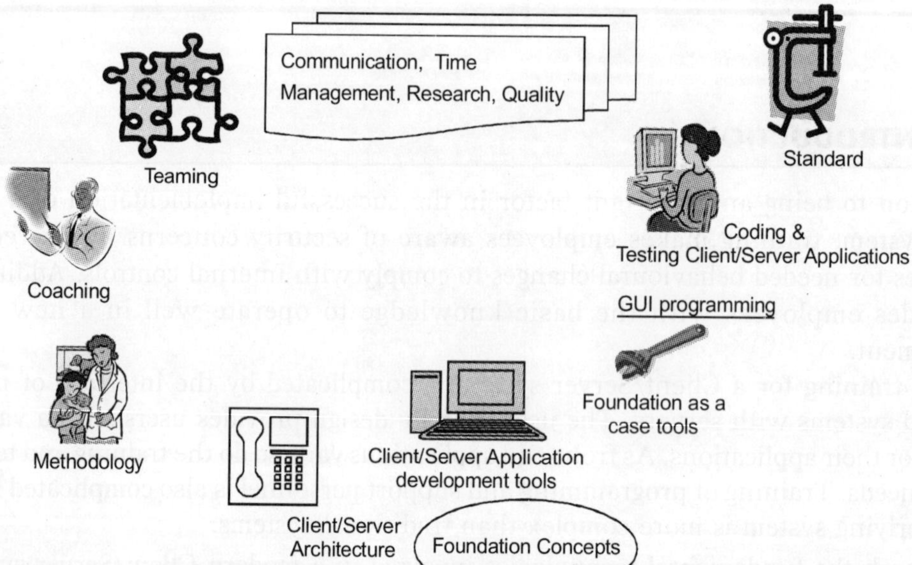

Fig. 7.1: Concept Map for Training in Client/Server Computer Application Development

7.2 TECHNOLOGY BEHIND TRAINING DELIVERY

7.2.1 Traditional Classroom

Most of you are familiar with the traditional face-to-face method of training and learning, given in a classroom or seminar. It is the oldest method for delivering training, and it can still get the job done effectively. In classical training delivery, learners and the instructor are present at the same time. Therefore, classroom training is defined as a synchronous training delivery vehicle. Face-to-face experience provides the trainer and participant with immediate feedback. It enables participants to discuss and share ideas with others in the classroom or seminar. The trainer presents materials, manages and guides discussion; responsibly ensuring that learning is constructive and positive. Traditional classroom delivery is thus termed teacher centric. The time commitment needed for traditional classroom delivery is increasingly considered a drawback in this kind of approach. With downsizing, rightsizing and outsourcing, there are fewer people with time to sit in a classroom. In addition, staff scheduling is often a nightmare when attendance is low or if the training must be scheduled according to employee commitments.

7.2.2 On-the-Job Training (OTJ)

On-the-job training is also a classical training delivery approach, dating back to the middle ages, when apprenticeship was dominant as a learning form, and little formal training existed. Often one of the most popular training delivery vehicles, OTJ training is frequently confused with informal office discussions, round table exchanges and brainstorming sessions. It is sometimes difficult to precisely define what makes up OTJ training. Frequently your coach, mentor, or trainer has a checklist of items which they must demonstrate to the learner, and validate learner's comprehension. Alternatively, informal styles consist of asking a learner to repeat an activity until the coach, mentor, or trainer is satisfied with the learner's performance.

7.2.3 Video Conferencing

There are many conferencing and virtual meeting tools, but most can be placed in one of two distinct categories: Conference room video conferencing, where two or more groups exchange information using one or two-way visual (image) and two-way audio (voice) transmission. Typically, wired conference rooms are voice activated. The person speaking dominates the audio lines. Students can see the instructor, and the instructor can often view the class groupings, sometimes with the capacity to focus in on the person speaking. Computer conferencing, where exchange information using one way visual (image) and two way (voice) transmission is employed. If all computers are equipped with cameras, peer to peer exchange—such as instructor to student and student to student allows both image and voice exchange. Streaming media technology will increasingly be used internally at companies and in business-to-business ventures and that will drive up corporate spending on the technology. This training delivery vehicle offers a live, immediate and synchronous experience, presenting a good discussion format in real time, with equipment that is relatively easy to operate.

7.2.4 Collaborative Tools

A host of conferencing tools can streamline and enrich a virtual business meeting experience, including, but not limited to, digital video, program and document sharing, and whiteboarding. These tools help the staff to find new ways to learn and collaborate online in real time. Digital whiteboards employ a board, a pen and an eraser to store every word, line and color on the computer. Using an Electronic Projection System (EPS), trainer can share this information electronically over the network with learners, creating an electronic flipchart in real time. In collaborative systems, learners can add comments to the flipchart that are visible to all session participants.

7.2.5 Virtual Groups and Event Calls

Computer technology allows training by using virtual groups in a cheap, accessible and easy-to-use fashion. Set up chat rooms where learning groups can discuss, debate and share information after training content has been distributed. Chat groups lack the face-to-face element and can be asynchronous if members are not asked to be simultaneously available. Voice intonation and body language cannot guide the learners. Virtual groups should be managed, focused and kept small, since superficial treatment of materials can be frustrating to learners. Some computers may be slower than others, so delays in communication should be expected. Other virtual groups include virtual office sites, where members of a company can interact using a computer, Web cam and modem to conduct meetings from any geographical location in the world. Event call training involves use of the telephone only rather than the computer. Training materials are often sent to event call locations in advance, and are delivered one-way by the instructor. Participants in many locations, connected via telephone conference, can ask questions. Again, telephone event calling offers no face-to-face element. However, it serves as an inexpensive, quick way to diffuse a uniform message to staff in different locations.

7.2.6 E-Learning

E-learning is the hot word on the block in training and investment circles. The term is elusive, and means something a little different to everyone. In terms of learning delivery approach e-learning is asynchronous: the learner does not receive instruction in the presence of an instructor or other students. The learner can repeat a lesson as many times as he needs, extracting the parts of the course he requires without wasting time going through material he has already mastered. Learners can proceed through an electronic program at their own pace, stopping and starting as desired. E-learning can be designed to offer different levels of complexity, targeting a wider training audience and customizing training accordingly. E-learning encompasses Computer Based Training (CBT), using a computer in combination with Compact Disks with Read-Only Memory (CD-ROMs), Digital Video Disks (DVDs) or browser driven, Web-Based Training (WBT). E-learning can be networked or single user based. E-learning vehicles depend on the technology available and bandwidth capacity. Lower bandwidth means that fewer graphic, animation, sound and video elements are possible.

7.2.7 Web-based Training

Web-based training is browser driven. For this reason, it is more accessible to many, but expensive for some because the Internet access is charged by the minute.

Accessibility to e-learning "is not currently as integral as an employee manual, a college syllabus or a 9th grade math textbook. Most industry observers and education practitioners believe that one day soon, it will be. Web-based content can be easily changed or updated so that learners receive the most recent version. When training is complete, feedback in the form of test or quiz results can be given online and stored in databases or Learning Management Systems. Instructor feedback and follow-up can take the form of online chat rooms or e-mail. Universal accessibility to the Web might require using limited bandwidth, which results in slower performance for sound and images. Avoid long downloading delays, since this can be a source of frustration for users. This module is a sample of low bandwidth, interactive, Web-based solution.

7.2.8 Learning Management Systems (LMS)

Learning Management Systems have been developed to record learner progress in computer and Web-based training. Some systems incorporate both asynchronous and synchronous training. Features generally include coordinating course registration, scheduling, tracking, assessment and testing learners while reporting to managers. Many systems interface with human resource development and enterprise wide systems. Learning Management Systems track and manage the learning process for each user. Some contain course and knowledge management modules. These are termed learning course management systems. There are approximately 600 currently on the market. Learning Management Systems can consume much of an infrastructure budget, so careful consideration should be given before selecting one. Another negative impact of implementing an LMS is that learners may feel policed. This may reduce learners' willingness to use this type of e-learning product.

7.2.9 Electronic Performance Support Systems (EPSS)

An Electronic Performance Support System provides task specific information, training, coaching, and monitoring to enhance job performance. The key to good EPSS tools is their simplicity and accuracy. An EPSS can be in the form of help files, glossary items, and task tools available on the Internet, or in print. EPSSs are concise, efficient to use, and provide clarification on tasks and procedures. An EPSS is part online help, part online tutorial, part database, part application program, and part expert system. In short, an EPSS is an integrated version of a lot of products that technical communicators produce. It is "an electronic system that directly supports a worker's performance when, how, and where the support is needed."

7.3 TO WHOM TRAINING IS REQUIRED?

7.3.1 System Administrator Training

System administrator is the person in Client/Server environment, who understands the availability of resources desired by client. He must understand the level of system performance and ease of use their users requirement. System Administrator concentrates on tasks that are independent of the applications running on adaptive server; he or she is likely to be the person with the best overview of all the applications. System administrator is responsible for managing server, client and as well as about all the applications running in the environment. Some of the important system administrator's tasks on that management must concentrate to prove sufficient training to system administrator.

1. Setting up and managing client server database, managing and monitoring the use of disk space, memory, and connections, backing up and restoring databases server, integration with back-end databases.
2. Setting up and managing user accounts, granting roles and permissions to Adaptive Server users and managing remote access.
3. Working with various control panels and hosting automation software and also day-to-day management of the equipment.
4. Diagnosing system problems along with fault management and performance management.

7.3.2 DBA Training

Client/Server environment consists of centralized or distributed data, so database administrator requires additional responsibilities. He must perform skilled operations with the help of technical staff while operating the application running on client server model. The additional complexity of the new environment requires some new training for database administration staff in that case design of Client/Server environment plays an important role in effecting the performance due to location of data. Here, Database Administrator (DBA) is an experienced senior member(s) of the computing staff who plan and co-ordinate the development and daily maintenance of the entire database environment. He has an extensive working knowledge of Client/Server environment. Usually the role of DBA is shared between 2 or 3 such employees for security purposes. A typical DBA's duties include:

- Installing and configuring the DBMS.
- Assisting in the implementation of information systems.
- Monitoring the performance of the database and tuning the DBMS for optimal performance.
- Ensuring data integrity is maintained and appropriate backups are made.
- Resource usage monitoring.
- Setting standards for system documentation.
- Facilitating end-users with required database facilities.
- Overseeing new database developments, database re-organisation.
- Maintaining an acceptable level of technical performance for database utilities.
- Educating the organization in the use, capabilities and availability of the database.

In other words, DBA prime basic duties are to manage administrative procedures like installation and configuration, backup, recovery, security administration and performance tuning that covers application, database, Client/Server, parallel, restructuring, crisis management, corruption repairs, long running and platform specific tuning.

7.3.3 Network Administrator Training

Network administrators training program specifically focuses on the design, installation, maintenance and management as well as implementation, and operating network services on LAN (Local-Area Network), WAN (Wide-Area Network), network segment, Internet, intranet of Client/Server system. The increasing decentralizes activities of network services makes coordinated network management difficult. To mange a network, let us see what the basic fundamentals are associated with a network management system. Basically, network management system is a collection of application, software, hardware and some tools for monitoring and controlling the system integration as shown in Fig. 7.2 given below. Then training of Network System Administrator requires training of following important areas like:

- Configuration management.
- Performance management.
- Accounting management.
- Security management.
- Fault management.

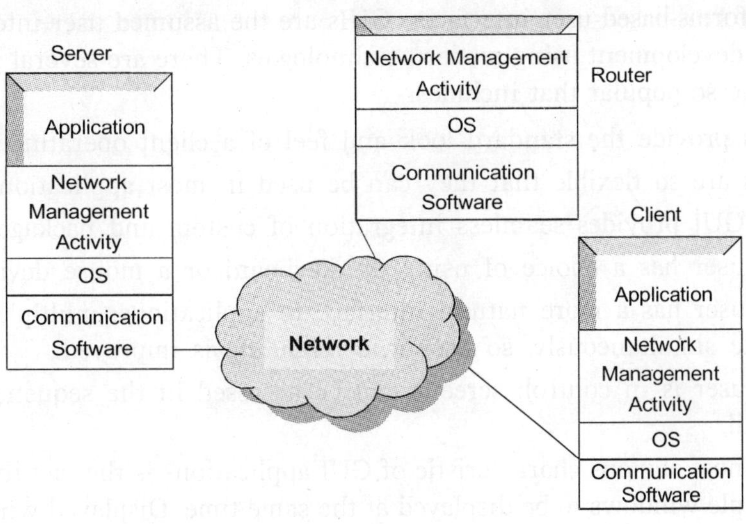

Fig. 7.2: Network System Elements

We can say, Network Systems Administrator are responsible for ensuring an organization's networks are used efficiently under the Client/Server environment. They provide day-to-day administrative support, monitor systems and make adjustments as necessary, and trouble-shoot problems reported by client and automated monitoring systems. They also gather data regarding customer needs, and then evaluate their systems based on those needs. In addition, they may also be involved in the planning and implementation of network security systems.

7.3.4 End-User and Technical Staff Training

End user's are the user's of Client/Server environment those how are already having sufficient knowledge about application running on the system. They are not technical persons but having enough function knowledge of system. They need to train about some new standards and functionality and technology of the applications being implemented in the system.

Technological component constituting the Client/Server system must be completely known to the supporting staff. There must a interface between high level administration and technical staff so that database access and communication technologies can be used in maximum potential by any client. Technical staff must be trained to respect the technological knowledge of user who is already familiar with existing system. The technical staff is the middle level of user of client server applications, then their corporate experience counts while a major fault occurs with system.

7.3.5 GUI Applications Training

Most clients in Client/Server systems deliver system functionality using a Graphical User Interface (GUI). When testing complete systems, the tester must grapple with the additional functionality provided by the GUI. GUIs have become the established alternative to traditional forms-based user interfaces. GUIs are the assumed user interface for virtually all systems development using modern technologies. There are several reasons why GUIs have become so popular that includes:

- GUIs provide the standard look and feel of a client operating system.
- GUIs are so flexible that they can be used in most application areas.
- The GUI provides seamless integration of custom and package applications.
- The user has a choice of using the keyboard or a mouse device.
- The user has a more natural interface to applications: multiple windows can be visible simultaneously, so user understanding is improved.
- The user is in control: screens can be accessed in the sequence the user wants at will.
- The most obvious characteristic of GUI applications is the fact that the GUI allows multiple windows to be displayed at the same time. Displayed windows are 'owned' by applications and of course, there may be more than one application active at the same time.

Windows provide forms-like functionality with fields in which text or numeric data can be entered. But GUIs introduce additional objects such as radio buttons, scrolling lists, check boxes and other graphics that may be displayed or directly manipulated. The GUI itself manages the simultaneous presentation of multiple applications and windows. Hidden windows in the same or different applications may be brought forward and used. There are few, if any, constraints on the order in which users access GUI windows so users are free to use the features of the system in the way they prefer, rather than the way the developers architected it. However, the sophistication and simplicity of a GUI hides the complexity from the user and where development frameworks are used, the programmers too. When trainers are presented with a GUI application to train, the hidden complexities become all too obvious. Consequently, training GUIs is made considerably more difficult. There are some key points that must be taken care while providing training to the various applications on Client/Server environment, in fact, these are the difficulties associated with GUI training.

- ***Event-driven nature:*** The event-driven nature of GUIs presents the first serious training difficulty. Because users may click on any pixel on the screen, there are many, many more possible user inputs that can occur. The user has an extremely wide choice of actions. At any point in the application, the users may click on any field or object within a window. They may bring another window in the same application to the front and access that. The window may be owned by another application. The user may choose to access an operating system component directly e.g., a system configuration control panel.
- ***Unsolicited events:*** Unsolicited events cause problems for trainers. A trivial example would be when a local printer goes off-line, and the operating system puts up a dialog box inviting the user to feed more paper into the printer. A more complicated situation arises where message-oriented middleware might dispatch a message (an event) to remind the client application to redraw a diagram on screen, or refresh a display of records from a database that has changed. Unsolicited events may occur at any time, so again, the number of different situations that the code must accommodate is extremely high. Training of unsolicited events is difficult.
- ***Hidden synchronization and dependencies:*** It is common for window objects to have some form of synchronization implemented. For example, if a check box is set to true, a text box intended to accept a numeric value elsewhere in the window may be made inactive or invisible. If a particular radio button is clicked, a different validation rule might be used for a data field elsewhere on the window. Synchronization between objects need not be restricted to object in the same window and its training must be done carefully.
- ***'Infinite' input domain:*** On any GUI application, the user has complete freedom to click with the mouse-pointing device anywhere on the window that has the focus. Although objects in windows have a default tab order, the user may choose to enter data values by clicking on an object and then entering data.

- ***Many ways in, many ways out:*** An obvious consequence of the event-driven nature of GUIs is that for most situations in the application, there may be 'many ways in' by which the user reached that point in the application. As many as possible, the ways must be known to the user.
- ***Window management:*** In a GUI environment, users take the standard features of window management and control for granted. These features include window movement, resizing, maximization, minimization and closure. These are usually implemented by standard buttons and keyboard commands available on every window. The trainer has control over which standard window controls are available, but although the operating system handles the window's behavior, the trainer must handle the impact on the application.

7.3.6 LAN/WAN Administration and Training Issues

For LAN administration there are various products available such as Network General Sniffer that enables administrator to monitor the network for capacity and problems without the need for detail knowledge of the applications. The biggest advantage of using such software is that they can be used to monitor LAN traffic, analyzing the data, and then to recommend actions based on data assessment. The software interpreter internal LAN message formats for LAN administrator to take action based on recommendations without the need for detailed knowledge of such message formats.

Before starting the training of any client/server system, the environment of system must be clearly known to administrator. Administrator must understand naming, security, help procedure etc., and able to implement them uniformly between applications and procedures. In case of large systems that are located in wide areas it requires administrator training as well as user training. Such training ensures that each of the installation operates in the same ways and also the support personal at remote can communicate with local administrator. All the software products should be installed on the entire client with uniform default setting and also the administrator should be an expert in the use of the product. Training document of product usage also revels that the administrator must understand, what the product requirements are? And arrange to have temporary and backup files created on volumes that can be cleaned up regularly.

WAN administrator must be trained in such a way that he can use and manage the remote management tools. Such tools enables administrator to remotely manage the LAN to WAN environment needed for many client/server applications. All the WAN network issues associated with remote terminal access to host system exist in the client/server to WAN access. Complexities arise when data is distributed to the remote LAN. The distributed application programs to remote servers present many of the same problems as do distributed databases. Then, the administrator must be trained in the software and in procedures to handle network definition, network management and remote backup and recovery. Due to wide impact of the WAN on communication issues, training developers in WAN issues becomes critical. And also due to availability of many optional configuration WAN's are complex to understand and optimized. Then the training of WAN administrators to understand all of the options available to establish an optional topology becomes more expensive.

In client/server application administrator must be expert in the operating system used by clients and servers. The network used in client/server implementations frequently runs several operating systems. Such diversity of platforms changes the administrator to have expertise not only in the particular of a single operating system but also in the interaction of the various operating systems. While designing and planning for a new client/server application, the training requirements should be considered carefully before an organization establishes too many operating systems on the network. The cost and implications of training in this area must not be overlooked.

7.4 IMPACT OF TECHNOLOGY ON TRAINING

Client/Server Systems were initially developed as a cost-effective alternative to hosting business applications on Mainframes. Client/Server Systems offer many advantages over traditional systems such as low cost, increased performance and reliability due to a distributed design, and easier interoperability with other systems etc. Over the last decade, the second generation of Client/Server Systems has seen a major technological evolution. The earlier Client/Server Systems based on the two-tier database centric design have evolved to incorporate middleware technologies (for application logic) such as CORBA, COM+ and EJBs in an N-tier architecture. These technologies provide enhanced scalability and robustness to the business application. In the last few years, the Client/Server applications have been web-enabled for easier access and manageability. The integration of web and Client/Server technologies has given rise to important applications such as Data Warehousing, Online Analytical Processing (OLAP) and Data Mining. The necessities to integrate and exchange information with other business systems have led to the recent development of "Web Services" using XML and SOAP protocols. And of course, with web enabling, the security issues with Client/Server computing have become more important than ever. There are a number of factors driving the education and training markets to increase the use of technology for learning delivery:

Technical obstacles in adoption are falling: Network and system infrastructures, hardware access, and limited bandwidth are rapidly becoming non-factors.

Penetration of the Internet: The pervasiveness and familiarity of the Internet and its related technologies is the number one driver behind the growth of e-learning.

Market consolidation and one-stop shopping: Corporations, educational institutions and students are increasingly demanding more of their educational providers.

Traditional players looking to get on the scene: Many big industries and technology players are watching and waiting for market opportunities.

Knowledge is the competitive weapon of the 21st century: Knowledge is now the asset that will make or break a company. To remain competitive, corporations and individuals themselves–are expected to increase the amount spent on education to increase the value of their human capital.

7.4.1 Client/Server Administration and Management

Administration and management of Client/Server environments is an important and challenging area. Client/Server administration includes a range of activities: software distribution and version management, resource utilization monitoring, maintaining system security, reliability, and availability. Centralized mainframe environments are relatively easy to manage and are typically associated with high-level of security, data integrity, and good overall system availability. The present lack of administrative control over Client/Server environments is a major de-motivating factor for many organizations, who are considering migration from mainframe based systems. Personal Computer based networks are particularly difficult to administer and significant resources are needed to maintain Personal Computer environments in operation.

Client/Server administrators need to continuously monitor and pro-actively manage the system to ensure system availability. The key to effective Client/Server administration is fast identification of problem areas and fast failure recovery. Ideally, administrators should be able to anticipate critical situations using information derived by monitoring important resources. This allows intervention before the problems escalate and affect users of the system. Because of the complexity of distributed environments and the interaction between various system components, it is no longer possible to rely on traditional techniques, where the administrator interacts directly with the system using operating system commands. Automation of systems administration is an essential pre-requisite for the successful implementation of Client/Server systems.

7.5 CLIENT/SERVER TESTING TECHNOLOGY

7.5.1 Client/Server Software

Client/Server Software requires specific forms of testing to prevent or predict catastrophic errors. Servers go down, records lock, Input/Output errors and lost messages can really cut into the benefits of adopting this network technology. Testing addresses system performance and scalability by understanding how systems respond to increased workloads and what causes them to fail. Software testing is more than just review. It involves the dynamic analysis of the software being tested. It instructs the software to perform tasks and functions in a virtual environment. This examines compatibility, capability, efficiency, reliability, maintainability, and portability. A certain amount of faults will probably exist in any software. However, faults do not necessarily equal failures. Rather, they are areas of slight unpredictability that will not cause significant damage or shutdown. They are more errors of semantics. Therefore, testing usually occurs until a company reaches an acceptable defect rate that doesn't affect the running of the program or at least won't until an updated version has been tested to correct the defects. Since Client/Server technology relies so heavily on application software and networking, testing is an important part of technology and product development. There are two distinct approaches when creating software tests. There is black box testing and white or glass box testing. Black box testing is also referred to as functional testing. It focuses on testing the internal machinations of whatever is being tested, in our case, a client or server program. When testing software, for example, black box tests focus on Input/Output. The testers know the input and predicted output, but they do not know how the program arrives at its conclusions. Code is not examined, only specifications are examined. Black box testing does not require special knowledge of specific languages from the tester. The tests are unbiased because designers and testers are independent of each other. They are primarily conducted from the user perspective to ensure usability. However, there are also some disadvantages to black box testing. The tests are difficult to design and can be redundant.

Also, many program paths go uncovered since it is realistically impossible to test all input streams. It would simply take too long. White box testing is also sometimes referred to as glass box testing. It is a form of structural testing that is also called clear box testing or open box testing. As expected, it is the opposite of black box testing. It focuses on the internal workings of the program and uses programming code to examine outputs. Furthermore, the tester must know what the program is supposed to do and how it's supposed to do it. Then, the tester can see if the program strays from its proposed goal. For software testing to be complete both functional/black and structural/white/glass box testing must be conducted.

7.5.2 Client/Server Testing Techniques

There are a variety of testing techniques that are particularly useful when testing client and server programs. Among them Risk Driven Testing and Performance Testing are most important.

(*a*) **Risk Driven Testing:** Risk driven testing is time sensitive, which is important in finding the most important bugs early on. It also helps because testing is never allocated enough time or resources. Companies want to get their products out as soon as possible. The prioritization of risks or potential errors is the engine behind risk driven testing. In risk driven testing the tester takes the system parts he/she wants to test, modules or functions, for example, and examines the categories of error impact and likelihood. Impact, the first category, examines what would happen in the event of a break-down. For example, would entire databases be wiped out or would the formatting just be a little off? Likelihood estimates the probability of this failure in the element being tested. Risk driven testing prioritizes the most catastrophic potential errors in the service of time efficiency.

(*b*) **Performance Testing:** Performance testing is another strategy for testing client and server programs. It is also called load testing or stress testing. Performance testing evaluates system components, such as software, around specific performance parameters, such as resource utilization, response time, and transaction rates. In order to performance test a client-server application, several key pieces of information must be known. For example, the average number of users working simultaneously on a system must be quantified, since performance testing most commonly tests performance under workload stress. Testers should also determine maximum or peak user performance or how the system operates under maximum workloads. Bandwidth is another necessary bit of information, as is most users' most frequent actions. Performance testing also validates and verifies other performance parameters such as reliability and scalability. Performance testing can establish that a product lives up to performance standards necessary for commercial release. It can compare two systems to determine which one performs better. Or they can use profilers to determine the program's behavior as it runs. This determines which parts of the program might cause the most trouble and it establishes thresholds of acceptable response times.

7.5.3 Testing Aspects

There are different types of software testing that focus on different aspects of IT architecture. **Three-testing** are particularly relevant to Client/Server applications. These are unit testing, integration testing, and system testing. A unit is the smallest testable component of a program. In object-oriented programming, which is increasingly influencing Client/Server applications. The smallest unit is a class. Modules are made up of units. Unit testing isolates small sections of a program (units) and tests the individual parts to prove they work correctly. They make strict demands on the piece of code they are testing. Unit testing documentation provides records of test cases that are designed to incorporate the characteristics that will make the unit successful. This documentation also contains positive and negative uses for the unit as well as what negative behaviors the unit will trap. However, unit testing won't catch all errors. It must be used with other testing techniques. It is only a phase of three-layer testing, of which unit testing is the first. Integration testing, sometimes called I&T (Integration and Testing), combines individual modules and tests them as a group. These test cases take modules that have been unit tested, they test this input with a test plan. The output is the integrated system, which is then ready for the final layer of testing, system testing. The purpose of integration testing is to verify functionality, performance, and reliability. There are different types of integration testing models. For example, the Big Bang model is a time saver by combining unit-tested modules to form an entire software program (or a significant part of one). This is the 'design entity' that will be tested for integration.

However, record of test case results is of the essence, otherwise further testing will be very complicated. Bottom up integrated testing tests all the low, user level modules, functions and procedures. Once these have been integrated and tested, the next level of modules can be integrated and tested. All modules at each level must be operating at the same level for this type of testing to be worthwhile. In object-oriented programming, of which client server applications increasingly are, classes are encapsulations of data attributes and functions. Classes require the integration of methods. Ultimately, integration testing reveals any inconsistencies within or between assemblages or the groupings of modules that are integrated through testing plans and outputs.

System testing is the final layer of software testing. It is conducted once the system has been integrated. Like integration testing, it falls within the category of black box testing. Its input is the integrated software elements that have passed integration testing and the integration of the software system with any hardware systems it may apply to. System testing detects inconsistencies between assemblages (thereby testing integration) and in the system as its own entity. System testing is the final testing front and therefore the most aggressive. It runs the system to the point of failure and is characterized as destructive testing. Here are some of the areas systems testing covers: usability, reliability, maintenance, recover, compatibility, and performance.

7.5.4 Measures of Completeness

In software testing, there are two measures of completeness, code coverage and path coverage. Code coverage is a white box testing technique to determine how much of a program's source code has been tested. There are several fronts on which code coverage is measured. For example, statement coverage determines whether each line of code has been executed and tested. Condition coverage checks the same for each evaluation point. Path coverage establishes whether every potential route through a segment of code has been executed and tested. Entry/Exit coverage executes and tests every possible call to a function and return of a response. Code coverage provides a final layer of testing because it searches for the errors that were missed by the other test cases. It determines what areas have not been executed and tested and creates new test cases to analyze these areas. In addition, it identifies redundant test cases that won't increase coverage.

7.6 TESTING CLIENT/SERVER APPLICATION

The structure of Client/Server Systems requires new approaches to testing them. A system can go wrong due to input/output errors, server down, records locked, lost messages and many more and then it requires to test the system response for these events. Performance and scalability testing is done to get valid results based on an insightful analysis of how systems respond to increasing load, and what makes them fail in various ways. With these information loads, testing is performed. Testing Client/Server applications requires some additional techniques to handle the new effects introduced by the Client/Server architecture. Testing Client/Server Systems is entirely different; still the testing of software is there, see Fig. 7.3 given below.

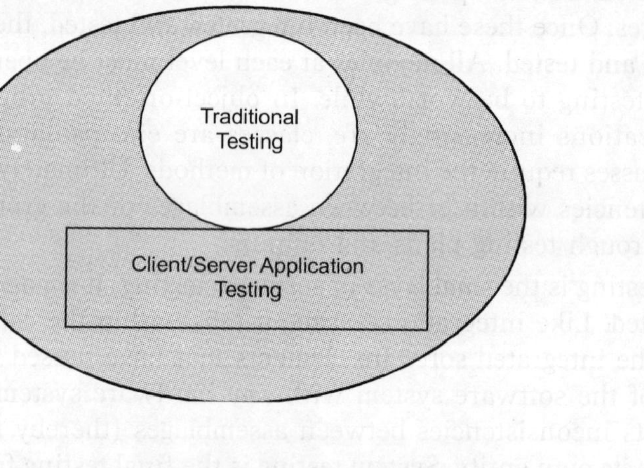

Fig. 7.3: Client/Server Testing

Such testing includes all the core testing techniques that are required to test *any* system, including systems that have a Client/Server design, *plus* the special techniques needed for Client/Server. Testing Client/Server applications is more challenging than testing traditional systems due to the following reasons:

- New kinds of things can go wrong: for example: Data and messages can get lost in the network.
- It's harder to set up, execute, and check the test cases: for example: Testing for proper responses to timeouts.
- Regression testing is harder to automate: for example: It's not easy to create an automated 'server is busy' condition.
- Predicting performance and scalability become critical: for example: It seems to work fine with 10 users. But what about with 1,000 users or 10,000 users?

Obviously, some new techniques are needed to test Client/Server systems. Most of these apply to distributed systems of all kinds, not just the special case of Client/Server architecture. The key to understanding how to test these systems is to understand exactly how and why each type of potential problem *arises*. With this insight, the testing solution will usually be obvious. For example, suppose Program A, (a client program, because it makes a request) asks Program B, a server program, to update some fields in a database.

Program B is on another computer. Program A expects Program B to report that either the operation was successfully completed or the operation was unsuccessful (for example, because the requested record was locked.). However, time passes and A hears nothing. What should A do? Depending on the speed and reliability of the network connecting A and B, there comes a time when A must conclude that something has probably gone wrong. Then, some possibilities are given as follow:

- The request got lost and it never reached B.
- B received the request, but is too busy to respond yet.
- B got the request, but crashed before it could begin processing it.
  B may or may not have been able to store the request before it crashed.
  If B did store the request, it might try to service it upon awakening.
- B started to process the request, but crashed while processing it.
- B finished processing the request (successfully or not), but crashed before it could report the result.
- B reported the result, but the result got lost and was never received by A.

There are more possibilities, but you get the idea. So what should A do?

Here the problem is that A can't tell the difference between any of the above cases (without taking some further action). Dealing with this problem involves complex schemes such as the Two Phases Commit. When to test the client program A, its needed to see whether it's robust enough to at least do something intelligent for each of the above scenarios. This example illustrates one new type of testing that have been done for Client/ Server systems. Testing the client program for correct behavior in the face of uncertainty. Now, let's look at the other new type of testing, this time on the server side with consideration of performance testing and scalability issues. There are some major reasons why Client/Server systems cause new effects:

(*i*) **Most of these systems are *event-driven*:** Basically, this means: "Nothing Happens Until Something Happens". Most program action is triggered by an event, such as the user hitting a key, some Input/Output being completed, or a clock timer expiring. The event is intercepted by an "event handler" or "interrupt handler" piece of code, which generates an internal message (or lots of messages) about what it detected. This means that it's harder to set up test cases than it is, say, to define a test case for a traditional system that prints a check. To set up a test case it requires to create events, or to simulate them. That is not always easy, especially, because it needed to generate these events when the system is in the proper state; but there are ways to do it.

(*ii*) **The systems never stop:** Many Client Server/Systems are set up to never stop running unless something goes really wrong. It is true for the servers, and in many cases, it is also true for the client machines. Traditional systems complete an action, such as printing a report, and then turn in for the night. When user restarts the program it is a whole fresh new day for it. In systems that don't stop (on purpose), things are different. Errors accumulate. As someone put it, sludge builds up on the walls of the operating system. So things like **memory leaks** that are wrong, but that probably would not affect the most traditional systems, will eventually bring non-stop systems down if they are not detected and corrected. One good way to minimize these effects is to use something called SOW and HILT variables in testing.

The system contains multiple computers and processors which can act (and fail) independently. Worse, they communicate with each other over less than perfectly reliable communication lines. These two factors are the root cause of the problem detailed above, where Program A makes a request of Program B, but gets no response.

EXERCISE 7

1. In Client/Server architecture, you are appointed as a system administrator. You have about 500 users and it is a mix of WinNT machine, Macintosh machine, and a very few DOS machine. Describe all the part given below with example, wherever necessary.
   (*a*) What all will you do so network runs smoothly?
   (*b*) What all will you do to make sure that data is secure?
   (*c*) What will be your Network Operating Systems for this particular configuration?
   (*d*) In a network arrangement, when you have several different machines, such as system in question, you need to watch for certain factors to keep network trouble-free. What are these factors?
   (*e*) Resource sharing architecture is not suitable for transaction processing in a Client/Server environment. Discuss.
2. What do you understand by Network Management and Remote System Management? How can security be provided to Network?
3. Explain System Administrator in Client/Server Application in detail.
4. Explain in detail, with help of suitable examples, the training advantages of GUI application.
5. Compare and contrast the system administrator training, database administrator training and end user training.
6. What are the responsibilities of the DBA? Also, discuss the capabilities that should be provided by a DBMS.
7. What are different LAN and Network Management issues? Explain with example.
8. Explain the term remote monitoring. What are different network management tools?

8

Client/Server Technology and Web Services

8.1 INTRODUCTION

The Internet and expanded network connectivity established Client/Server models as the preferred form of distributed computing. When talking about Client/Server models of network communication using web services the broadest components of this paradigm become the web browser (functioning as the client) and web server. So, by introducing web services into the equation, Client/Server models become browser/server models. These models are Server-Centric, which make applications easy to load and install, but reduces rich user interaction. Server-Centric applications are currently available from standard browsers, making them convenient and popular with developers. Therefore, a way of enriching user experience is an essential frontier that must be developed for using browser/server models of distributed computing. One of the revolutions of the personal computer was usability or the ease with which humans could communicate with and configure their computers. This usually occurred through individual configuration and the User Interface (UI). Administratively, this was a nightmare because administrators had to install and maintain applications one machine at a time and manage multiple platforms. Individual installation and maintenance across platforms made web services seem like a good solution. Using HTML tools, developers moved toward giving applications global potential and a uniform protocol for management and deployment. The evolving trend was for developers to create applications that run on the server side, while web browsers became, for all intents and purposes, the standard client interface. Client processing power atrophied as execution of programs took place on central servers and output or responses were transmitted back to the browser through standard IP (Internet Protocols). This improved installation, administration, and maintenance. However, to be intelligible to the wide-array of platforms being targeted, web developers had to write in the lowest common denominator or the most widely accepted standards. This affected user experience negatively, while ensuring that applications could be deployed to the most users.

8.2 WHAT ARE WEB SERVICES?

8.2.1 Web Services History

The World Wide Web was developed by Tim Berners-Lee for his employer CERN or the European Organization for Nuclear Research between 1989-1991. In 1990, he wrote the program for the World Wide Web. This program created the first web browser and HTML editor. It was the first program to use both FTP and HTTP.

FTP (File Transfer Protocol) is used to transfer data over a network. Protocol is the set of standards that defines and controls connection, communication, and the transfer of data between two computer endpoints. It determines the format and defines the terms of transmission. HTTP is the protocol that supports hyper-text documents. Both of these protocols are necessary for communication over the Internet or World Wide Web. The source code for the World Wide Web was made public in 1993, making it available to everyone with a computer. The technology continued to develop and between 1991-1994, extended from communication only between scientific organizations, to universities and, finally, to industry. By 1994, computers could transfer data between each other through a cable linking ports across various operating systems.

The first web server, also written by Berners-Lee, ran on NeXTSTEP, the operating system for NeXT computers. The other technology authored by Berners-Lee that is required for Web communication is URLs (Universal Resource Locators). These are the uniform global identifiers for documents on the Web allowing for easily locating them on the Web. Berners-Lee is also responsible for writing the initial specifications for HTML. The first web server was installed in the United States on December 12, 1991 and at SLAC (Stanford Linear Accelerator Center), which is a U.S. Department of Energy laboratory. In 1994, Berners-Lee created the World Wide Web Consortium (WWC) to regulate and standardize the various technologies required for Web construction and communication. It was created to ensure compatibility between vendors or industry members by having them agree on certain core standards. This ensures the ability for web pages to be intelligible between different operating systems and software packages. After 2000, the web exploded. Till date, there exist more than 110 million web sites on the World Wide Web.

8.2.2 Web Server Technology

At the most basic level, the process for web communication works as follows: a computer runs a web browser that allows it to request, communicate and display HTML documents (web pages). Web browsers are the software applications that allow users to access and view these web pages and they run on individual computers. The most popular web browsers are Internet Explorer, Mozilla, Firefox, and Safari (for Mac). After typing in the URL (or address) and pressing return, the request is sent to a server machine that runs the web server. The web server is the program that delivers the files that make up web pages. Every web site or computer that creates a web site requires a web server. The most popular web server program is Apache. The server machine then returns the requested web page. See the Fig. 8.1(*a*) and 8.1(*b*), depicting the Web Technology yesterday and today.

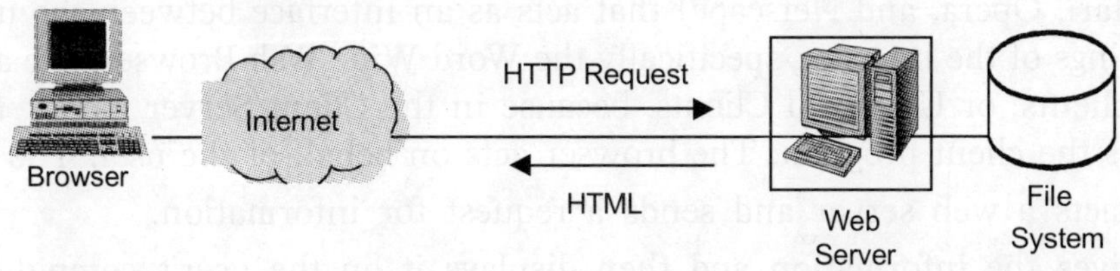

Fig. 8.1(*a*): Web Technology Yesterday

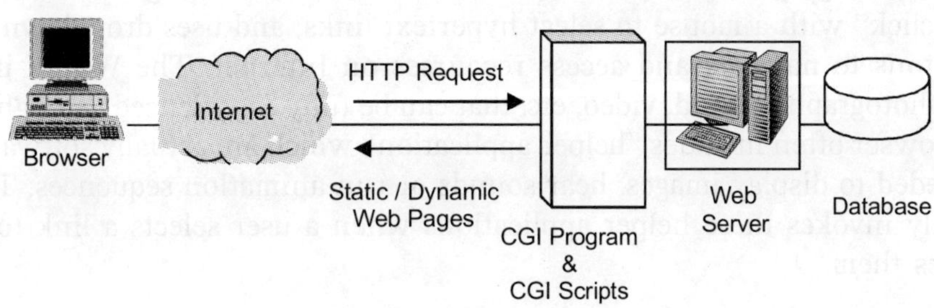

Fig. 8.1(*b*): Web Technology Today

Communication over the Internet can be broken down into two interested parties: clients and servers. The machines providing services are servers. Clients are the machines used to connect to those services. For example, the personal computer requesting web pages according to search parameters (defined by key words) does not provide any services to other computers. This is the client. If the client requests a search from, for example, the search engine Yahoo!. Yahoo! is the server, providing the hardware machinery to service the request. As previously mentioned, each computer requesting information over the Internet requires a web server program like Apache to render the search result intelligible in HTML.

Web servers translate URL path components in local file systems. The URL path is dependent on the server's root directory. The root directory is the top directory of a file system that usually exists hierarchically as an inverted tree. URL paths are similar to UNIX-like operating systems.

The typical client request reads, for example, "http://www.example.com/path/file.html". This client web browser translates this request through an HTTP request and by connecting to "www.example.com", in this case. The web server will then add the requested path to its root directory path. The result is located in the server's local file system or hierarchy of directories. The server reads the file and responds to the browser's request. The response contains the requested documents, in this case, web sites and the constituent pages.

Web Browser (Web Client)

A browser is a software (the most popular web browsers are Internet Explorer, Mozilla Firefox, Safari, Opera, and Netscape) that acts as an interface between the user and the inner workings of the internet, specifically the Word Wide Web Browsers are also referred to as web clients, or Universal Clients, because in the Client/Server model, the browser functions as the client program. The browser acts on behalf of the user. The browser:

- Contacts a web server and sends a request for information.
- Receives the information and then displays it on the user's computer.

A browser can be text-based or graphical and can make the internet easier to use and more intuitive. A graphical browser allows the user to view images on their computer, "point-and-click" with a mouse to select hypertext links, and uses drop-down menus and toolbar buttons to navigate and access recourses on Internet. The WWW incorporates hypertext, photographs, sound, video, etc. that can be fully experienced through a graphical browser. Browser often includes "helper application" which are actually software programs that are needed to display images, hear sounds or run animation sequences. The browser automatically invokes these helper applications when a user selects a link to a resource that requires them.

Accessing Database on the Web Page

Generally, it has been observed that a remote user's web browser cannot get connected directly with database system. But in most of the cases, the browsers are a program running on the web server that is an intermediary to the database. This program can be a common Gateway Interface (CGI) script, a Java servlet, or some code that lives inside an Active Server Page (ASP) or Java Server Page (JSP) document. The program retrieves the information from the page is an ordinary HTML document or the output of some script that Web-based database system. All these activities happen in number of steps explained below and also shown in figure 8.2:

Step1: The user types in a URL or fills out a form or submits a search on a Web page and clicks the Submit button.

Step 2: The browser sends the user's query from the browser to the Web server, which passes it on to a CGI script.

Step 3: The CGI script loads a library that lets it talk to an SQL database server, and it uses that library to send SQL commands to the database server.

Step 4: The database server executes the SQL commands and sends the request information to the CGI script.

Step 5: The CGI script generates an HTML document and writes the HTML document to the Web server.

Step 6: The Web server sends the HTML page back to the remote user.

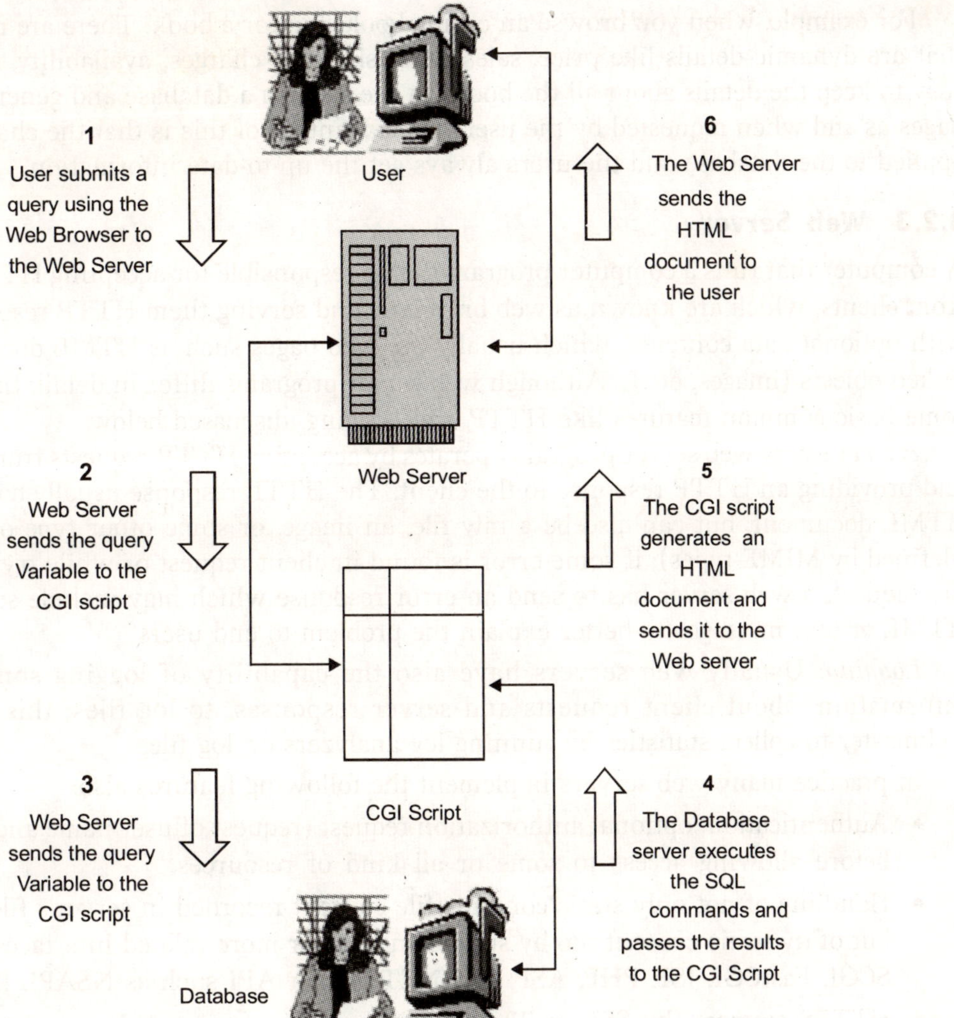

Fig. 8.2: Information Exchange between User and a Web-based Database

If the user has send some information to update a database. Then the CGI Script will generate the appropriate SQL commands and send it to the database server. The database server will execute the SQL commands and then inform the user about the result of execution. A typical example of a database query is search that you perform using a search engine. An example for an insert operation will be filled up a form on your browser to do an online registration for seminar. An example for an update operation will be updating your profile on a portal like naukari.com. In many web sites, even when you type a URL, web pages are generated for you using the information retrieved from a database.

For example, when you browse an online bookshop for a book. There are many details that are dynamic details like price, sales rank, shipping charges, availability, etc. So, it is easy to keep the details about all the books in the shop in a database and generate the web pages as and when requested by the user. The advantage of this is that the changes can be applied to the database and the users always get the up-to-date information.

8.2.3 Web Server

A computer that runs a computer program that is responsible for accepting HTTP requests from clients, which are known as web browsers, and serving them HTTP responses along with optional data contents, which usually are web pages such as HTML documents and linked objects (images, etc.). Although web server programs differ in detail, they all share some basic common features like HTTP and Logging, discussed below.

HTTP: Every web server program operates by accepting HTTP requests from the client, and providing an HTTP response to the client. The HTTP response usually consists of an HTML document, but can also be a raw file, an image, or some other type of document (defined by MIME-types); if some error is found in client request or while trying to serve the request, a web server has to send an error response which may include some custom HTML or text messages to better explain the problem to end users.

Logging: Usually web servers have also the capability of logging some detailed information, about client requests and server responses, to log files; this allows the webmaster to collect statistics by running log analyzers on log files.

In practice many web servers implement the following features also:

- Authentication, optional authorization request (request of user name and password) before allowing access to some or all kind of resources.
- Handling of not only static content (file content recorded in server's filesystem(s)) but of dynamic content too by supporting one or more related interfaces (SSI, CGI, SCGI, FastCGI, JSP, PHP, ASP, ASP.NET, Server API such as NSAPI, ISAPI, etc.).
- HTTPS support (by SSL or TLS) to allow secure (encrypted) connections to the server on the standard port 443 instead of usual port 80.
- Content compression (i.e., by gzip encoding) to reduce the size of the responses (to lower bandwidth usage, etc.).
- Virtual hosting to serve many web sites using one IP address.
- Large file support to be able to serve files whose size is greater than 2 GB on 32 bit OS.
- Bandwidth throttling to limit the speed of responses in order to not saturate the network and to be able to serve more clients.

Although web servers differ in specifics there are certain basic characteristics shared by all web servers. These basic characteristics include HTTP and logging. As previously, mentioned HTTP is the standard communications protocol for processing requests between client browsers and web servers. This protocol provides the standardized rules for representing data, authenticating requests, and detecting errors.

The purpose of protocols is to make data transfer and services user-friendly. In computing, the protocols determine the nature of the connection between two communicating endpoints (wired or wireless) and verify the existence of the other endpoints being communicated with. It also negotiates the various characteristics of the connection. It determines how to begin, end, and format a request. It also signals any errors or corruptions in files and alerts the user as to the appropriate steps to take. HTTP is the request/response protocol used specifically for communicating. HTML documents which is the language hypertext or web pages are written in. However, responses can also return in the form of raw text, images or other types of documents. The other basic web server characteristic is logging. This is a feature that allows the program to automatically record events. This record can then be used as an audit trail to diagnose problems. Web servers log detailed information recording client requests and server responses. This information is stored in log files and can be analyzed to better understand user behavior, such as key word preferences, generate statistics, and run a more efficient web site.

There are many other practical features common to a variety of web sites. Configuration files or external user interfaces help determine how much and to what level of sophistication users can interact with the server. This establishes the configurability of the server. Some servers also provide authentication features that require users to register with the server through a username and password before being allowed access to resources or the execution of requests. Web servers must also be able to manage static and dynamic content. Static content exists as a file in a file system. Dynamic content is content (text, images, form fields) on a web page that changes according to specific contexts or conditions. Dynamic content is produced by some other program or script (a user-friendly programming language that connects existing components to execute a specific task) or API (Application Programming Interface the web server calls upon). It is much slower to load than static content since it often has to be pulled from a remote database. It provides a greater degree of user interactivity and tailor responses to user requests. To handle dynamic content, web servers must support at least any one of interface like JSP (Java Server Pages), PHP (a programming language that creates dynamic web pages), ASP (Active Server Pages) or ASP.NET (it is the successor of ASP).

8.2.4 Web Server Communication

Web servers are one of the end points in communication through the World Wide Web. According to its inventor, Tim Berner-Lee, the World Wide Web is "*the universe of network-accessible information, an embodiment of human knowledge.*" The World Wide Web is the global structure of electronically connected information. It refers to the global connections between computers that allow users to search for documents or web pages by requesting results from a web server. These documents are hyper-text based (written in HTML-Hypertext Markup Language), allowing users to travel to other pages and extend their research through links. They are delivered in a standardized protocol, HTTP (Hypertext Transfer Protocol, usually written in lower case letters), making HTML documents intelligible across hardware and software variations.

This information travels through web servers and web browsers. The communication initiates from a user request through a web browser. The request is delivered to a web server in 'HTTP' format. The server then processes the request, which can be anything from a general search to a specific task, and returns the results in the same format. The results are written in HTML, which is the language web pages are written in that supports high-speed travel between web pages. HTML is also essential for displaying many of the interactive features on web pages, such as linking web pages to other objects, like images. An important distinction when defining web servers is between hardware and software. A web server is also a computer program (software) that performs the functions outlined above.

8.3 ROLE OF JAVA FOR CLIENT/SERVER ON WEB

Client server models provide the essential mechanisms for working with the Internet. In fact, most of the World Wide Web is built according to this paradigm. In client server models the web browsers run by millions of users are the clients. On the other side of the equation, is the web hosting systems that run at host sites and provide access to processes and data requested by the client. In this case, these hosting systems are the server. This definition is based on software programs, where the client is a program running on a remote machine that communicates with a server, a program running at a single site and providing responses to client requests, such as web pages or data.

Java is a programming language that has been developed specifically for the distributed environment of the Internet. It resembles C++ language, but is easier to use. C++ is a high level programming language that performs low level functions. In computing, low level functions are those that focus on individual components and the interaction between them as opposed to abstracted and systemic features (high level). Java, like C++, is a language that is multi-paradigm and supports object-oriented programming (OOP), procedural programming, and data abstraction. Object-oriented programming is increasingly being used in client server technology. It refers to a programming language model that is organized by objects rather than actions, data rather than logic. OOP identifies objects (sets of data) and defines their relationship to each other. These objects are then generalized into a class. Methods or sequences of logic are applied to classes of objects. Methods provide computational instructions and class object features provide the data that is acted upon. Users communicate with objects and objects with each other through specifically defined interfaces called messages. Java can create applications that are distributed between clients and servers in a network. Java source code (signaled by .java extension) is compiled (source code transformed into object code) into byte code (signaled by .class extension). A Java interpreter then executes this byte code format. Java interpreters and runtime environment run on Java Virtual Machines (JVMs).

The portability and usability that characterizes Java stems from the fact that JVMs exist for most operating systems, from UNIX, to Windows, to Mac OS.

Java is one of the most well-suited languages for working on the World Wide Web and the client server model is the primary models for working on distributed networks, of which the World Wide Web is just one. There is natural affinity between the two and this article will discuss some major characteristics of Java and how it can be utilized in building client server systems.

To understand how Java is used in client server systems it becomes essential to understand the major characteristics of Java. Syntactic of Java are similarity to C and C+ + languages, Java is simple, simpler, in fact, than the languages it emulates. Java is also a robust programming language, which means it creates software that will identify and correct errors and handle abnormal conditions intelligently. Another major characteristic of Java is that it is object oriented programming, which was described above. OOP is characterized by three properties also present in Java programming: inheritance, encapsulation, and polymorphism. Inheritance is a major component in OOP which defines a general class and then specializes these classes by adding additional details in the already written class. Programmers only have to write the new features since the specialized class inherits all the features of the generalized class.

In OOP, encapsulation is the inclusion of all methods and data required for an object to function. Objects publish their interfaces and other objects communicate with these object interfaces to use them without having to understand how the encapsulated object performs its functions. It is the separation of interface and implementation. Polymorphism in OOP in general and Java specifically, is the ability to assign a different set of behaviors to an object in a subclass from the methods describe in the more general class. Therefore, subclasses can behave differently from the parent class without the parent class having to understand why for change itself. Multi threading is also an important characteristic of Java that increases interactive responsiveness and real time performance. Threading is the way a program splits or forks itself into two or more tasks running simultaneously. This allows for thread based multi tasking. Multi threading creates the effect of multiple threads running in parallel on different machines simultaneously.

Socket-based Client Server Systems in Java

Java builds client server systems with sockets. Sockets are the endpoints of two-way communication between programs running in a network. They are software objects that connect applications to network protocols, so they become intelligible. For example, in UNIX a program opens a socket that enables it to send and receive messages from the socket. This simplifies software development because programmers only have to change or specify the socket, while the operating system is left intact. In client/server models, the server contains sockets bound to specific port numbers. Port numbers identify specific processes that are to be forwarded over a network, like the Internet, in the form of messages to the server. The server only has to monitor the socket and respond when a client requests a connection. Once connections have been made and bound to port numbers, the two endpoints, client and server, can communicate through the socket. Java sockets are client side sockets, known simply as sockets and server side sockets known as server sockets. Each belong to their own class within a Java package. The client initiates the socket, which contains a host name and port number, by requesting connections.

The server socket class in Java allows for servers to monitor requests for connections. As the socket communicates over the network, Java's server socket class assigns a one port number to each client in the server and creates a socket object or instance. This server socket instance creates a connection and produces a thread or string of processes through which the server can communicate with the client through the socket. Java web servers are built according to this model. TCP (Transmission Control Protocol) works in conjunction with IP (Internet Protocol) to send messages between computers over the Internet. When communicating over the Internet, the client program and the server program each attach a socket to their end of the connection. Then the client and server can read from and write to the socket. Java provides operating system sockets that allow two or more processes to send and receive data, regardless of computer location.

Java's RMI System

The other method for using Java to build client server systems is RMI. RMI stands for Remote Method Invocation. By using Java language and functions, programmers write object oriented programming, so that objects that are distributed over a network can interact with each other. RMI allows for client objects in JVMs to request services through a network from another computer (host or server). Client objects included with the request may call upon methods in the remote computer that change the results. Methods are programmed procedures attributed to a class that are contained in each of its objects (or instances). It is a characteristic of object-oriented programming.

Classes and, therefore, objects can have more than one method and methods can be used for more than one object. Responses then run as if they were local (on the same computer.) This passing back and forth of objects and methods attached to objects is called 'object serializations'. Simply put, RMI requests call upon the method of a remote object. As previously stated, it uses the same syntax it would locally. To make this intelligible to the servers or sites being called upon requires three layers: a client side stub program, a remote reference layer, and a transport connection layer. Each request travels down the layers of the client computer and up the layers of the server. The client side stub program initiates the request. Stub programs are small sections of programs containing routines from larger programs. It is a substitute for programs that may take too long to load or are located remotely on a network. They are provided by the server at the client's request. Stubs accept client requests and communicate requested procedures (through another program) to remote applications. They also return the results to the client or requesting program. These stubs mimic the program being called for service.

In Java, stub programs are also referred to as 'proxy'. Remote reference layers manage reference variables for remote objects, using the transport layer's TCP (Transmission

Control Protocol) connection to the server. Reference variables contain class data and therefore include methods. The transport layer protects and maintains end to end communication through a network. The most used transport layer is TCP. After the client requests pass through the transport layer, they pass through another remote reference layer before requesting implementation of the request by the server from a skeleton. These skeletons are written in high level IDL (Interface Definition Language). The server receives the request and sends the response along the same channels, but in the other direction.

8.4 WEB SERVICES AND CLIENT/SEVER/BROWSER—SERVER TECHNOLOGY

Web services and Client/Server technology made it possible for applications to integrate of separate components. These components might exist on separate machines, but they work together through network (Internet) communication. Applications using web services demonstrate the integration of components coming from multiple sources. This makes version management important. One of the benefits of having to focus on version management is to make developers aware of component dependencies and specific areas that require maintenance in each version. This allows developers to customize maintenance for application deployment. These distributed application components use universal formats provided by such programming languages as XML (Extensible Markup Language) and WSDL (Web Standard Description Language).

XML is the W3C standardized language that allows information and services to be written in a structurally and semantically intelligible way that both humans and machine on different platforms can understand. It can be customized with user or industry tags. WSDL uses an XML format to describe network services. These services are described as endpoints that use messages to transmit documents or procedure-oriented information. These operations and messages are abstract, but then they are attached to specific network protocols and message formats to enable communication. Distributed application components also use universal protocols like HTTP (Hypertext Transfer Protocol) and SOAP (Simple Object Access Protocol).

HTTP is the standard protocol for transmitting HTML files or documents. SOAP is a message-based protocol formatted in XML and using HTTP. It is a way for a program running in one operating system to communicate with a program running in another. For the purposes of this discussion, applications that take advantage of web services will be understood as 'balanced computing model' because these applications are designed to take the fullest advantage of both client and server capabilities in the most efficient way. This model of balanced computing improves traditional Client/Server model by not stressing one part of the system and ignoring the capabilities of other parts.

For example, traditional browser-server models were Server-Centric. They could handle user demands but did not take advantage of client-side processing that could predict user behaviour. To predict the behaviour from a diverse customer base requires headroom. Headroom is also known as the attenuation crosstalk ratio. It ensures the network connections are strong and that signals on the receiving end of a communication are strong enough to overcome any interference. This provides a consistent and customized user experience regardless of unpredictable behaviour in the network.

8.5 CLIENT/SERVER TECHNOLOGY AND WEB APPLICATIONS

There is a gap in user experience between desktop applications and web applications. Desktop applications run on a single computer, while web applications run on the Internet. Since the invention of the Web, developers have been trying to design web applications that demonstrate the speed and interactivity of applications running on the client machine of a LAN (Local Area Network). Despite the explosion of web based applications in the 1990's (and continuing today), many users still prefer desktop applications. Like web sites, desktop applications access up to date information by connecting to the Web through the Internet.

However, desktop applications are designed with a much more refined sensibility and use PC power to customize requests from information stored on the desktop. This user experience is significantly better than when using remote web sites. Many are arguing that desktop applications will be the next wave in the Internet revolution.

So, with desktop applications breathing down their necks, web applications need to keep up the pace. Web applications are accessed by web browsers and run over a network, like the Internet. They are popular because of the power dominance of web browsers serving as thin clients.Thin clients are client applications or devices that simply initiate requests and provide input. They do very little of the processing, letting the server handle the heavy lifting by forwarding requests and contacting different nodes and networks. Web applications are responsible for web based e-mail applications like Hotmail, online shopping sites, online auction sites, wikis, and blogs. In traditional client server computing, every application contained a client program that provided the User Interface (UI) through which users would interact with/make requests from the applications. Each client program had to be installed individually on each user workstation. Web applications are different.

Web applications dynamically generate web documents. These are HTML/XHTML (Hypertext Markup Language/Extensible Hypertext Markup Language) documents transmitted over the Internet through HTTP (Hypertext Transfer Protocol). These documents or pages make up the web site. Using a standard server side scripting language like JavaScript allows for more interactive features in the user interface. Usually, each page is delivered as a static document, but the sequence in which they are presented is interactive. User web forms are embedded in the page markup, customizing responses. The web browser, acting as "universal client", interprets and displays the dynamic web pages. Web application UIs offer a variety of features. For example, the drag and drop feature allows for virtual objects to be moved from location through the mouse. This can create all sorts of actions, from copying to associating two objects to create a new action. By using application specific technologies like Java, JavaScript, DHTML (Dynamic HTML), and Flash, all sorts of graphic and audio interactive features may be added to a UI. As previously stated, web developers are currently looking for ways to improve user experiences with web applications so they may closely resemble the performance of desktop applications. Remember, the user experience is the most often gauged by the usability of the UI or GUI (Graphic User Interface).

1st Generation Web Applications

The applications that are available now are typified by the technology used/presented in the 1st Generation Web Application; see the Fig. 8.3 shown. This might be characterized as a new form of electronic publishing, but it's richer in some ways than books because it's multimedia publishing. Today most home pages consist of text, photos, and graphics. By early 1997, however, it's likely that animation and 3D applications will be available. This technology is already very useful in information dissemination. Companies are replacing human resources manuals and maintenance manuals with browsers connected over intranets or the Internet to a server which contains the latest information sought.

A primary limitation of first generation applications is that there is no database management system, connected to the web server and the software does not keep the track of who is requesting information or of the last request from that user. It is a stateless connection. The addition of DBMS capabilities to the HTML processes on the server will allow HTML servers to have memory. As the leading DBMS vendors add connections for Web servers, it becomes possible for that server to remember who you are and what you have done from page to page and from visit to visit. The interaction, then, becomes a lot more intelligent and useful.

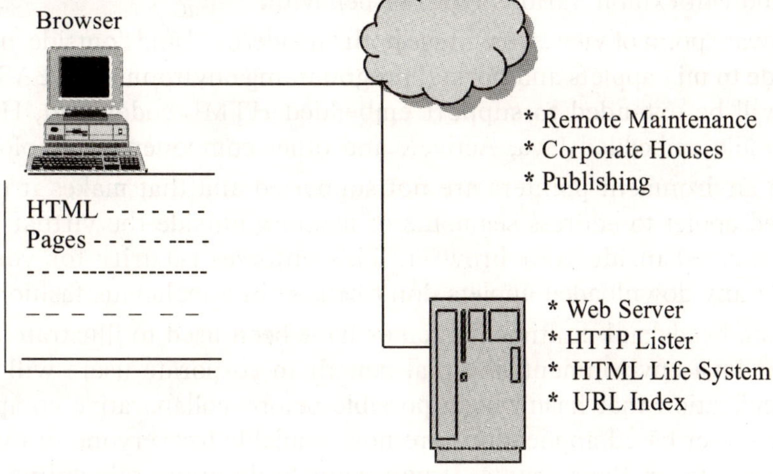

Fig. 8.3: Architecture of Ist Generation Web Application

2nd Generation Web Applications

First Generation Web Applications are quickly going to be joined by newer more capable environments that perhaps we can call the second generation. Several things will define this newer generation that are given as below:

- Support for active clients via downloadable applets (software components),
- Live DBMS links that enable the server to know who you are from page to page, and visit to visit, and
- True interactivity between the client and server (indicated by the two-headed arrow).

2nd generation Web applications have live DBMS connections on the server. Today what is mostly available for such support are SQL DBMS engines from companies like Sybase, Informix, IBM and Oracle. A problem with these engines is that SQL supports traditional business data types such as alphanumeric, date and time. No major SQL product supports extended and complex data types such as voice, maps or video at this time. That is a defect that will be remedied (probably) in the 1997 timeframe. All of the major DBMS vendors are making important strides in this direction.

This software component type of operation will be the first example of widespread use for distributed object computing. Sun's Java technology is the best known example of this approach. Sun describes its Hot-Java browser/Java language technology as "simple, object-oriented, distributed, interpreted, robust, secure, architecture-neutral, portable, high performance, multi-threaded and dynamic." The way this will work is for your browser on the client to have a Java (or ActiveX or C++) interpreter that can activate a component that has been downloaded to your client from the Web server. Your browser, then, becomes event driven and can exhibit various types of behavior.

From a software point of view, we will see both "inside/out" and "outside/in" approaches to write the code to mix applets and normal programming environments. BASIC compilers, for example, will be extended to support embedded HTML code. And, HTML will be extended to handle embedded Java, ActiveX and other component technologies.

In the Java environment pointers are not supported and that makes it impossible for any downloaded applet to address segments of memory outside the virtual Java machine that has been created inside your browser. This enforces security for your client and makes sure that any downloaded applets don't behave in a malicious fashion.

While talking heads and multimedia demos have been used to illustrate the operation of the Java/Hot Java environment, the real benefit to corporate users will come from a new type of application that hasn't been possible before–collaborative computing among strangers. Your server based applications are now available to everyone in the world; your programs can execute on their clients. If you want to do group scheduling, for example, until now everyone in the effort had to have the same client, something like Lotus Notes. With this new environment, it will be easy to accomplish wide area, multi-platform group scheduling via the Internet. The scheduling applet can be downloaded and executed in the component enabled browser.

8.6 BALANCED COMPUTING AND THE SERVER'S CHANGING ROLE

In balanced computing, processing is shared between clients, servers, and any other devices connected via a network. This distribution is inherent in the design since applications are already spread out on different machines and connected through web services. In balancing, the processing required by each new use is often shifted back to the user's system, thereby taking fuller advantage of client-side processing power. This allows for improved scalability, since the processing load is increased insignificantly by the addition of users.

Load balancing can also be achieved by building Service-Oriented Applications (SOAs) where components run on different nodes in multiple locations duplicate services on multiple nodes. This duplicating of services on multiple nodes also improves reliability since there is no single point of failure that will topple the entire application. Through balanced computing, platforms can take maximum advantage of computing and display capabilities on each platform. The virtual application which is balanced across multiple nodes remains transparent (its complex functions hidden) while the user utilizes his or her own collection of devices to run and view the application on the user end.

Balanced computing not only distributes the processing load, but changes the role of the server as well. Instead of computing so heavily, the server primarily directs traffic. Given rich clients and decent Internet connectivity, users directly contact databases instead of requiring server intervention. Rich clients are applicants in user computers that retrieve data through the Internet. As previously discussed, the proliferation of web-based applications replaced the user interface with the web browser. Scripting languages, like JavaScript or VBScript, were embedded into HTML to improve user interfaces (among other things). Java applets were also added. But nothing could compete with the user experience of using an application built from its local environment. Developing technologies like improved web-page scripting languages and AJAX (Asynchronous JavaScript and XML), made web browsers function more like rich client applications.

Another method used to reduce demands on the server uses a connecting device to re-direct previously server-side processing to the client. This depends on the client device capability and Internet connectivity. If these are weak, the server picks up the slack, making application performance consistent on both the client and server ends.

User Experience and Development

Balanced distributed computing models improve user experience and expand development. Developers can focus on user experience by examining devices and customizing features. For example, different user interfaces can be customized for different departments that require different resources to perform their function. Different roles would have their own user interface. Well-defined user roles and profiles that are stored on user machines make more efficient use of server computation. It allows the server to pull customized responses based on the identity/role of the user. To further reduce server demand, clients can communicate directly with databases by requesting information for the user role profile. This eliminates the web server as middleman for the request and computation on the output side.

Data integration on user platforms offers new opportunities to build applications that draw data from a variety of sources and can add different contexts. In a balanced distributed computing model, web services send information that is usually stored on databases or servers (like financial information) to the user's machine. It accomplishes this by using the client-side's processing power. These responses are formatted in the increasingly popular, universal XML. Desktop applications (on the user's system) can take that information and analyze it in different contexts.

The decentralization of distributed browser-server models also improves security and protects privacy. For example, data repositories are often located in a different location from the server. This makes it more difficult for external attackers to find. It also makes it less accessible to internal attackers. Also, it is safer for user profiles to be stored on individual machines, rather than on a central database.

Distributed computing models address the future of IT architecture and application. Organization must aim to create independent and flexible applications that can respond quickly to a variety of contexts. Connections must be agile. Loosely coupled applications, characteristic of distributed computing models, withstand broken connections and slow Internet performance. This protects core technologies from customer demands and lack of Internet bandwidth.

EXERCISE 8

1. Explain an object web model based on java client and CORBA ORB's on the basis of following points:
   (*i*) Web client
   (*ii*) Protocol used
   (*iii*) Web server
2. Explain end-to-end working of Client/Server web model. (Hint: Use CGI, GET, POST, Web browser and Web server)
3. Explain, with the help of block diagram and example, the Common Object Request Broker Architecture.
4. Discuss the role of traditional and web databases in handling Client/Server based applications.
5. Discuss the role of web browser for providing web service in Client/Server environment.
6. Explain how the Database is being accessed on the Web. Or how the information exchange take place between User and a Web-based Database.
7. Discuss the development of Client/Server Technology based web applications.

9

Future of the Client/Server Computing

9.1 INTRODUCTION

Development of Client/Server technologies is still evolving. From year to year, project-to-project, technocrats are not doing anything the same way twice. Today, we are busy moving our Client/Server assets to the intranet. In a few years, who knows where we'll take Client/Server and distributed development? Spotting trends is not only a nice thing to do, it's a career skill. For instance, those who saw the rise of the intranet early on, and obtained the skills they needed to leverage the technology, were the same people who cashed in when the Web took off. The same can be said about three-tier Client/Server, and now about the rise of distributed objects. We may also see the rise of user agents, or point-to-point networking.

In this chapter, we shall discuss the bright future of Client/Server technologies, including technology that will be seen in the near and distant future. Furthermore, we will discuss about some of the trends that you can latch on today, and where to catch the next wave of Client/Server technology.

9.2 TECHNOLOGY OF THE NEXT GENERATION

Predicting technology is like predicting the weather. While it's safe to say that processors will be faster and disk space cheaper, it's much more difficult to predict the way we'll use and develop software. Developers don't create the trends, they follow them. For example, the interest in the intranet came from the millions of users who found a friendly home in their Web browser, and wanted a way to run their business applications with the Disney and CNN Home Pages. The same could be said about traditional Client/Server computing a few years ago. Users wanted to run business applications with their new GUI desktop applications.

Using the past as our guide, we can make an intelligent gives about the future of Client/Server computing. The predictions can be broken up into a few categories: networking, development tools, processors and servers, paradigms, and enabling technologies.

9.2.1 Networking

The pipe between the client and server is still too narrow, and bandwidth has not kept up with the development of technology and modern architecture. With the advent of ATM and switched networks, we can finally count on a pipe wide enough to push tons of data through. It will take a few years before we bring this wide pipe down to the desktop.

Client/Server developers must become networking gurus as well. The performance of the network dictates the performance of the Client/Server system. What's more, with the advent of application-partitioning technology (such as application-partitioning tools and distributed objects), the network not only links the client to the server, but links all the application objects together to form the virtual (partitioned) application. Clearly, the network is the infrastructure of the distributed application.

In addition to upgrading the speed and reliability of enterprise network technology, we are looking for ways to upgrade the speed of WAN technology. Frame relay and other global networking solutions will create high-performance virtual systems, available throughout the world. Let us hope this technology will extend to the Internet. If you haven't noticed, it's creaking under the strain of thousands of additional users, who start surfing every day.

9.2.2 Development Tools

Client/Server development tools are finally delivering on promises made initially, but there is a lot of room for improvement. Some of the areas where tools can be made to perform better include:

- Use of true compilers.
- Native links to the distributed objects and TP monitors.
- Better component development capabilities.
- Use of standards.
- Consistent language support.
- True application-partitioning capabilities.
- Consistent approach to the intranet.

Use of true compilers: With the advent of Delphi, developers saw the benefit of a specialized development tool that cannot only do RAD, but create small, efficient, and speedy applications. The use of a true compiler allows developers to create native executables and avoid the overhead of dealing with an interpreter.

In the past, specialized Client/Server development tools counted on the fact that processors increased in speed every year to mask the inefficiencies of their deployment mechanisms. But users did notice, and they labeled PowerBuilder, Visual Basic, and other specialized development tool applications "dogs" on low-end PCs. Upgrading the hardware in the entire company to run a single application costs millions, and there is something to be said about efficient application development (such as is offered by most C++ development environments).

Today we see a trend in specialized Client/Server development tools that offers a true compiler. Besides Delphi, PowerBuilder runs close to native, and Visual Basic (version 5) will also provide a true compiler. Other specialized tool vendors are bound to head in that direction. Tool vendors should have done this from the start, and it's about time they got their act together.

Native links to the distributed objects and transaction processing monitors: Despite the fact that distributed objects and TP monitors are key enablers for multi-tier Client/Server development, few Client/Server tools exist that can easily use them. For instance, if we want to use a specialized Client/Server tool with a TP monitor, we have to load and invoke the services of a DLL (in most cases), or limit the selection of tools to those few that support TP monitors (e.g., Prolific, EncinaBuilder). The same can be said about distributed objects.

As mentioned above, the number of multi-tiered Client/Server applications keep growing, and so will the need for Client/Server tools that can access the services of TP monitors and distributed objects. With demand comes innovation, and most tool vendors plan to provide links to the distributed objects and TP monitors. With the advent of Transaction Server, for example, TP monitors come as close to a DCOM connection as any COM-enabled Client/Server development tools.

As IIOP makes intranet development easier, we'll see a rise in the number of tools that support traditional Client/Server development and integration with distributed objects. Thus, as a byproduct of links to Web technology, we'll see the use of CORBA-compliant distributed objects as a part of most Client/Server development tools. Already, any Windows-based Client/Server development tool that does OLE automation can also link to DCOM, and thus, COM-enabled ORBs. The movement toward the use of distributed objects will continue.

Better component development capabilities: The other side of distributed objects is the ability to assemble Client/Server applications from rebuilt components. While most Client/Server tools support the integration of components (e.g., ActiveX or Java), they don't support them well. Many components don't work and play well with others, and don't provide developers with enough granularity.

If component development is to work, tool vendors must provide consistent support for components that will allow developers to modify the interfaces, and easily link components together to create an application. What's more, the same tools should create components. We have many examples of tools today (such as Visual Basic and PowerBuilder) that can both create and use components. The future lies in tools that can easily create and share components, as well as mix and match tools to construct an application from a very low level (e.g., middleware) to a very high level.

If current indicators continue to hold true, ActiveX will provide the component standards we need for Windows, while OpenDoc will have limited success on non-Windows platforms. A lot will depend on Microsoft's ability to parlay ActiveX into a legitimate open standard. Right now, developers view ActiveX as a proprietary standard, still bound to Windows. They are right.

Use of standards: Of course, the use of distributed objects, TP monitors, and components leads to a discussion of standards. While many standards and standards organizations exist today, standards are only as good as the number of developers who use them.

Key Client/Server standards include CORBA, COM, and SQL92, but many others run with the wolves. A common problem in the industry is our failure to use and enforce standards. The tradeoff is the exclusive advantage that vendors enjoy while they employ proprietary features versus the benefits they could reap if they would provide developers with standards they support in other tools. While many Client/Server technology vendors give lip service to the idea, standards are not yet a priority.

The movement toward standards really depends on the users/developers. If we demand that tool and technology vendors employ standards, and agree that interoperability is of great value, the vendors will respond. The standards organizations (such as OMG) also need to work harder to bring standards to the technology. It took five years before the OMG had a standard that actually spelled out a way for CORBA-based distributed objects to work together. That's just too long for this business.

Despite the slow movement, I think we'll continue to move toward a standard technology that will let everyone and everything work together. The trick now is to pick the standard(s) you think will win.

Consistent language support: Until recently, the mantra of Client/Server tool vendors was 'build a tool, build a proprietary language.' Fact is, we have more development languages today than ever before, with languages proprietary to particular tools. The reasons are the same as with our previous standards discussion.

The most recent trend is for Client/Server tool vendors to employ non-proprietary languages in their tool, or to use the same language throughout a product line. For example, Delphi is based on Pascal, rather than a proprietary scripting language like PowerBuilder. Optima++ and VisualAge C++, use C++ as their native language. Visual Basic shares VBA with Access, Microsoft Office products, and even third-party tools such as Oracle's PowerObjects. VBA is licensed by Microsoft to over forty vendors. This trend will continue. While developers are happy to learn a new IDE, they aren't nearly as thrilled when they must learn a new programming language.

True application-partitioning capabilities: Along with links to the distributed objects, tools will continue to provide more sophisticated proprietary application-partitioning capabilities. Many traditional two-tier tools, such as Power Builder and Unify, are heading in this direction (albeit slowly), while Forte, Dynasty, and IBI's Cactus are learning to do a better job with their existing partitioning tools.

There is also a movement in the application-partitioning world toward the use of open technologies. For instance, distributed objects and TP monitors now work with the proprietary ORBs of application-partitioning tools. Proprietary ORBs are not a long-term solution, and the opening of these environments to non-proprietary technology will only increase their value to developers.

Consistent approach to the intranet: The enabling technology of the intranet must settle down to a few consistent approaches. For example, now we have HTML, SGML, VRML, CGI, NSAPI, ISAPI, Java, JavaScript, VBScript, ActiveX, Java, IIOP, and the list goes on. Although this provides developers with an arsenal of technologies and techniques, it results in a few too many standards to follow, and confusing for developers.

Over the next year, we'll see the list of intranet-enabling technologies shorten, as the market naturally removes the technologies that do not capture the hearts and minds of the developers and that offer redundant technologies. Redundant technologies include Java and ActiveX, JavaScript and VBScript. We'll also see a movement toward ISAPI and NSAPI, or back to CGI. Finally, we need to go with a single HTML standard, and move away from the proprietary extensions of Netscape and Microsoft.

9.2.3 Processors and Servers

We can expect processing power to increase; without any slowdown in that area. The power of servers will be keeping up increase in future, up with the requirements of your application, and we can now run mainframe class systems on commodity hardware.

We'll also see the rise of symmetric multi-processing computers and operating systems for use as clients as well as servers. When Windows 95 and Windows NT merge, clients will have a powerful operating system that can make the most of this new hardware. Clients can once again become a location for application processing.

Servers will become more component-based. Architects will be better able to customize servers around particular application server and database server requirements, adjusting the cache, memory, processors, and disk size to the exact specifications of the application. The operating system that will run these servers will have to keep up. Advanced multi-processing operating systems (such as Windows NT and Unix) will provide better load balancing and fault-tolerant capabilities, including, for instance, the ability to better work through memory, disk, and processor failures without service interruptions.

Despite the religious implications of operating systems and an anti-Microsoft sentiment, Windows NT will take more market share away from the traditional server operating system for Client/Server: Unix. Windows NT is almost as powerful, supports multi-processing, and can run on a number of processors. What really drives the movement toward Windows NT is the ease of use it offers, as well as its ability to support the majority of off-the-shelf software. While Sun servers will run Oracle, they won't run Word for Windows as a native application. Web servers for use on intranets or the Internet will become the domain of NT as well as Microsoft is giving its Web server away with NT, which is a convenient situation.

9.2.4 Paradigms

Today we are well into the object-oriented development paradigm, and this will remain true. In fact, as we become better at using object Client/Server tools, we will dig deeper into their support for the object-oriented development model.

The use of components will become more of an issue too. We really can't build an application by mixing and matching today's components. However, as component standards finally take off, we'll be able to snap in many application components, and even mix and match components with the native objects of the tools.

9.3 ENABLING TECHNOLOGY

We must consider the evolution of the enabling technologies of Client/Server. Enabling technologies are the combinations of hardware and software that can be used to assist in creating a particular kind of application system. These technologies include TP monitors, databases, and middleware, Expert systems, Point-of-Services (POS), imaging, intranet and extranet.

Transaction-processing monitors: As we move headlong into large-scale, mission-critical distributed computing, we need an "ace in the hole." TP monitors are that ace. Now developers have begun to understand the benefits of the TP monitors with other alternatives (such as proprietary application-partitioning tools) proved themselves to be a bit less popular. With the advent of Microsoft's Transaction Server, we now have a TP monitor that fits easily into commodity Windows environments, built from the ground up for ActiveX and the intranet. With the success of Transaction Server, We may see more TP monitors heading into the market.

Databases: Databases will continue to dazzle us with better performance and new features. The big three players (Oracle, Sybase, and Informix) will continue to dominate share, and the relational database model will remain. The concept of the universal server will enlarge the database market by allowing databases to be a "jack of all trades" for developers (object-oriented, relational, Web, binary, etc.). Databases vendors will find, as Oracle is finding now, that working with distributed objects provides a competitive advantage as the rest of the world moves there.

Middleware: Finally, middleware will evolve too. While middleware is powerful and necessary, it's difficult to use and deploy. In the next few years, we'll see a rise of middleware solutions—both message and RPC-based—that provide "snap-in" functionality and consistent interfaces. Microsoft's Falcon message-oriented middleware will once again prove that Microsoft can turn a high-end product into a consumer commodity, and other, more aggressive vendors will have to keep up.

9.3.1 Expert Systems

Expert system is a branch of artificial intelligence that makes extensive use of specialized knowledge to solve problem at the level of human expert. Expert systems are intelligent computer programs that use knowledge and inference process to solve problems that are difficult enough to require significant human expertise for their solution. That is, an expert system is a computer system that emulates the decision-making ability of a human expert. The term expert system is often applied today to any system that uses expert system technology that includes special expert system languages, programs and hardware design to aid in the development and execution of expert systems. The knowledge in expert systems may be either expertise or knowledge that is generally available from books, magazines, and knowledgeable persons. The terms expert system, knowledge based system, or knowledge based expert system are often used synonymously. Fig. 9.1 given below, illustrates the basic concepts and the architecture of knowledge based expert system that consists of two main components internally. The knowledge base contains the knowledge based on which the *inference engine* draws conclusion.

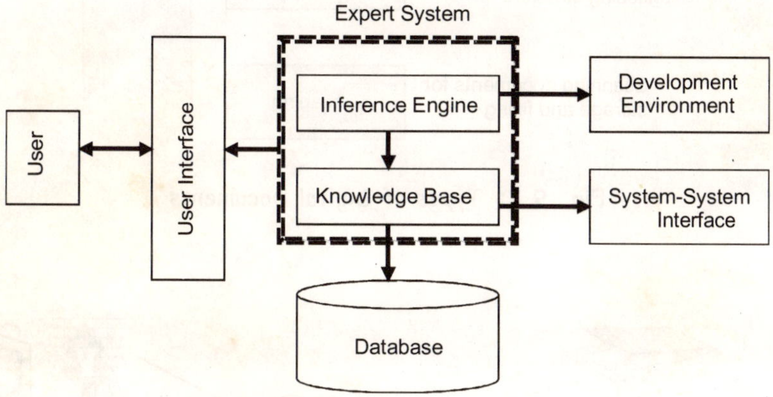

Fig.9.1: Basic Concept of Expert System

Applications of expert system are widely accepted and well-suited for the Client/Server models. The *user interface* provides some rule based advantages related with the processing power and some of the benefits at the workstations. Mostly the rules are managed by knowledgeable user and not by a professional programmer, because the user only knows how his job works (a job the expert system emulates). The inference engine, a CPU-intensive process that takes advantage of low-cost processing and RAM available with Client/Server technology, enforces the rules. Most applications will be implemented using existing databases on host-based DBMS's. The Client/Server model provides the necessary connectivity and services to support access to this information.

Expert system provides an advantage in business world by encapsulating the rules and object of the trade. Objects are created by expert knowledge hence can be reused throughout the organization. The outcomes of the expert system can frequently be used in integrated business systems.

9.3.2 Imaging

Widely used digital documents are imaging, structured documents, and distributed hypertext, active or compound. Fig. 9.2 given below, illustrates the various forms of existing digital documents).

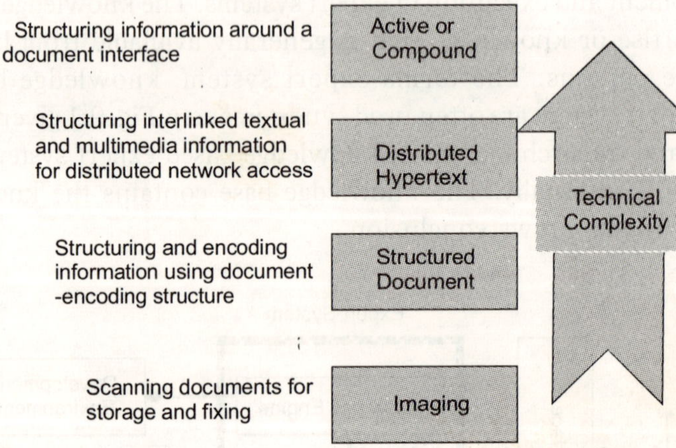

Fig. 9.2: Types of Digital Documents

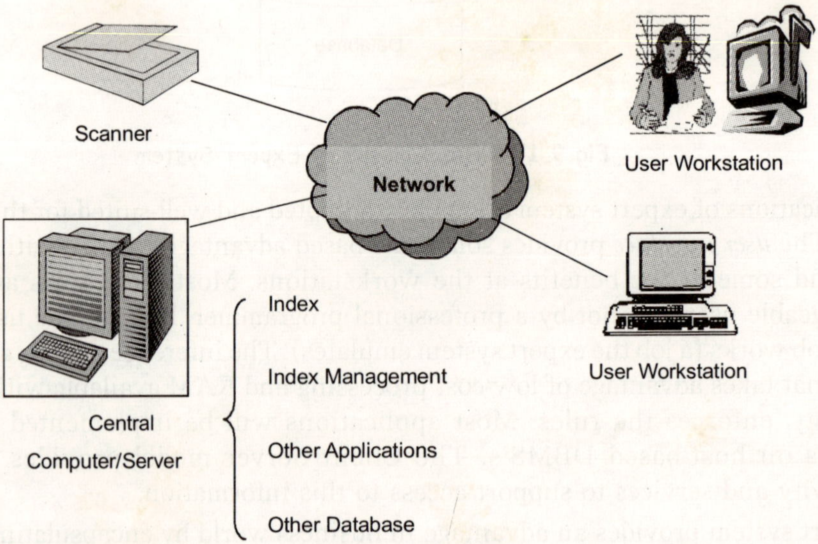

Fig. 9.3: Imaging System

Now, imaging is the method of getting digital documents from physical ones. An imaging system passes a paper document through a scanner that renders it digital and then stores the digital data as a bit mapped image of the document. Fig. 9.3 illustrates the imaging system. This image is stored on a permanent medium (magnetic tape, disk or optical disk). The keyword for each document that helps in indexing and retrieval are entered during scanning. The index usually is stored in a relational database on a high-speed magnetic disk. Access to stored image is always initiated by an index search. These image documents can be accessed by any workstation, which accesses the image server.

9.3.3 Point-of-Service

POS is one of the most widely installed examples of Client/Server technology, also known as Point of Sale. POS's represents the best model for the implementation of Client/Server applications by combining information technology, management information and trade processes on a single platform. For product distribution, inventory control, pricing, accounting, staff management, the POS's are used everywhere at the supermarket, hotel, restaurants, stores and auto-service stations. POS systems record each sale in a central database (server), using a scanner which reads the bar code on the products, so that retailers no longer have to wait for a periodic inventory check to find out what they need to reorder. Centralized buying ensures price through volume purchasing and efficient distribution chains.

Point-of-sale scanning is the starting point in the EDI chain that allows the retailer to track merchandise at the item level and provides detail information for demand forecasting. This way of managing inventory can eliminate the need to remark merchandise for discount and promotions to reduce inventory levels. POS systems feed data to automatic replenishment systems that constantly monitor inventory levels and trigger EDI transactions. These systems support smaller, more frequent deliveries, which improve in-stock positions and reduce on-hand inventory. Scanning is a valuable part of warehouse operations, as this expedites the rapid flow of goods through the distribution center by reducing manual receiving and checking procedures.

9.4 CLIENT/SERVER COMPUTING AND THE INTRANET

9.4.1 Intranet

Due to sheer numbers, the intranet will continue to be the main area of interest for Client/Server development. Intranet is a term used to refer to the implementation of Internet technologies within a corporate organization, rather than for external connection to the global Internet. Or in other words, the term Intranet refer to the whole range of internet base applications, including network news, gopher, web technology. An intranet-based approach to corporate computing includes the following advantages:

- Supports a range of distributed computing architecture (few central server or many distributed servers).
- Open architecture means large number of add-on applications available across many platforms.
- Can be implemented on virtually all platforms with complete interoperability.
- Rapid prototyping and deployment of new services.
- Structure to support integration of "legacy" information sources.
- Support a range of media types (Audio, video, interactive applications).
- Inexpensive to start, requires little investment either in new software or infrastructure.
- Virtually no training required on the part of users and little training required to developers, because the user services and user interfaces are familiar from the Internet.

9.4.2 Is the Intranet Killing Client/Server?

Some people think that there is so much interest in the intranet that Client/Server will fall by the wayside. Actually, the opposite is true. The intranet and Client/Server complement rather than compete. In fact, the migration to the intranet is actually a process of simply deploy Client/Server technology using the commodity Web technology. What the intranet brings to the table is a new platform, interface, and architectures. The intranet can employ existing Client/Server applications as true intranet applications, and integrate applications in the Web browser that would not normally work and play well together. The intranet also means that the vast amount of information on the Internet becomes available from the same application environment and the interface which is a valuable advantage. The intranet also puts fat client developers on a diet. Since most intranet applications are driven from the Web server, the application processing is moving off the client and back onto the server. This means that maintenance and application deployment become much easier, and developers don't have to deal with the integration hassles of traditional Client/Server (such as loading assorted middleware and protocol stacks).

There is a drawback to the intranet movement. The interest in the Web has taken most R&D funds away from traditional Client/Server. In many respects, the evolution of traditional Client/Server technology (middleware, databases, and front-end development tools) remained static while the technology vendors moved their products to the Web.

Moving to Proprietary Complexity: While the sheer simplicity of the intranet has driven its success, we are now in danger of driving this technology the same way we are driving client servers: to proprietary complexity. Where HTML and CGI were once commoly held standards, we now have proprietary APIs such as NSAPI and ISAPI that are pushing CGI aside. Java was considered the only way to program dynamic web applications, but now we have ActiveX as an alternative. Even Netscape now touts the standard HTTP as "legacy technology."

> It's difficult at this time to determine if this movement to proprietary technology is a good thing. One thing for sure is that the simple architecture of just a few years ago is gradually disappearing. In many respects, intranet development is becoming as complex as Client/Server development. The trend is going to continue. We could see even more complexity in the world of Web development than we ever saw with Client/Server.

As interest in the Web shifts towards creating successful applications, we'll see more links between the intranet and traditional Client/Server. Right now, the tool vendors' fear that they will miss a large portion of the market puts them in a reactive rather than a proactive mode.

9.4.3 Extranet

Extranet is the similar concept to the intranet, using TCP/IP protocols and applications, especially the Web. The distinguished feature of the extranet is that it provides the access to corporate resources by outside clients (suppliers and customers of the organization). This outside access can be through the Internet or through other data communication networks. An extranet provides a simpler Web access and more extensive access to corporate resources, enforcing some security policies becomes a necessity. As with the intranet, the typical model of operation for the extranet is Client/Server. Some of the communication options available for operating intranet to outsiders to create an extranet.

- Long distance dialup access.
- Internet access to intranet with security.
- Internet access to an external server that duplicates some of a company's intranet data.
- Internet access to an external server that originate database queries to internal servers.
- Virtual private network.

9.5 FUTURE PERSPECTIVES

9.5.1 Job Security

Client/Server developers and application architects have a bright future. IDC (International Data Corporation) says that 33 per cent of organizations are already committed to Client/Server computing, despite the long break-in period. The Strategic Focus reports that three-tier Client/Server applications will grow from 4.9 per cent to 18.7 per cent in just two years. This growth will also fuel the rise of three-tier and n-tier Client/Server technology (such as TP monitors and distributed objects). Forrester Research estimates that the Client/Server market place will rise to $7.5 billion in 1996. Finally, the Gartner Group predicts that 65 per cent of all applications created in the next five years will employ Client/Server technology.

Clearly, the growth of Client/Server is steady, and as time goes on, the vast majority of applications we build for businesses will employ Client/Server technology. We still have a way to go, and many problems to solve, but it is certain that the Client/Server development game will always have room for talented people.

Look around today's "corporate downsized" job market. Those in Client/Server development have little reason to worry. There are more job openings than candidates, and that's been a pretty steady trend for several years.

9.5.2 Future Planning

Planning for the future is simply a matter of establishing the strategy and the tactics of our application development environment. From time to time, we need to consider the following:

- Re-evaluate our business objectives.
- Re-evaluate the current technology infrastructure.
- Determine the differences (what's missing?).
- Adjust our technology infrastructure to meet your objectives.

In most cases, this is a process of looking at new enabling technologies and paradigms that will better serve our needs. For example, if we need access to many applications for a single multi-platform user interface, then we may want to set a course for the intranet. Or, if we need to access a number of legacy resources as a single virtual system, then TP monitors and DCE are worth using. Of course, we would need to consider which enabling technology to employ, and then select the tools that support the enabling technology of choice.

While working out the plan for enabling technologies it is worth remembering that Vendors usually deliver 80 per cent of their promises up front, and the other 20 per cent shows up a few years later. For example, while Visual Basic and Power Builder offer proprietary application-partitioning mechanisms, they were so difficult to set up and so limited in what they could do that many development organizations abandoned them in their search for a quicker, easier way to move to n-tier. Visual Basic is fixing its limitations with DCOM and integration with Falcon and Transaction Server, but it took a few years.

It is always safer to follow the technology curve. While distributed objects were new and unproven a few years ago, they are proven today. DCOM is not yet proven, and proprietary application-partitioning tools such as Forte or Dynasty are almost there.

9.5.3 Conclusion

We can conclude some key features about client/server computing that are:

- Client/server distributes processing among computers on a network.
- In client/server environment most of the client provides GUI's facilities.
- Most of the servers provide SQL processing.
- Business rules can run either on the client or the server.
- Clients are typically programmed with a visual programming tool.

- Transaction processing is on of the biggest challenges of client/server computing.
- Middleware is the layer between clients and servers.
- Client/server standards are emerging.

In near future, cheap and powerful workstation technologies will be available to all with truly distributed applications using processing power where available, and providing information where required. Also information will be available for use to owners and authorized users without a constant need for system development by professional and their complex programming languages. The future will see information being captured at its source, and made available immediately to authorized users. Users will be able to avail information in original forms of data, such as image, video, audio, graphics, documents and spreadsheet without the need to be aware of various software requirements for information presentation. Successful organizations of the future, that those are market driven and competitive will be the ones that use client/server as an enabling technology to add recognized value to their products and services.

9.6 TRANSFORMATIONAL SYSTEM

The working environment of many of the organizations has been greatly affected by applications of Client/Server technologies. Following are the examples of technologies that have changed the trade processes.

(*i*) Electronic mail.

(*ii*) Client/server and user security.

(*iii*) Object oriented technology: CORBA.

(*iv*) Electronic data interchange.

9.6.1 Electronic Mail

Electronic mail is already the most heavily used network application in the corporate world. It is a facility that allows users at workstations and terminals to compose and exchange messages. However, the traditional e-mail is generally limited and inflexible. Intranet mail products provide standards, simple methods for attaching documents, sound, images, and other multimedia to mail messages.

The simplest form of electronic mail is the single system facility allowing the users of a shared computer system to exchange messages (see the Fig. 9.4 (*a*) given). The electronic mail facility is an application program available to any user logged onto the system. A user may invoke the electronic mail facility, prepare a message, and "send" it to any other user on the system. The act of sending simply involves putting the message in the recipient's mailbox. Mailbox is actually an entity maintained by the file management system and is in nature of a file directory. Any incoming mail is simply stored as a file under that user's mailbox directory. One mailbox is associated with each user.

With a single system electronic mail facility, messages can only be exchanged among users of that particular system. For a distributed mail system, a number of mail handlers (mail servers) connect over a network facility (e.g., WAN or internet) and exchange mail. That is illustrated in Fig. 9.4(b) given below:

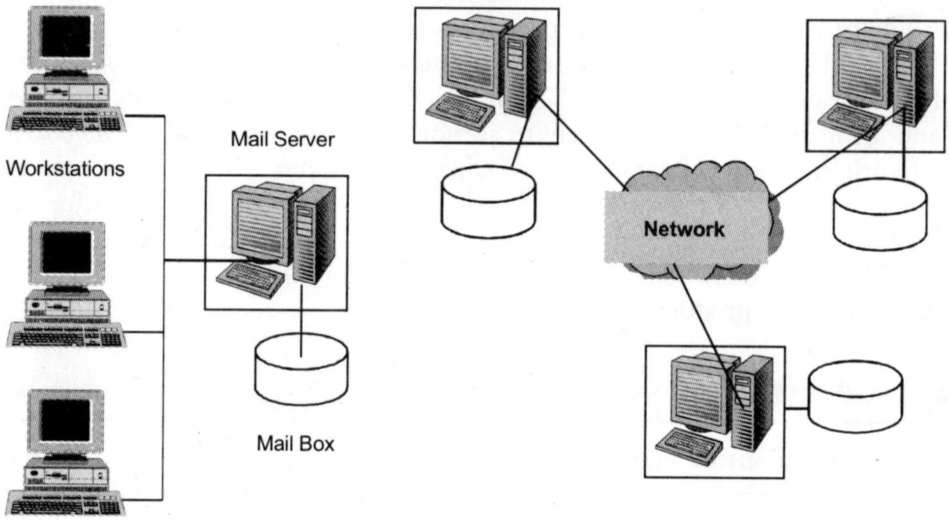

(*a*) Single System (*b*) Networks of Mail System

Fig. 9.4: Electronic Mail Configurations

Intranet mail system creates and manages an electronic mailing list that is an alias to multiple destinations. Mailing list is usually created to discuss specific topics. Any one interested in that topic may join that list, once a client has been added to the list. A user can ask question or respond to some one else's question by sending a message to the list address.

9.6.2 Client/Server and User Security

However, the very characteristic that make Client/Server popular are also what make it the most vulnerable to breaches in security. It is precisely the distribution of services between client and server that open them up to damage, fraud, and misuse. Security consideration must include the host systems, personal computers (PCs), Local Area Networks (LANs), Global Wide Area Networks (WANs), and users. Because security investments don't produce immediately visible returns and Client/Server buyers sometimes don't educate themselves about security, this area of development is often overlooked until a problem occurs.

Desktops are the front-end system devices, the ones that deal most directly with user input. They are also the least secure environments in Client/Server models. Clients connect to servers and these connections, if left open or not secured, provide entry points for hackers and other intruders that may use data for nefarious purposes. Aside from physical client security in the form of disk drive locks or diskless workstations that prohibit the loading of unauthorized software or viruses, accessibility to all files stored on a workstation operating system is the other gaping security hole in clients. For example, the machine assumes that whoever turns on the computer is the owner of all the files stored on it. They even have access to configuration files. This could result in sabotage or the leaking of sensitive data. The transmission of corrupted data may also occur on the level of the operating system, outside the realm of Client/Server application security, as data is transferred to different tiers of the architecture.

However, the primary culprits of breaching client security are not hackers or viruses, but the users themselves. The front-line of defense in client security is user identification and authentication. The easiest way to gain illegal access to computers is to get users' login ID and passwords. Sometimes users pick short or easily guessed passwords or share their passwords with others. Password management provides a security measurement for this by requiring a minimum amount of characters to be used in passwords checking passwords for guess ability, and regularly asking users to change their passwords. For example, more organizations are adopting policies of 'pass phrases' rather than passwords that are more complicated and harder to identify or guess. The system contains a scheme (minimalist, multi-paradigm programming language) that proactively detects and blocks spyware. It also updates daily. Gateways are nodes on a network that create entrances to other networks. It routes traffic from workstations to broader networks. Therefore, securing the gateways will prevent malware from ever reaching the client.

Using Client/Server computing some of the secure systems can also be implemented, having a goal to provide secure services to clients with maximum possible performance. Emergency response vehicle can be quickly dispatched by dispatch operator to an incident and at the same time dealing can also be reported over the phone. This functionality can be provided 24 hours. It is now possible to duplicate all of the functionality of such an existing traditional design with the additional advantages of better performance, a Graphical User Interface (GUI), a single point of contact, higher reliability, and lower costs. With the help of a Client/Server-based system, the dispatch operator is empowered to oversee how staff and equipment are allocated to each incident. The operator uses a GUI to dynamically alter vehicle selection and routing. Maps may be displayed that show the location of all incidents, emergency response centers, and vehicles. Vehicles are tracked using Automatic Vehicle Locator (AVL) technology. Obstacles, such as traffic congestion, construction, and environmental damage (such as earthquakes) are shown on the map so the dispatcher can see potential problems at a glance. Workstation technology provides the dispatcher with a less stressful and more functional user interface. The dispatcher can respond quickly to changes in the environment and communicate this information immediately to the vehicle operator. The system is remarkably fault-tolerant. If a single workstation is operating, the dispatcher can continue to send emergency vehicles to the incident.

9.6.3 Object-oriented Technology: CORBA

As object oriented technology becomes more prevalent in operating system design; Client/Server designers have begun to embrace this approach. Here client and servers ship messages back and forth between objects. Object communication may rely on an underlying message or Remote Procedure Call (RPC) structure or be developed directly on top of object oriented capabilities in the operating system. Clients that need a service send a request to an object request broker, which acts as a directory of all the remote services available on the network. The broker calls the appropriate object and passes along any relevant data. Then the remote object services the request and replies to the broker, which returns the response to the client. There are several object oriented approach for standardization of these object mechanism are COM (Common Object Model), OLE (Object Linking and Embedding), Common Object Request Broker Architecture (CORBA, see the Fig. 9.5).

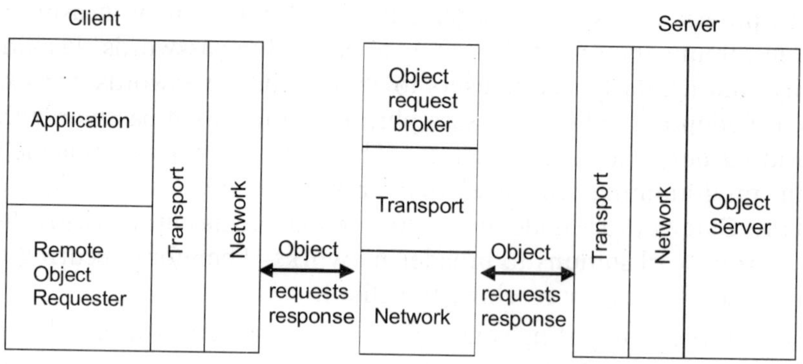

Fig. 9.5: Object Request Broker

An Overview of CORBA

The Object Management Group (OMG) was created in 1989. The OMG solicited input from all segments of the industry and eventually defined the CORBA standards.

CORBA specification has been implemented by numerous hardware and system software manufacturers, provides a rich and robust framework that operates across the heterogeneous computing platform. CORBA is a specification for an emerging technology known as distributed object management (DOM). DOM technology provides a higher level, object oriented interface on top of the basic distributed computing services.

At its most basic level, CORBA defines a standard framework from which an information system implementer or software developer can easily and quickly integrate network resident software modules and applications to create new, more powerful applications. It combines object technology with a Client/Server model to provide a uniform view of an enterprise computing system-everything on the network is an object. The highest level specification is referred to as the object management architecture (OMA), which addresses four architectural elements (ORB, CORBA services, CORBA facilities and CORBA domains are also defined as a part of specifications. The term CORBA is often used to refer to the object request broker itself, as well as to the entire OMG architecture.

The role of ORB is to route request among the other architectural components. CORBA services, CORBA facilities and CORBA domains are also defined as a part of specifications. The key to integrating application object is the specification of standard interfaces using the interface definition language (IDL). Once all applications and data have an IDL-compliant interface, communication is independent of physical location, platform type, networking protocol, and programming language. An information system is created by using CORBA to mediate the flow of control and information among these software objects.

CORBA an Introduction

Mechanism that allows various clients to share/call the object (applications) over a mixed network, more specifically CORBA is a process of moving objects over network providing cross platform for data transfer.

CORBA compliance provides a high degree of portability. Within CORBA, objects are an identifiable entity which provides one or more services to clients. CORBA manages the identity and location of the objects, transport the request to the target object, and confirms that the request is carried out. A client that needs a service sends a request to an object request broker (which acts as a directory) of all the remote services available on the network, illustrated in Fig. 9.6.

The broker calls the appropriate object and passes along any relevant data, and then the remote object services the request and replies to the broker, which returns to the client. The object communication may rely on an underlying message or RPC structure or be developed directly on top of object-oriented capability in the operating system.

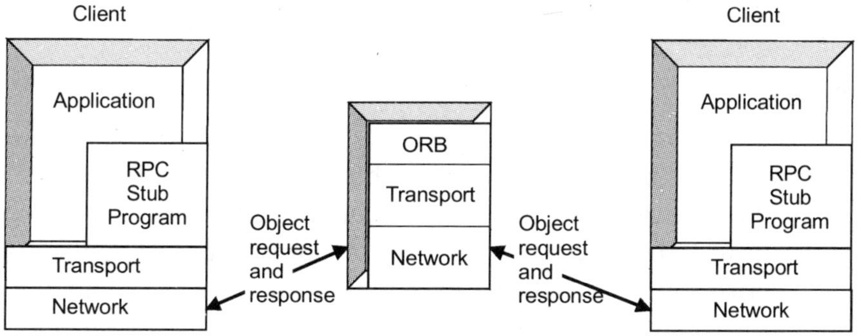

Fig. 9.6: *CORBA Remote Services*

CORBA Client and Servers

Like the Client/Server architecture, CORBA maintains the notions of Client and Server. In CORBA, a component can act as a client and as a server. Morever a component is considered a server if it contains CORBA objects whose services are accessible to other objects. Similarly, a component is considered a client if it accesses services from some other CORBA object.

Thus, a component can simultaneously provide and use various services, and so a component can be considered as a client or a server depending on the way.

More specifically, in CORBA application, any component that provides an implementation for an object is considered as a server, at least where that objects are concerned. If a component creates an object and provides others components with visibility to that object (or in other words, allows other components to obtain references to that object), that component acts as a server for that object; any requests made on that object by other components will be processed by the component that created the object. Being a CORBA server means that the component (the server) executes methods for a particular object on behalf of other components (the clients).

An application component can provide services to other application components while accessing services from other components. Here, the component is acting as a client of one component and as a server to the other components; see the Fig. 9.7 given below, illustrating those two components can simultaneously act as clients and servers to each other. In a CORBA application, the term client and server might depends on the context of the method being called and in which component that method's object resides. Although an application component can function as both a client and a server.

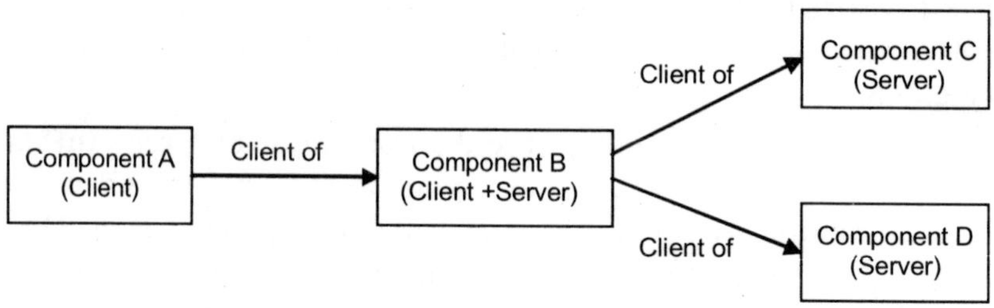

Fig. 9.7: Acting as a Client and a Server

CORBA Concepts

The basic idea is distributed computing, nowadays, most of the application are across the open environment, based on the connection of heterogeneous platforms. All modern business systems employ a network to connect a variety of computers, facilitating among applications. In the future, there will be continued evolution toward applications that exist as components across a network, which can be rapidly migrated and combined without significant effort. This is where CORBA shines, by providing unified access to applications, independent of the location of each application on network, also it provides:-

- Uniform access to services.
- Uniform discovery of resource/object.
- Uniform error handling methods.
- Uniform security policies.

These capabilities facilitate the integration and reuse of systems and system components, independent of network location and the details of underlying implementation technology. CORBA can be theoretically described based on the following three important concepts:

(*i*) Object-oriented model.

(*ii*) Open distributed computing environment.

(*iii*) Component integration and reuse.

(*i*) Object-oriented model: CORBA's object model is based on complete object approach in which a client sends a message to an object. The message identifies an object, and one or more parameters are included. The first parameter defines the operation to be performed, although the specific method used is determined by the receiving object. The CORBA object model comprises of:

Objects: An encapsulated entity that provides services to a client.

Request: An action created by a client directed to a target object that includes information on the operation to be performed and zero or more actual parameters.

Object creation and destruction: Based on the state of request, objects are created or deleted.

Types: An identifiable entity defined over values.

Interfaces: The specification of operations that a client can request from an object.

Operations: An identifiable entity that defines what a client can request from an object.

Object implementation in CORBA can be constituted in two parts, illustrated in the Fig. 9.8, first one is construction part and second one is execution part.

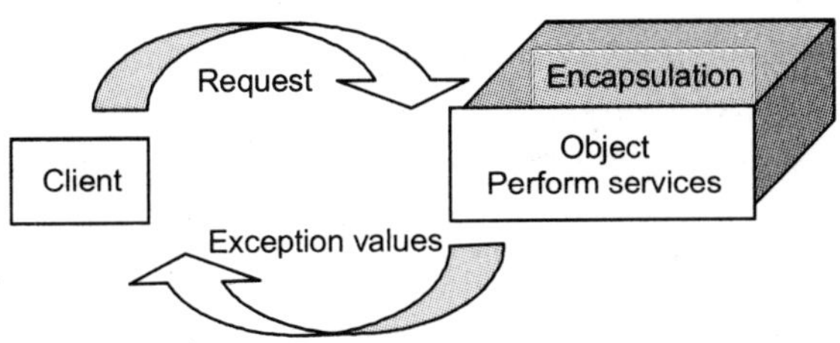

Fig. 9.8: Object Implementation

(*ii*) Open distributed computing environment: As we have earlier discussed that CORBA is based on a client server model of distributed computing. Within the Client/Server model, requests for services are made from one software component to another on a network. CORBA adds an additional dimension to this model by inserting a broker between the client and server components. The main objective of the broker is to reduce the complexity of implementing the interaction between the client and server. The broker plays two major roles. Primarily, it provides common services, including basic messaging and communication between client and server, directory services, meta-data description, security services, and location transparency. Secondly, it insulates the application from the specifics of the system configuration, such as hardware platform and operating system, network protocol, and implementation languages.

(iii) **Component integration and reuse:** The integration is the combination of two or more existing components. With a good integration techniques and tools, reuse can be achieved up to significant degree. Broker defines custom interfaces for each interaction between components. Each interface is defined just once and subsequent interactions are handled by the broker. With CORBA IDL, these interfaces can be defined in a standardized, platform independent fashion.

9.6.4 Electronic Data Interchange

Electronic data Interchanged uses direct link between computers, even computers on different sites, to transmit data to eliminate data sent in printed form. It is a controlled transfer of data between business and organizations via established security standards. One of the examples of EDI is shown in Fig. 9.9.

EDI is generally thought of as replacing standardized documents such as order forms, purchase orders, delivery notes, receiving advices and invoices in a standardized electronic message format. EDI documents are electronically exchanged over communication networks which connect trading partners to one another. These documents are stored in user mailboxes on the networks' EDI server from where they can be downloaded/uploaded at the user is convenience from any one of the workstations. But it differs from electronic mail in that it transmits an actual structured transaction (with field such as the transition date, transaction amount, senders name and recipient name) as opposed to unstructured text message such as a letter.

The main purpose of EDI is cost reduction by eliminating paper document handling. Faster electronic document transmission further saves time and man power by avoiding the need to re-key data. And the data arrival rate is much faster that mail.

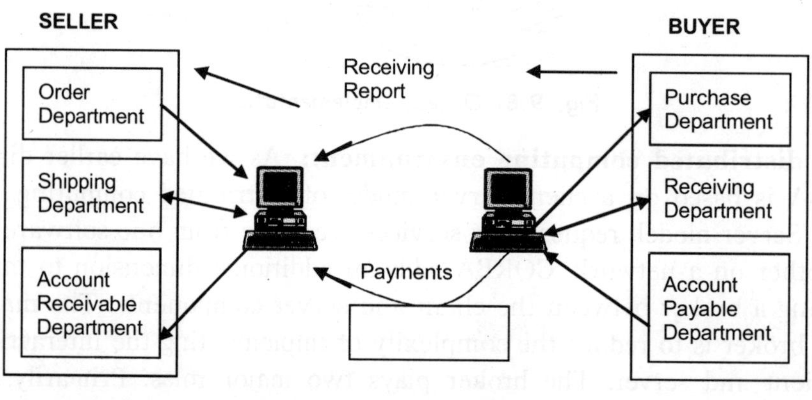

Fig. 9.9: EDI as an Example

EXERCISE 9

1. What is the future of Client/Server computing in the following technologies:-
   (*i*) Geographic Information System (GIS).
   (*ii*) Point of Service Technology (POS).
   (*iii*) Electronic Data Interface Technology (EDI).
   (*iv*) Multimedia.
2. What is the future of Client/Server computing in the following technologies?
   (*i*) Electronic Document Management.
   (*ii*) Full Text Retrieval.
   (*iii*) Geographic Information System.
3. What are different enabling technologies? Explain Expert System, Imaging and Electronic Document Management.
4. Discuss the changing role of Server's to provide the balance computing in Client/Server environment.

References

Alapali, Sam. R. *Expert Oracle Database 10g Administration*, A Press Burkeley, USA.

Bhattacharjee, Satyapriya. *A Textbook of Client/Server Computing.*

Comer, Douglas. E. *Computer Networks and Internets.*

Comer, Douglas. E. *Internetworking with TCP/IP.*

Coronel, R. *Database System,* Pearson Education, New Delhi.

Coulouris, George, et al. *Distributed System : Concepts and Design*

Crowley, Charles. *Operating System a Design Oriented Approach*, Tata McGraw-Hill Pub., New Delhi.

CSI Communications, *A Comparative Study on 2-tier and 3- tier Client/Server Architecture*, September, 2001.

CSI Communications, *Client/Server Technology, A Polymorphic Visage*, June, 2002.

Date, C. J. *An Introduction to Database Systems*, Pearson Education, New Delhi.

Desai, Bipin C. *An Introduction to Database Systems*, Galgotia Pub., New Delhi.

Dhamdhere, D. M. *Operating Systems* , Tata McGraw-Hill Pub., New Delhi.

Edward and Jerry. *3-Tier Client/Server at Work.*

Elmarsi, Ramez and Navathe, Shamkant. B. *Fundamentals of Database System.*

Eversest, Gordon C. *Database Management*, Tata McGraw-Hill Pub., New Delhi.

Forouzan, Behrouz A. *Data Communication and Networking*, Tata McGraw-Hill Pub., New Delhi.

Gallo, Michael. A. and Hancock, William. M. *Computer Communications and Networking Technology*, Books/Cole Pub. Company, Singapore.

Godbole, Achynt S. *Operating Systems*, Tata McGraw-Hill Pub., New Delhi.

Greenwald, Rick. et al. *Oracle Essantials.*

Haecke, Bernard Van. *Java-Database Connectivity.*

Hahn, Harley. *The Internet Complete Reference*, Tata McGraw-Hill Pub., New Delhi.

Halsall, Fred and Kulkarni, Lingana. *Computer Networking and the Internet*, Pearson Education, New Delhi.

Halsall, Fred. *Data Communication, Computer Networks & Open Systems.*

Harvey, Dennis and Beitler, Steve. *The Developer's Guide to Oracle Web Application* Server 3.

Hutehinson, Sarah, E. and Sawyer, Stcey. C. *Computer Communications, Information*,Tata McGraw-Hill Pub., New Delhi.

Jani, Madhulika and Jain , Satish. *Data Communication and Networking*, BPB Publications, New Delhi.

Kalakota, Ravi and Whinston, Andrew B. *Frontiers of Electronic Commerce.*

Kurose, James. F. and Ross, Keith. W. *Computer Networking*, Pearson Education, New Delhi.

Leon Alexis & Leon Mathews. *Data Base Management System.*

Majumdar, Arun K. and Bhattacharyya, Pritimoy. *Database Management Systems*, Tata McGraw-Hill Pub., New Delhi.

Martin, James. *Principles of Database Management*, PHI, New Delhi.

Milenkovic, Milan. *Operating System: Concepts and Design*, Tata McGraw-Hill Pub., New Delhi.

Miller, Michael A. *Data and Network Communications*, Thomson Asia Pvt. Ltd, Singapore.

Nutt, Gary. *Operating System: A Modern Perspective*, PHI, New Delhi.

Powell, Gavin. *Beginning Database Design*, Wiley Publishing Inc., USA.

Prabhu C. S. R. *Object-oriented Database Systems*, PHI, New Delhi.

Ramakrishnan, Raghu and Gehrke, Johannes. *Database Management Systems*, McGraw-Hill, Boston.

Ritchie, Colin. *Operating Systems in Corporating Unix and Windows*, PBP Publication, New Delhi.

Rosenberger, Jeremy.: *Teach Yourself CORBA,* Techmedia, New Delhi.

Scqnk, Jeffrey D. *Novell's Guide to C/S Design and Implementation.*

Silberchatz, Abraham, et al. *Operating System Principles*, John Wiley & Sons, Singapore.

Silberchatz, Abraham. et al. *Database System Concepts.*

Sinha, Pradeep K. *Distributed Operating System Concepts and Design*, PHI Pub., New Delhi.

Smith, Pattric N. and Ganguarich, Evan. *Client Server Computing*, PHI, New Delhi.

Perry, James T. and Laler Joseph G. *Understanding ORACLE.*

Sperik, Mark and Sledge, Orryn. *SQL-Server 7.0 DBA Survival Guide.*

Stalling, William. *Business Data Communication.*

Stalling, William. *Operating Systems*, PHI, New Delhi.

Tanenbaum, Andrew S. and Woodhull, Albert S. *Modern Operating System*, PHI, New Delhi.

Tanenbaum, Andrew S. and Woodhull, Albert S. *The MINIX book Operating System Design and Implementation*, Pearson Education, New Delhi.

Tanenbaum, Andrew S. *Computer Networks*, Pearson Education, New Delhi.

Shay, William A. *Understanding Data Communications and Networks*, Books/Cole Pub. Company, Singapore.

Thomas, Robert. M. *Introduction to Local Area Network.*

Travis, Dawna D. *Client/Server Computing.*

Vaskevitch, David. *Client/Server Unleashed.*

URLS

http://www.ssuet.edu.pk/taimoor/books/0-672-30473-2/csc09.htm
http:/www.ssuet.edu.pk/taimoor/books/0-672-30473-2/index.htm
http:/www.corba.ch/e/3tier.html
http:/www.acs.ncsu.edu/~nacsrjm/cs_stnd/cs_stnd.html
http://www-bfs.ucsd.edu/systems/cs/standrd.htm
http://www.sei.cmu.edu/str/descriptions/clientserver_body.html
http://www.softis.is
http://www.dciexpo.com/geos/
http://www.byte.com/art/9504/sec11/art4.htm
http://www.iterrasoft.com/ClientServer.htm
http://www.dpu.se/CTR/ctrcli_e.htm
http://www.tietovayla.fi/borland/techlib/delvpowr.html
http://www.opengroup.org/dce/successes/case_kredbank.htm
http://linuxtoday.com/developer/2001120600920OSSW
http://www.freeos.com/articles/2531/
http://www.linuxgazette.com/issue68/swieskowski.html
http://www.hrmanagement.gc.ca/gol/learning/interface.nsf/engdocBasic/1.html
http://www.conceptsystems.com
http://www-staff.it.uts.edu.au/~chin/dbms/cs.htm
http://www.exforsys.com
http://www.testingcenter.com/oviewtc.html
http://www.education-online earch.com
http://orca.st.usm.edu/~seyfarth/network_pgm/net-6-3-3.html
http://www.se.cuhk.edu.hk
http://www.gerrardconsulting.com/GUI/TestGui.html

Index